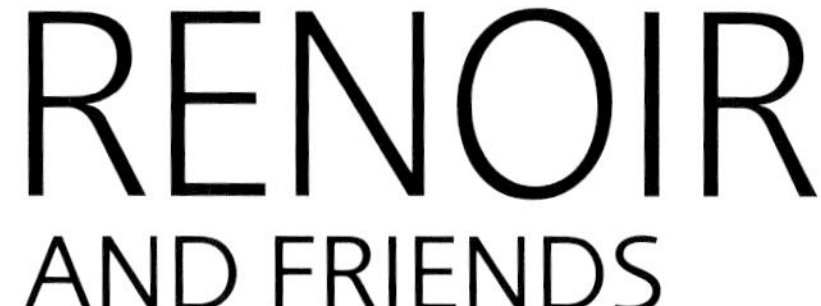

RENOIR
AND FRIENDS

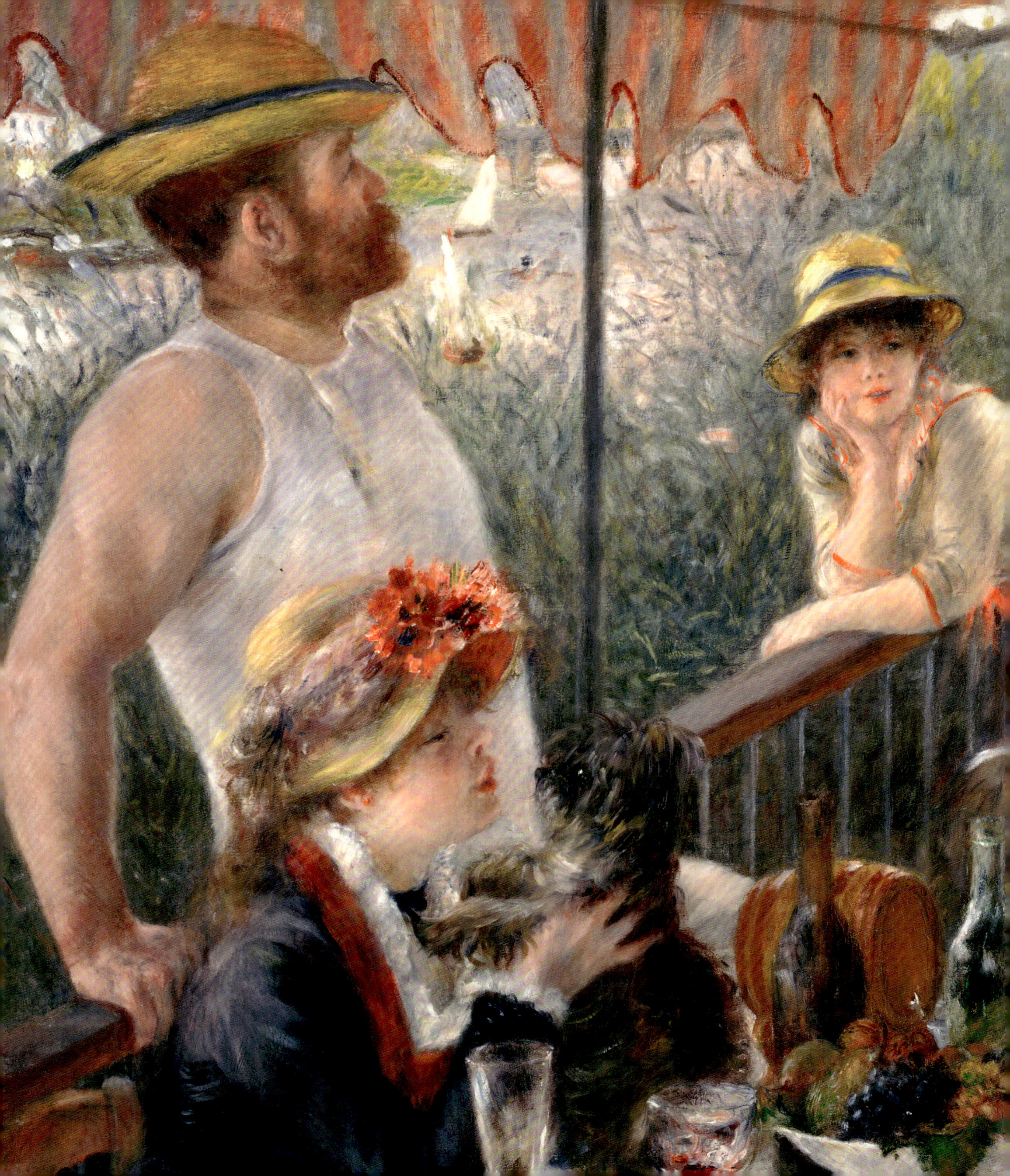

RENOIR
AND FRIENDS

LUNCHEON OF THE BOATING PARTY

ELIZA E. RATHBONE

WITH CONTRIBUTIONS BY MARY MORTON, SYLVIE PATRY, AILEEN RIBEIRO, ELIZABETH STEELE, AND SARA TAS

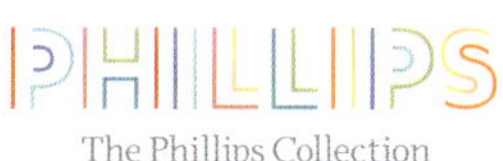 The Phillips Collection

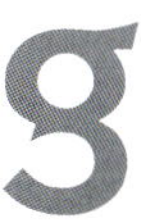

THE PHILLIPS COLLECTION, WASHINGTON, D.C., IN ASSOCIATION WITH D GILES LIMITED, LONDON

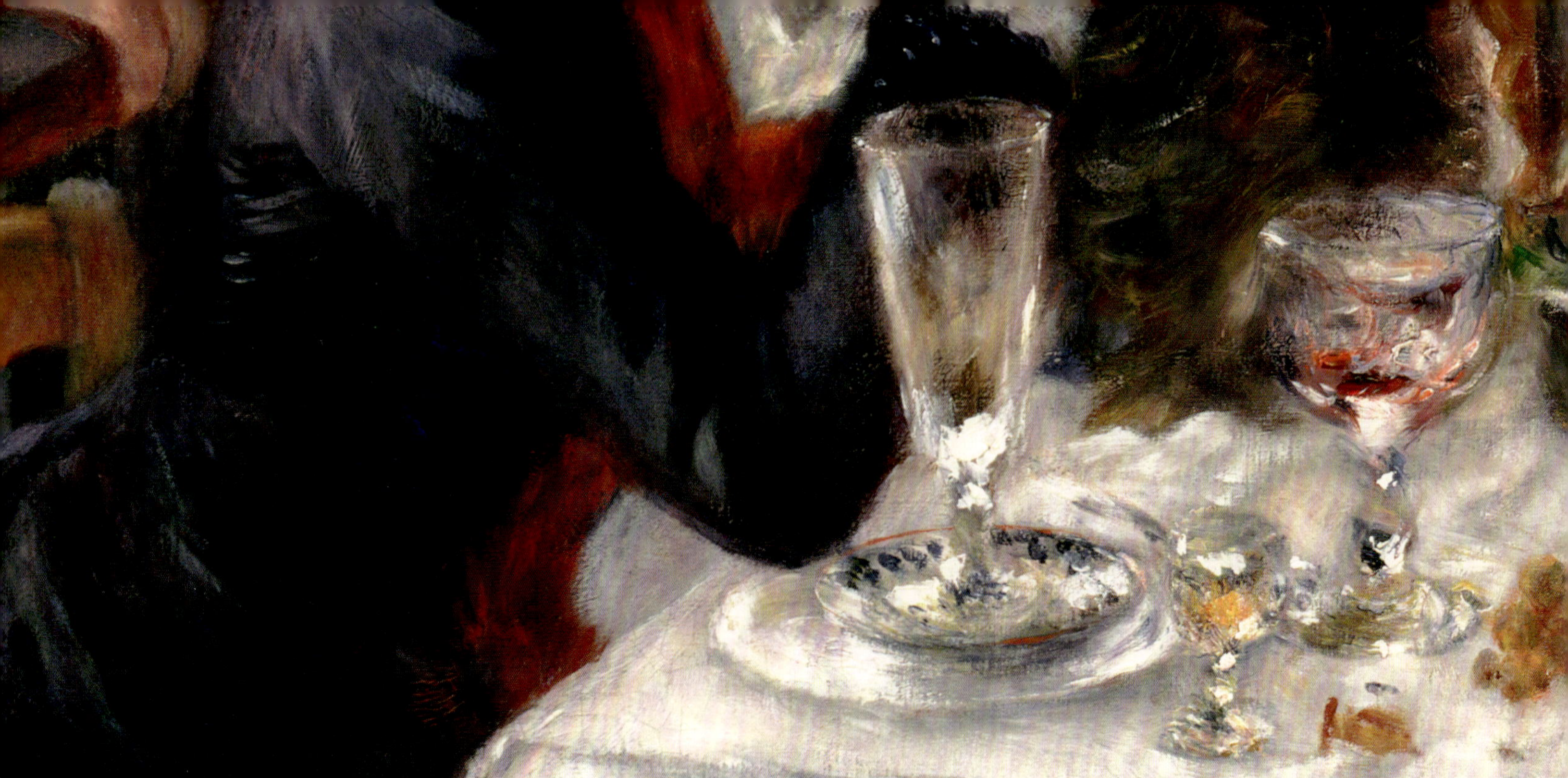

This catalog accompanies the exhibition *Renoir and Friends: Luncheon of the Boating Party* on display at The Phillips Collection, Washington, D.C. from October 7, 2017 – January 7, 2018

First published in 2017 by
The Phillips Collection
1600 Twenty-first Street, NW
Washington D.C., 20009-1090
www.phillipscollection.org

In association with GILES
An imprint of D Giles Limited
4 Crescent Stables, 139 Upper Richmond Road
London SW15 2TN, UK
www.gilesltd.com

ISBN 978-1-911282-00-6 (hardcover edition)

For The Phillips Collection:
Project management and editing by Eliza E. Rathbone and Liza Key Strelka

For D Giles Ltd:
Copy-edited and proofread by Sarah Kane
Sylvie Patry's essay translated from the French by Sarah Kane
Designed by Helen Swansbourne
Produced by D Giles Limited, London
Printed and bound in China

Library of Congress Cataloging-in-Publication Data
Names: Rathbone, Eliza E., 1948- author. | Morton, Mary G., writer of supplementary textual content. | Patry, Sylvie, writer of supplementary textual content. | Ribeiro, Aileen, 1944- writer of supplementary textual content. | Steele, Elizabeth (Conservator), writer of supplementary textual content. | Tas, Sara, writer of supplementary textual content. | Renoir, Auguste, 1841-1919, artist. | Phillips Collection, host institution, issuing body.
Title: Renoir and friends : Luncheon of the boating party / Eliza E. Rathbone ; with contributions by Mary Morton, Sylvie Patry, Aileen Ribeiro, Elizabeth Steele, and Sara Tas.
Description: Washington DC, : The Phillips Collection, in association with GILES, an imprint of D Giles Limited, 2017. | "This catalog accompanies the exhibition Renoir and Friends: Luncheon of the Boating Party on display at The Phillips Collection, Washington, D.C., from October 7, 2017 - January 7, 2018."--Colophon. | "Taking as its focus The Phillips Collection's celebrated Luncheon of the Boating Party (1880- 1881) by Pierre-Auguste Renoir, this exhibition uncovers the circumstances leading up to the painting's creation and the diverse and fascinating circle of friends who inspired it."--Foreword. | Includes bibliographical references and index.
Identifiers: LCCN 2017018024 | ISBN 9781911282006 (hardcover)
Subjects: LCSH: Renoir, Auguste, 1841-1919. Luncheon of the boating party--Exhibitions. | Renoir, Auguste, 1841-1919--Friends and associates --Exhibitions. | Phillips Collection--Exhibitions.
Classification: LCC ND553.R45 A69 2017 | DDC 759.4-- dc23 LC record available at https://lccn.loc.gov/2017018024

The exhibition is organized by The Phillips Collection.

With support from The Florence Gould Foundation, the MARPAT Foundation, the National Endowment for the Arts, the Robert Lehman Foundation, and Sotheby's.

Additional in-kind support provided by Farrow & Ball.

Front cover illustration:
Pierre-Auguste Renoir, *Luncheon of the Boating Party* (*Le Déjeuner des Canotiers*), 1880–1881, oil on canvas, 51¼ × 69⅛ in. (130.2 × 175.6 cm), detail. The Phillips Collection, Washington, D.C., Acquired 1923.

Back cover illustration:
Pierre-Auguste Renoir, *Portrait of Madame Renoir – Aline Charigot* (*Portrait de madame Renoir – Aline Charigot*), c. 1885, oil on canvas, 25¾ × 21¼ in. (65.4 × 54 cm), detail. Philadelphia Museum of Art, Purchased with the W.P. Wilstach Fund, 1957.

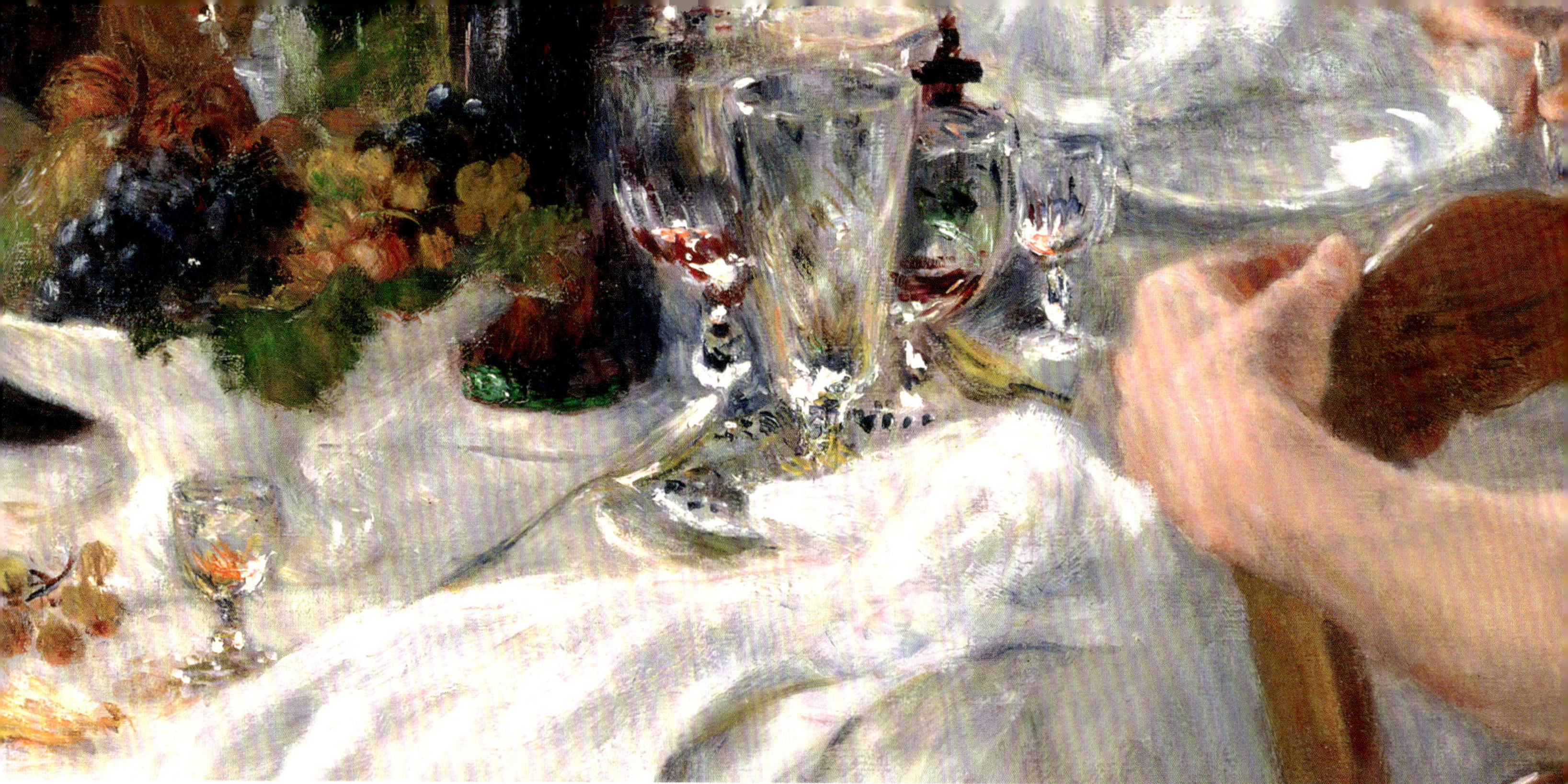

Contents

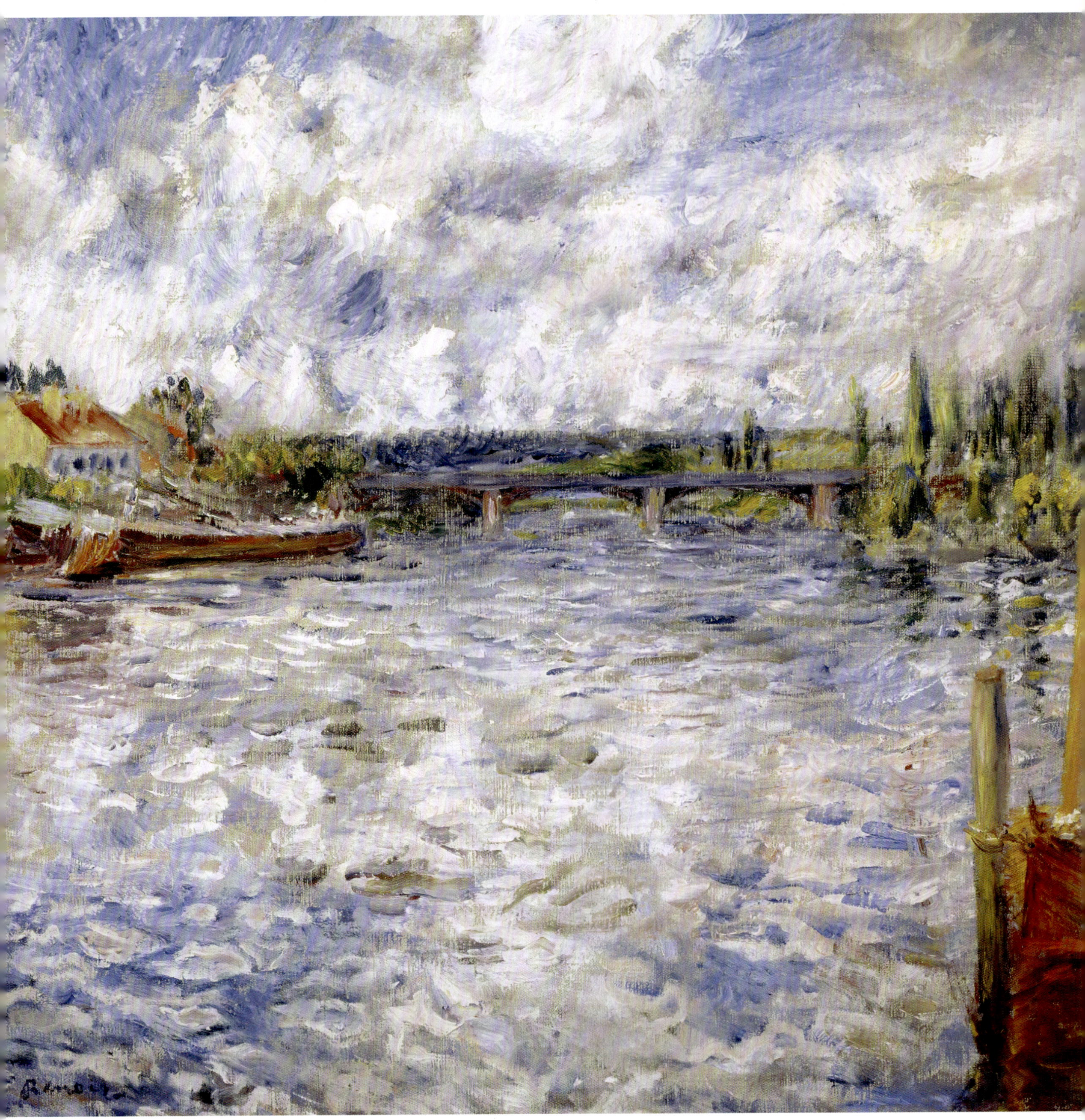

Lenders to the Exhibition

Art Gallery of Ontario, Toronto

The Art Institute of Chicago

The Baltimore Museum of Art

Dallas Museum of Art

Larry Ellison Collection

The J. Paul Getty Museum, Los Angeles

Institut national d'histoire de l'art, Paris

Musée de l'Orangerie, Paris

Musée d'Orsay, Paris

Museum of Art, Rhode Island School of Design, Providence, RI

Museum of the City of New York

Museum of Fine Arts, Boston

National Gallery of Art, Washington

The Norton Simon Foundation, Pasadena, CA

Philadelphia Museum of Art

Portland Art Museum, Oregon

Private collection c/o Durand-Ruel & Cie

Private collection c/o Simon Dickinson Ltd., London

Private collections

Mr. and Mrs. Felipe Propper de Callejon

Saint Louis Art Museum

Sterling and Francine Clark Art Institute, Williamstown, MA

Bruce Toll

Mr. and Mrs. G. Duane Vieth

Virginia Museum of Fine Arts

Edmund de Waal

Wallraf-Richartz-Museum & Fondation Corboud, Cologne

Yale University Art Gallery, New Haven, CT

Detail of Cat. 2, Pierre-Auguste Renoir, *The Seine at Chatou* (*La Seine à Chatou*), 1874.

Foreword

TAKING AS ITS FOCUS The Phillips Collection's celebrated *Luncheon of the Boating Party* (1880–1881) by Pierre-Auguste Renoir, this exhibition uncovers the circumstances leading up to the painting's creation and the diverse and fascinating circle of friends who inspired it. Duncan Phillips purchased *Luncheon of the Boating Party* from the Durand-Ruel gallery in 1923 for the record sum of $125,000. It was a stroke of genius for his fledgling institution that put the Phillips Memorial Gallery on the map. He had opened his doors to the public just two years earlier, in 1921. The only painting by Renoir in the collection, *Luncheon of the Boating Party* has remained its greatest treasure, the one Phillips knew would draw visitors from around the world. Recognized as one of the greatest achievements of the artist's career, the work is a marvel of plein-air painting on a grand scale.

This exhibition is the first in a Centennial Series that examines the history and legacy of The Phillips Collection as we speed toward 2021—the museum's 100th anniversary. Moreover, it is the first exhibition to highlight this masterwork in over twenty years, following the museum's 1996 exhibition, *Impressionists on the Seine*. It is fitting that the Centennial's opening show focuses on a work so central to the museum's identity.

Chief Curator Emerita Eliza Rathbone carefully chose paintings, drawings, pastels, prints, books, and photographs for the show. We are grateful to her for proposing this project, and for her willingness to assemble detailed research into the conditions and circumstances under which the painting was made. Elizabeth Steele, head of conservation, agreed to reexamine the painting with new techniques and equipment, and made unexpected discoveries. Their findings are enriched by the insights of contributing authors Mary Morton, Sylvie Patry, Aileen Ribeiro, and Sara Tas, each of whom has brought deep knowledge and a unique perspective to this inquiry.

Over a quarter of the exhibition comes from private collections, giving us an opportunity to see pictures not usually on public view. The generous loan of these pieces endows the exhibition with a depth that would not have been achievable without them. I extend special thanks to Larry Ellison, Mr. and Mrs. Felipe Propper de Callejon, Bruce Toll, Mr. and Mrs. G. Duane Vieth, Edmund de Waal, and other private collectors. We are equally indebted to the public institutions that have shared exceptional works from their collections. I also extend sincere thanks to Stephan Jost, director of the Art Gallery of Ontario, Toronto; Matthew Teitelbaum, Ann and Graham Gund Director of the Museum of Fine Arts, Boston, and his predecessor, Malcolm Rogers; Earl A. Powell, director of the National Gallery of Art; John W. Smith, director of the Rhode Island School of Design Museum; Timothy Rub, director of the Philadelphia Museum of Art; Brent R. Benjamin, director of the Saint Louis Art Museum; Guy Cogeval, former director of the Musée d'Orsay; James Rondeau, President and Eloise W. Martin Director of the Art Institute of Chicago and his predecessor, Douglas Druick; Christopher Bedford, Dorothy Wagner Wallis Director of the Baltimore Museum of Art and his predecessor, Doreen Bolger; Marcus Dekiert, director of the Wallraf-Richartz-Museum & Fondation Corboud; Timothy Potts, director of the J. Paul Getty Museum, Los Angeles; Antoinette Romain, general director, Institut national d'histoire de l'art, Paris; Hope Alswang, executive director and CEO of the Norton Simon Museum, Pasadena; Agustín Arteaga, Eugene McDermott Director of the Dallas Museum of Art; Laurence des Cars, director of the Musée d'Orsay; Whitney W. Donhauser, director of the Museum of the City of New York; Brian J. Ferriso, Marilyn H. and Dr. Robert B. Pamplin, Jr. Director, Portland Art Museum, Oregon; Olivier Meslay, Felda and Dena Hardymon Director, Sterling and Francine Clark Art Institute, Williamstown; Alex Nyerges, director of the Virginia Museum of Fine Arts; and Jock Reynolds, director of Yale University Art Gallery.

For their generous support of this exhibition, The Phillips Collection is grateful to the Florence Gould Foundation, the MARPAT Foundation, the Robert Lehman Foundation, and Sotheby's. In addition, I heartily thank our painting sponsors: Sam and Ruth Alward, Alan S. Inouye, Robert and Debra Drumheller, Molly and Fred Rolandi, Patricia Squires and Patrick Spann, and G. Duane Vieth.

I want to recognize the invaluable contributions of the many Phillips staff members who have worked on this exhibition: Liza Strelka, manager of exhibitions; Trish Waters, associate registrar for exhibitions; Amanda Hunter, director of marketing and communications; Bridget Zangueneh, director of institutional giving; Charlotte Mikk, deputy director of development, major gifts; Suzanne Wright, director of education; Bill Koberg, chief of installations; Alec MacKaye, manager of installations; Patricia Favero, associate conservator; Sylvia Albro, conservator of art on paper; Laura Tighe, collections care manager; Shelly Wischhusen, chief preparator; Klaus Ottmann, deputy director for curatorial and academic affairs; Laith Alnouri, deputy director, development, partnerships and corporate relations; Kelley Daley, head of public programming; and Caitlin Hoerr, executive assistant to the director and board of trustees.

Dorothy M. Kosinski
DIRECTOR

Preface and Acknowledgments

ANYONE MIGHT WONDER IF there could be more to know about Pierre-Auguste Renoir's famed *Luncheon of the Boating Party*. In the 135 years since its completion, various authors—Julius Meier-Graefe, Georges Rivière, John House, and Martha Carey, to name a few—have looked at it in some detail. Yet this is the first in-depth focus exhibition around the painting. Traditionally, such an exhibition would comprise preparatory works and studies. However, Renoir astonishingly made none, mostly creating this large oil on canvas *en plein air* at the Maison Fournaise at Chatou. I had to find another avenue into the process of its creation. The approach became to investigate the people who modeled for the painting as well as the artist's familiarity with the site. Though the method is different, the aim is the same, to gain new insight into this work that has mesmerized its audience for so long. Is it a celebration of the Third Republic that enabled various classes and stations in life, men and women, to enjoy a beautiful day by the river, completely at ease in each other's company? Or simply a vision of utopia, a charmed reality that Renoir perceived more readily than others? Here is an attempt to clarify the circumstances of this work's creation and to separate fact from fiction. Our line of inquiry offers an unusually personal

vantage point, and the artist's process gains in complexity as we come to a more intimate understanding of the people he knew. This backstory is enhanced by a technical analysis of the painting's execution. Some widely accepted ideas about Renoir's models can be confirmed, others remain speculative; certain friends gain in clarity and importance as others recede or remain elusive. Indeed, in spite of our best efforts, much remains elusive given the limits of time and space for this project, leaving intriguing material for further investigation.

Assistance with our research came from many quarters. In recent years, Edmund de Waal's *The Hare with Amber Eyes* created new and widespread interest in his forebear Charles Ephrussi, who appears to have a starring role in Renoir's painting. Study of the life and work of Gustave Caillebotte, also a principal player in Renoir's life, has continued apace. Nineteenth-century French fashion has attracted increased interest, and Renoir's painting begs to be looked at from this point of view. I am grateful to Edmund de Waal for allowing me to visit him in his south London studio; he shared with me his collection of Ephrussi-related publications and steered me to other works relating to the Ephrussi family, saying he was "beguiled" by the project. Sylvie Patry, formerly chief curator at the Musée d'Orsay, now deputy director for collections and exhibitions and Gund Family Chief Curator at the Barnes Foundation, not only wrote her own essay about Aline Charigot but led me to Sara Tas, curator of exhibitions at the Jewish Historical Museum in Amsterdam, who was intrigued by Charles Ephrussi and contributed her insights to this publication. Mary Morton, curator and head of the Department of French Paintings at the National Gallery of Art, organized for that institution a Gustave Caillebotte retrospective in 2015, and contributed an essay on Renoir's close friend, whose love of boating appears to have rivaled his love of painting. Aileen Ribeiro, professor emerita of the Courtauld Institute of the University of London and an authority on the history of dress, offered her take on Renoir's approach to fashion. She put me in touch with Phyllis Magidson at the Museum of the City of New York, whose loan of hats from their collection is a first adventure into this form of material culture for The Phillips Collection. I am deeply grateful to all of them for enriching this exhibition and publication.

For the first time, the materials, techniques, and evolution of *Luncheon of the Boating Party* are shown on the walls of an exhibition as well as in its publication, presenting the findings of The Phillips Collection's head of conservation, Elizabeth Steele. On her behalf, we would like to thank Stephanie Barnes, Patricia Favero, Inge Fiedler, Thomas Lam, Nicole Riesenberger, Christine Romano, Annie Schrandt, and Jai-Sun Tsang.

The effort to gain deeper insight into Renoir's painting and its models led to a search for works of art that have never been exhibited together, including many from private collections. I am indebted to all those who helped locate these key works. For their assistance, support, and generosity, my heartfelt thanks go to friends and colleagues Lynne Addison, Lauren Anderson, Ronni Baer, Colin Bailey, Suzanne Borsh, Sylvie Brame, Laurie Brewer, Anna Brooke, Katya Chelli, Teresa Ciapparoni La Rocca, Michael Conforti, Alina Davey, Lilly Dawson, Lamia Doumato, Edith Eustis, Jessica Fertig, Caitlin Frank, Isabelle Gaetan, Anne Galloyer, Wendy Garner, Davide Gasparotto, Hugh Gibson, Gloria Groom, Anika Guntrum, Johanna Halford-MacLeod, Grace Hernandez, Marie Caroline van Herpin, Genevieve Hulley, Jemima Johnson, David Kleiweg de Zwaan, Elizabeth and Timothy Llewellyn, Yuri Long, Jessica McFadden, Phyllis Magidson, Daniel Marchesseau, Mitchell Merling, Maureen O'Brien, Van Ogden, Ariana Panbechi, Michael Pantazzi, Joseph Rishel, Katherine Rothkopf, James Roundell, Barbara Schaefer, George T. M. Shackelford, Marjorie Shelley, Amanda Shore, Simon C. Dickinson Limited, Susan Stein, Jennifer Thompson, Carol Togneri, Mr. and Mrs. G. Duane Vieth, Edmund de Waal, Helen Waters, and Barbara Ehrlich White. For their invaluable assistance with records in the Durand-Ruel archives, I especially thank Paul-Louis Durand-Ruel and Flavie Durand-Ruel. For their persistent research and enthusiasm for this project, I am grateful to Katherine Brennan and Manon Hasselmann. From the Phillips Collection, I wish to thank more people than space allows, but cannot fail to mention Sylvia Albro, Colleen Hennessey, Christine Hollins, Klaus Ottman, Karen Schneider, Elizabeth Steele, Elizabeth Temme, Shelly Wischhusen, Bridget Zangueneh, and especially Trish Waters and Liza Strelka. My thanks to Dorothy Kosinski for the opportunity to take on this project.

Our editor, Claire Aelion-Moss, did a thorough and splendid job for which we are truly thankful. We are fortunate to work with Dan Giles, Allison McCormick, Liz Japes, Louise Ramsay and Helen Swansbourne, who have produced this beautiful book. For their unfailing support, I am forever grateful to Claudia, Emma, and James Hamilton, and to Emma especially for her insightful reading of the text.

Eliza E. Rathbone
CHIEF CURATOR EMERITA AND PROJECT DIRECTOR

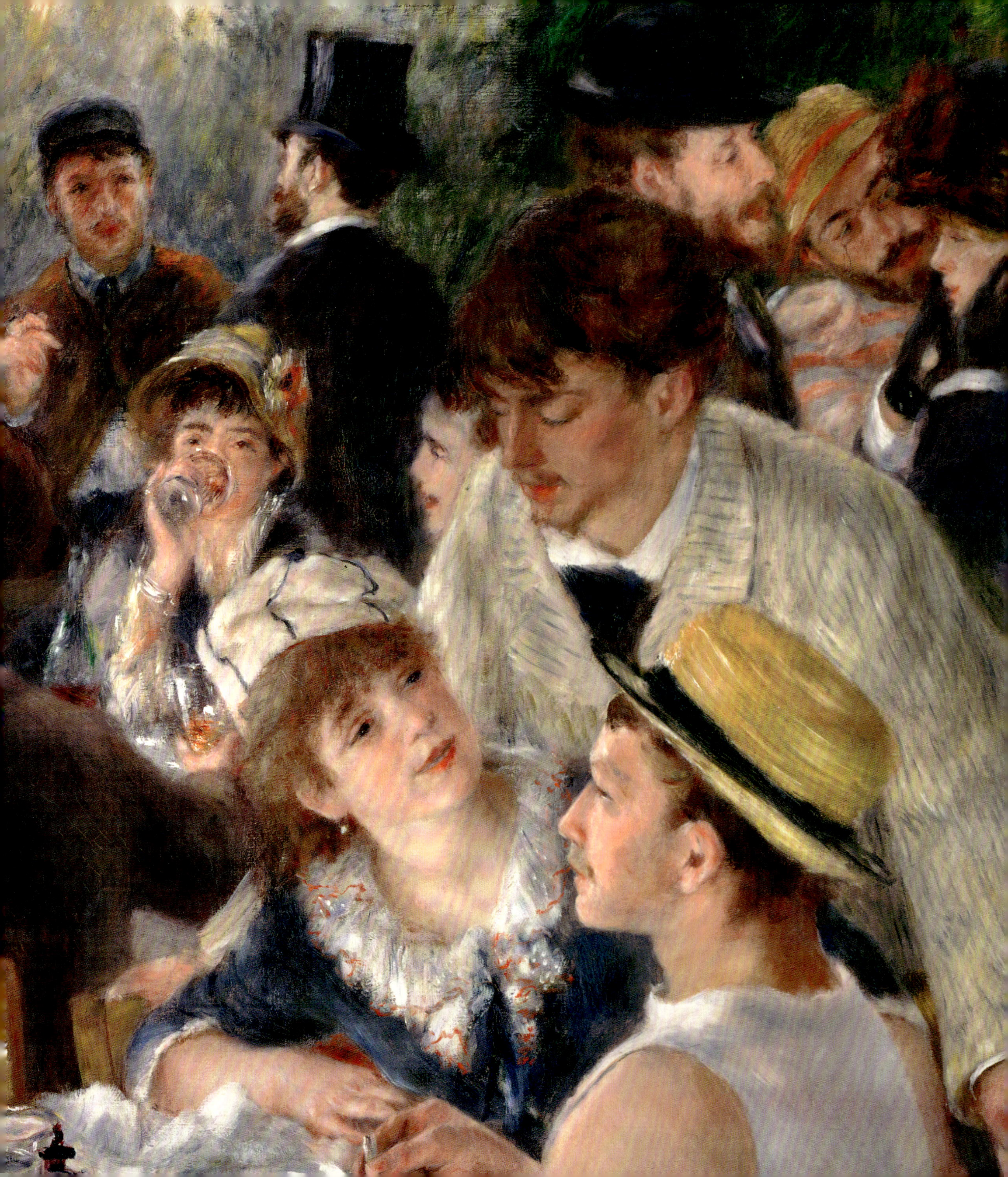

Renoir's *Luncheon of the Boating Party*: "Le dernier grand tableau"

ELIZA E. RATHBONE

ON VIEW AT THE impressionist exhibition of 1882, Renoir's *Luncheon of the Boating Party* (Cat. 1), which he had sworn would be his "last big painting,"[1] was received for the most part with tremendous enthusiasm: Armand Silvestre declared it "one of the best things he has painted; shaded by an arbor, bare-armed boatmen are laughing with some girls. . . . It is one of the most beautiful pieces that this insurrectionist art by Independent artists has produced. For my part, I found it absolutely superb."[2] Only the day before, critic Paul de Charry described Renoir's painting as "a charming work, full of gaiety and spirit, its wild youth caught in the act, radiant and lively, frolicking at high noon in the sun, laughing at everything, seeing only today and mocking tomorrow. For them eternity is in their glass, in their boat, and in their songs. It is fresh and free without being too bawdy." He went on to declare that the Renoir "share[s] the honors of the exhibition"[3] with Gustave Caillebotte's *Game of Bezique* (fig. 25), also a large group composition.

Gaining an audience

Such praise must have warmed the heart of the artist, who had gone all out to achieve this major work. His letters to Paul Berard in the summer of 1880 make vivid the enormous investment of time and money involved; in one of them, he explained to his friend that one must, from time to time, attempt things beyond one's capacity.[4] Soon after Renoir completed his ambitious painting destined for the Salon, he sold it to Paul Durand-Ruel, who decided to lend it to the seventh impressionist exhibition. Renoir had not shown with the impressionists at their independent exhibitions since the third, in 1877. Even then, when he showed *The Swing* (Musée d'Orsay, Paris) and *Dance at Le Moulin de la Galette* (fig. 15), several critics laughed at his work, finding it "ridiculous." Reveling in derision, one described "pompoms" where Renoir had painted patches of light.[5] The year before, a Renoir nude was called a "mass of decomposing flesh," "depressing."[6] The 1870s were an arduous decade for the impressionists (and for Renoir in particular), strained by lack of sales and deplorably low prices.[7] While in retrospect it was the great decade of impressionism, when the group was at its most cohesive, by its end there were challenges to this cohesion. In 1879, in defense of Renoir openly favoring the official Salon over their independent exhibitions in hopes of finding a wider audience, Pissarro expressed sympathy, noting that "poverty is so hard."[8] Renoir increasingly sought the support of writers who understood and praised his work and collectors who purchased, and soon, in greater numbers, commissioned portraits and decorations. Shifting his sights from the small impressionist group exhibitions to the huge official Salon meant submitting his work to the possibility of unfortunate placement, lost on a triple-hung wall, and to the certainty of being among pieces by painters who subscribed to traditional subjects and established techniques. Although some of Renoir's paintings had been accepted at the Salon in previous years, this had not resulted in any significant increase in sales or recognition. It was his success at the Salon of 1879, when his portrait of Marguerite Charpentier and her children was advantageously shown, that confirmed his commitment to this much larger venue and spurred him to create a work of equal size and greater complexity: *Luncheon of the Boating Party*. How he came to choose the site and the friends to model for his ambitious project is the subject of this exhibition and publication.

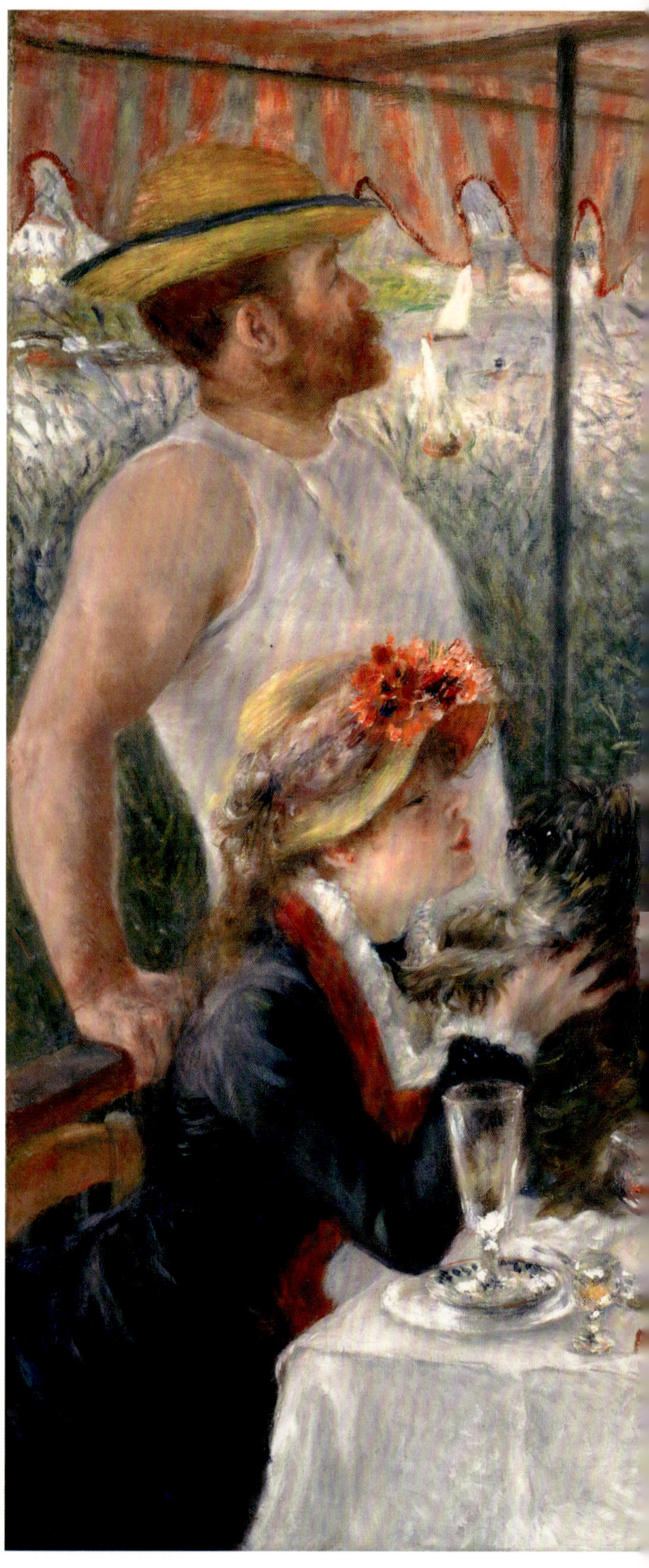

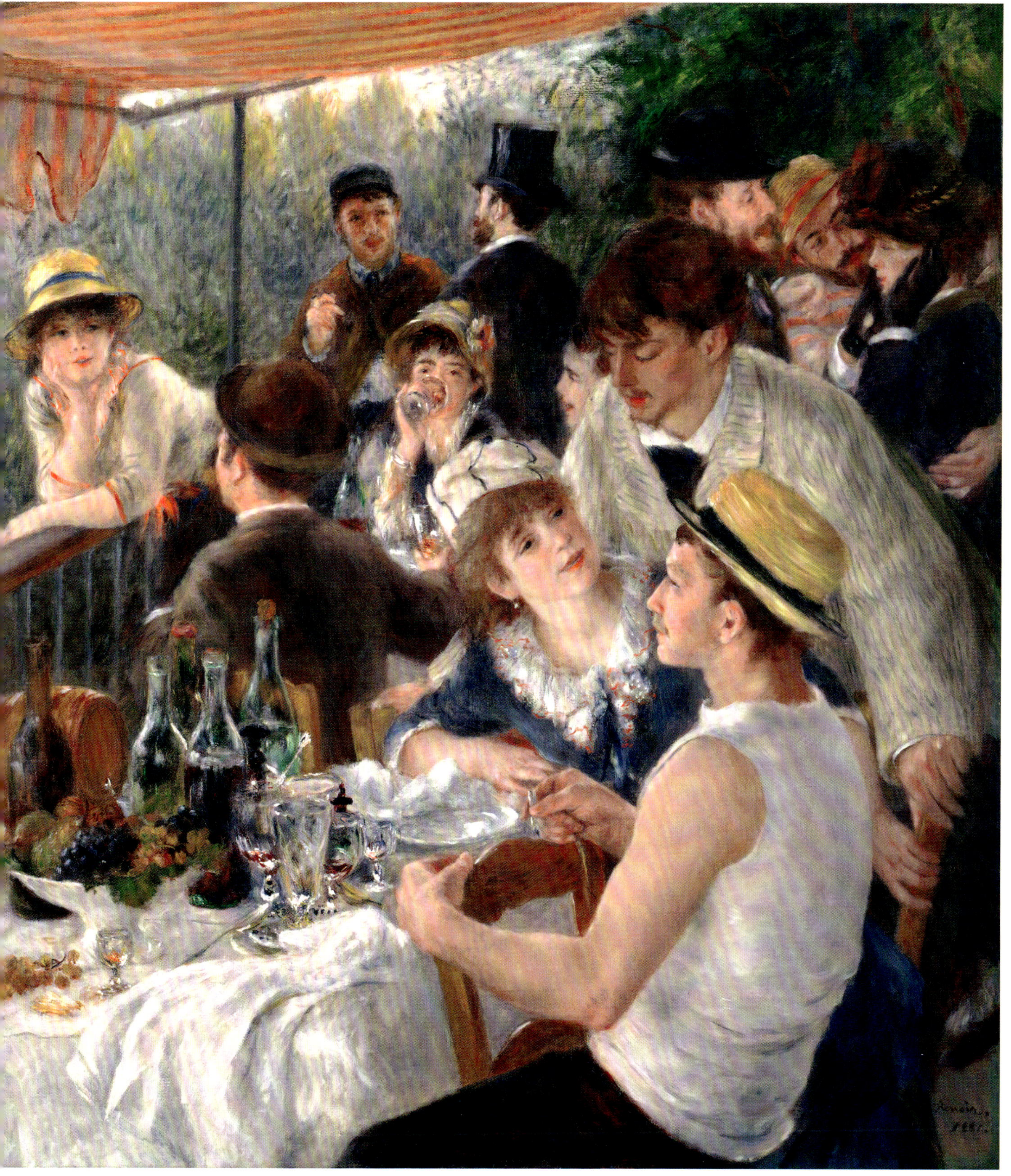

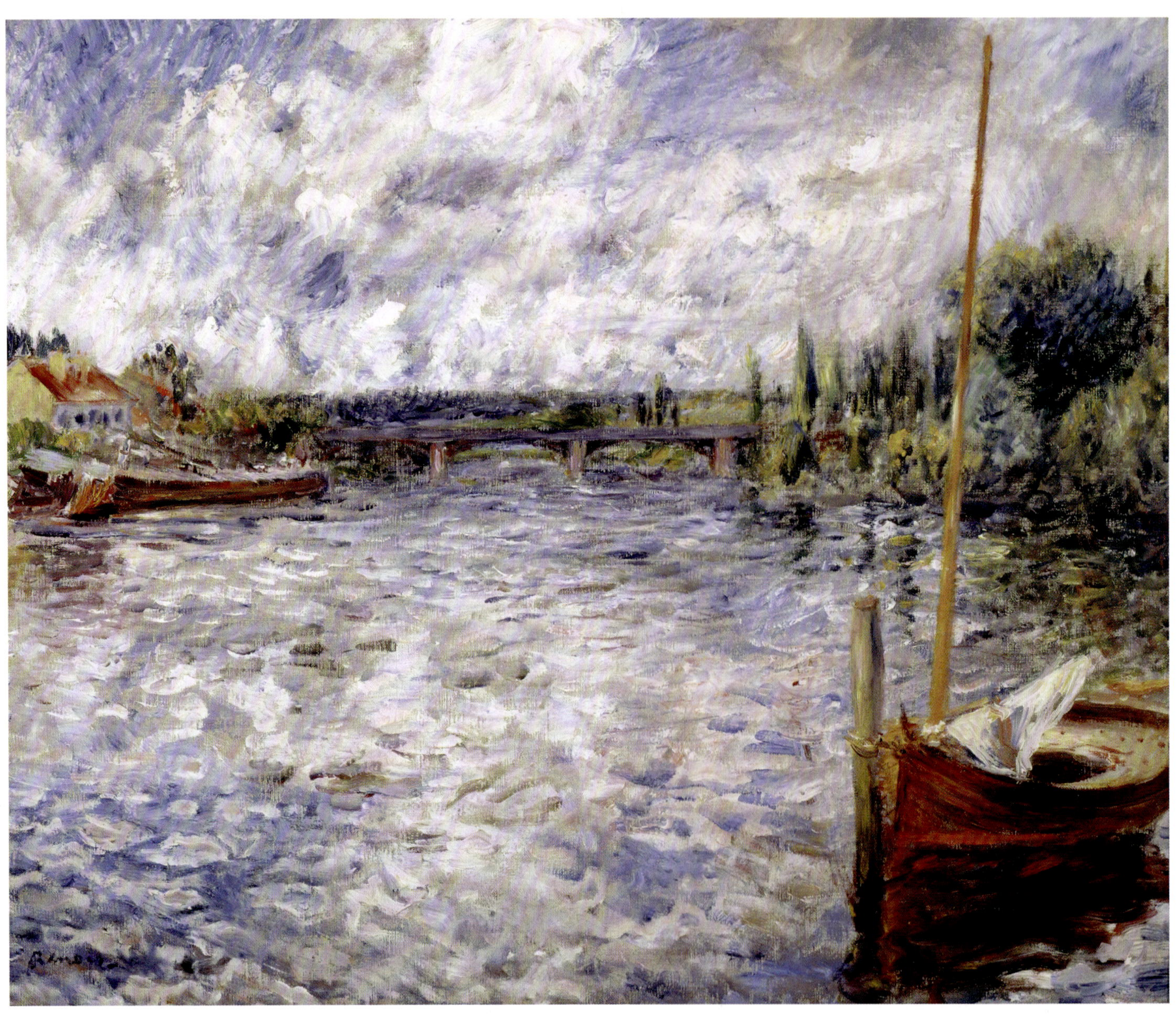

CAT. 2. Pierre-Auguste Renoir, *The Seine at Chatou* (*La Seine à Chatou*), 1874, oil on canvas, 20 × 25 in. (50.8 × 63.5 cm). Dallas Museum of Art, The Wendy and Emery Reves Collection.

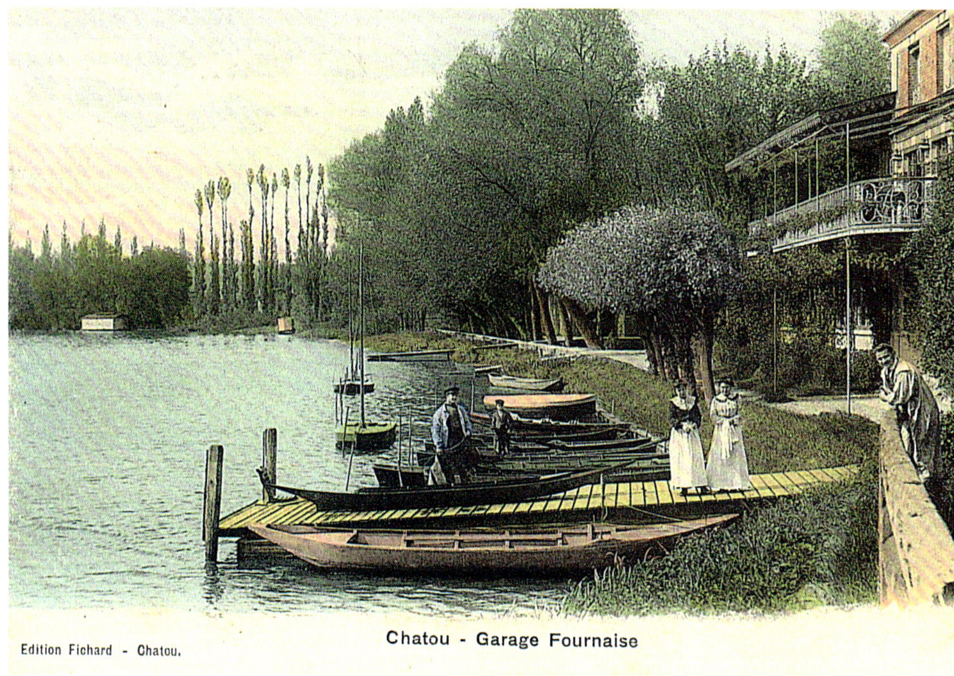

FIG. 1. *Chatou – Garage Fournaise*, digital print from an early 20th-century postcard. Via Joconde – Portail des collections des musées de France.

Social connections

Virtually all those who are believed to have modeled for *Luncheon of the Boating Party* emerged as key players in Renoir's life in the late 1870s. In 1876, Renoir painted the work (fig. 15) that became a source for several major paintings of the early 1880s, including *Luncheon of the Boating Party* and three life-size pictures of dancing couples. For this panorama of a Sunday afternoon at the Moulin de la Galette on the outskirts of Paris, he rented a studio in rue Cortot in Montmartre, near the site. Corralling his models and friends who frequented the Moulin, Renoir aimed to create an authentic image of his own time, as animated and naturalistic in its atmosphere of changing light and movement as possible—a modern history painting, as his friend Georges Rivière called it. His good friends Paul Lhote and Eugène-Pierre Lestringuez posed for the piece, dancing in the crowd in the middle distance. Among the models for seated figures was Rivière, who praised Renoir's work lavishly when it was shown at the third impressionist exhibition, saying, "Noise, laughter, movement, sunshine, in an atmosphere of youth. . . .

Never has he been more inspired. It is a page of history."[9] What delighted Rivière was Renoir's ability to appeal to the senses; as he wrote in *L'Impressionniste* of another of Renoir's works, a "superb" landscape of the Seine, "no one before has so strikingly given the feeling of a windy autumn day." *Dance at Le Moulin de la Galette* was purchased from the exhibition by Renoir's friend and fellow artist Gustave Caillebotte, who included it in the background of an 1879–1880 self-portrait (fig. 12). Since Caillebotte bought many works by other impressionists, his reference to this painting in his self-portrait seems a deliberate symbol of their mutual admiration and friendship. During these days of struggle and ambition, Rivière and Caillebotte emerged as stalwart advocates for Renoir, and both became lifelong supporters of his work.

Keenly aware of the value of personal contacts and social connections, Renoir cultivated the friendships of those who understood and supported him. Among those who helped him in the mid-1870s when he badly needed it were Georges and Marguerite Charpentier and Théodore Duret, who responded on numerous occasions to Renoir's requests for financial support. Georges Charpentier had acquired his first painting by Renoir (*The Angler* [*Le Pêcheur à la ligne*]), private collection, 1874) for a song in 1875, and wanted to meet the artist. Often accompanied by Rivière, Renoir attended gatherings at the Charpentiers', meeting a circle that included actors and artists, as well as naturalist writers like Gustave Flaubert, Guy de Maupassant, and Émile Zola, whose books were literary equivalents of realism and impressionism in painting. For the prominent Charpentiers, this diversity of opinion and background was a socially daring mix.[10] Duret was born to a family in the cognac business; an author, a critic, and an early supporter of Manet and the impressionists, he was socially well connected. He traveled to Asia with Henri Cernuschi, who was forming a collection of Asian art. Through Duret, Renoir met Cernuschi and eventually his friend also entranced by Asian art, Charles Ephrussi. Duret wrote favorably about the work of the impressionists in 1878, finding in it parallels with art of the Far East.

Though Renoir had painted occasional large-scale paintings and had shown at the Salon before, it was in 1879 that the Charpentiers' early support was borne out, as his portrait of Madame Charpentier and her two children (fig. 33) brought critical and commercial success, precipitating a marked increase in commissions. In advance of the show, Ephrussi had expressed interest in seeing the recent portrait, and Renoir gladly took him to the Charpentiers' house for a viewing. Ephrussi, who had purchased work by Renoir for his collection, emerged as a vocal advocate for impressionism in 1880 when he praised Caillebotte's paintings in the fifth impressionist exhibition, and, in a review of the sixth, deplored the absence of Manet, Monet, Sisley, and Renoir.[11] "A man of the world, devoted to the study

of art," as Duret described him, Ephrussi used his influence to get Renoir an advantageous hanging at the Salon—that Marguerite Charpentier was a prominent member of Parisian society did not hurt the placement of her portrait either, nor its critical reception. The following year, Ephrussi suggested that Renoir be commissioned to paint a portrait of his aunt, Thérèse Prascovie Ephrussi (Madame Léon Fould) (Cat. 41), and over time he made introductions for Renoir that led to further commissions, especially from prominent Jewish members of society like the Cahen d'Anvers. Renoir did a portrait of the daughters of Louise Cahen d'Anvers that was shown at the Salon of 1881—an entry he left entirely in Ephrussi's hands.[12] Ephrussi must also have recommended Renoir to Albert Cahen d'Anvers, brother-in-law of Louise (she married his brother Louis), whose portrait he painted in 1881 (Cat. 3). Without the support of Marguerite Charpentier, Théodore Duret, and Charles Ephrussi, the tide might not have turned for Renoir.

How was it that Renoir came to be embraced by these individuals, many of a very different background from his? One of five children born to a tailor father and seamstress mother, Renoir began working for a living at a young age. How did this young man, who had few possessions (and liked it that way), befriend those born to far more than the proverbial silver spoon in their mouths? We can look to two people who knew him well during these years when he was establishing himself as an artist in Paris: Duret and Rivière. The former his age and the latter his junior by fourteen years, they provide a picture of his temperament and manner (Cat. 4). Amiable, kind, generous, and unpretentious, Renoir was by their accounts a pleasure to have around.[13] Endowed with a sense of humor, he was given to witticisms, quips, and amusing references to things as mundane as plants on sale (of which he writes to

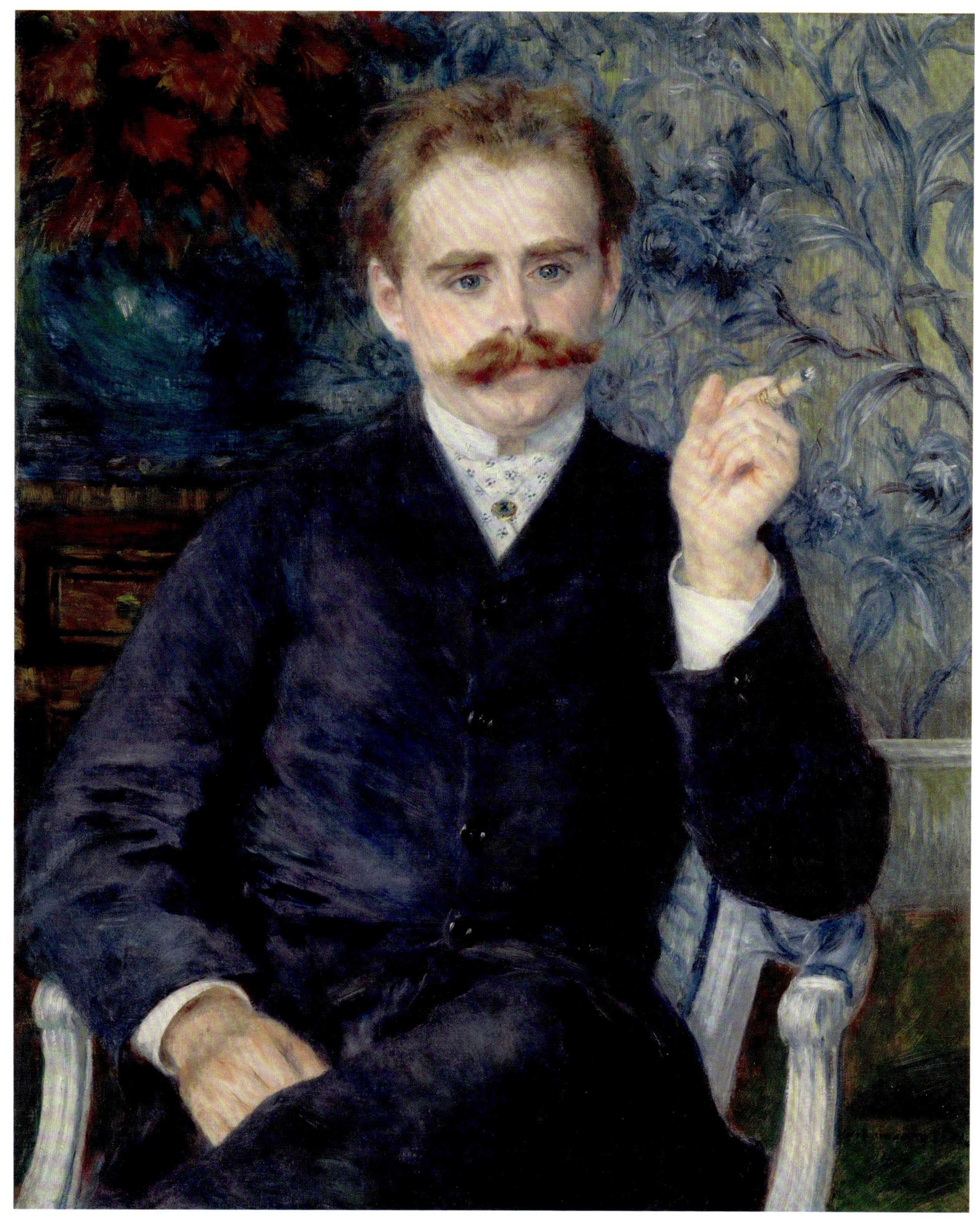

CAT. 3. Pierre-Auguste Renoir, *Albert Cahen d'Anvers*, 1881, oil on canvas, 31½ × 25⅛ in. (80 × 63.8 cm). The J. Paul Getty Museum, Los Angeles.

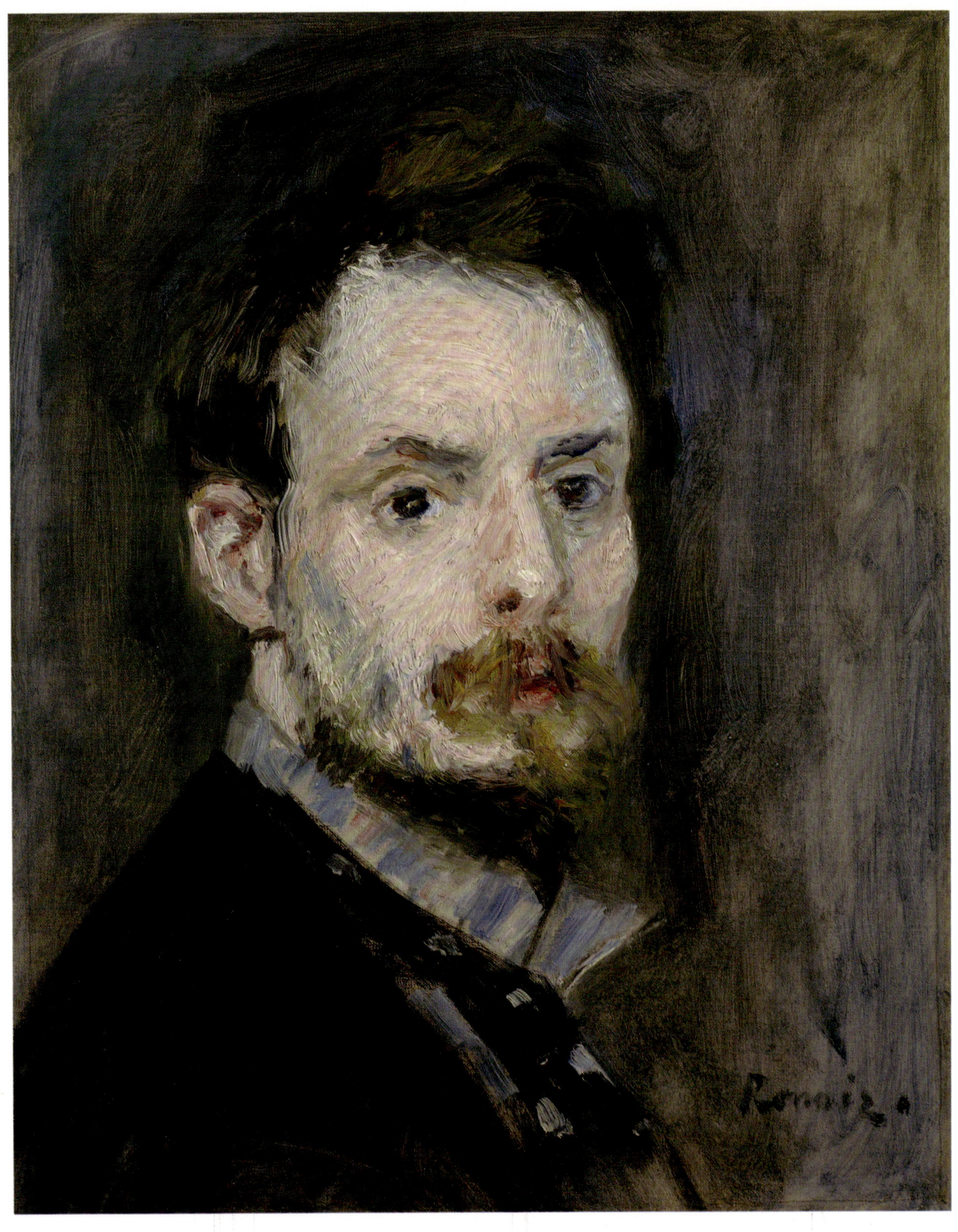

CAT. 4. Pierre-Auguste Renoir, *Self-Portrait* (*Autoportrait*), c. 1875, oil on canvas,
15⅜ × 12⁷⁄₁₆ in. (39.1 × 31.6 cm). Sterling and Francine Clark Art Institute, Williamstown, MA.

Madame Charpentier) or as significant as art, architecture, and history, about which he could voice strong opinions.[14] Another significant contact for Renoir that reflects the breadth of his social circle was Paul Berard, who invited him to his summer house on the Normandy coast, the Château de Wargemont, every summer from 1879 for at least six years. At this grand country establishment Renoir could settle in for a stay of many weeks, painting portraits and decorations. He was at home with everyone, happily joining the cook for a trip to the market or the gardener to tend the beautiful grounds. But he also became one of Paul Berard's close friends. A wealthy banker who led a glamorous life in Paris, Berard was relaxed and informal at Wargemont, slipping into country life like a comfortable shoe. While Jacques-Émile Blanche, who visited the Berards from his house near Dieppe, described Renoir as "not at all sociable," he says he "became quite cheerful among his genuine admirers at the Château de Wargemont."[15] Duret describes Renoir as "a man full of kindness. . . . The charm Renoir put into his works came, first of all, from his technique, but also from his conduct. . . . He looked at life on the bright side, and therefore was easy to meet and to live with."[16] Rivière, too, describes Renoir's acts of kindness to those less fortunate than he.[17] With Caillebotte, Renoir could engage in animated debates, teasing his more literate friend in discussions of art, politics, and history.[18] One more source deserves special mention: Paul Durand-Ruel. Although the dealer came to appreciate Renoir's work later than that of some of the other impressionists, he developed a closer, warmer relationship with him than with any other. Without a doubt this gift of friendship affected Renoir's success as a portrait artist: one testimony to this is that the extremely numerous sessions he required to paint the portrait of Madame Charpentier and her children produced, rather than irritation,

a warm friendship. He wrote engagingly to Georges Charpentier to "have the goodness to thank Mme Charpentier on behalf of her most devoted artist, and to say that if I eventually achieve success it will be owing to her, for I am certainly not capable of it alone."[19] This friendship and critical support may be the subject Renoir celebrated in his major undertaking yet to come, *Luncheon of the Boating Party*.

Modeling for Renoir

For over a century a name has been attached to most of the figures in *Luncheon of the Boating Party*. Julius Meier-Graefe, whose monograph on Renoir was published in German in 1911 and in French in 1912, updated and expanded these early editions twice, in 1920 and 1929. In the 1929 edition, he attached names to nine individuals in the painting, adding seven to the two specified in his first edition (the woman to become the artist's wife and Charles Ephrussi). It is tempting to imagine that Meier-Graefe sat down with Renoir during the late years of the artist's life to ask him about his work and some of his most important paintings. The identifications cited by Meier-Graefe in 1929 precisely match those inscribed on a photograph in the archives of Durand-Ruel & Cie (fig. 2); that they correspond so exactly suggests that one was a source for the other.[20] The early photograph dates from c.1891 when the painting was still in the possession of Durand-Ruel; and the inscriptions around the edge are thought to be from about that time. These identifications of models were subsequently carefully transferred to the back of another photograph, probably dating from the early 1920s, perhaps around the same time that The Phillips Collection was acquiring the painting and added by the hand of Charles Durand-Ruel (grandson of Paul).[21] Paul Durand-Ruel, who was so close to

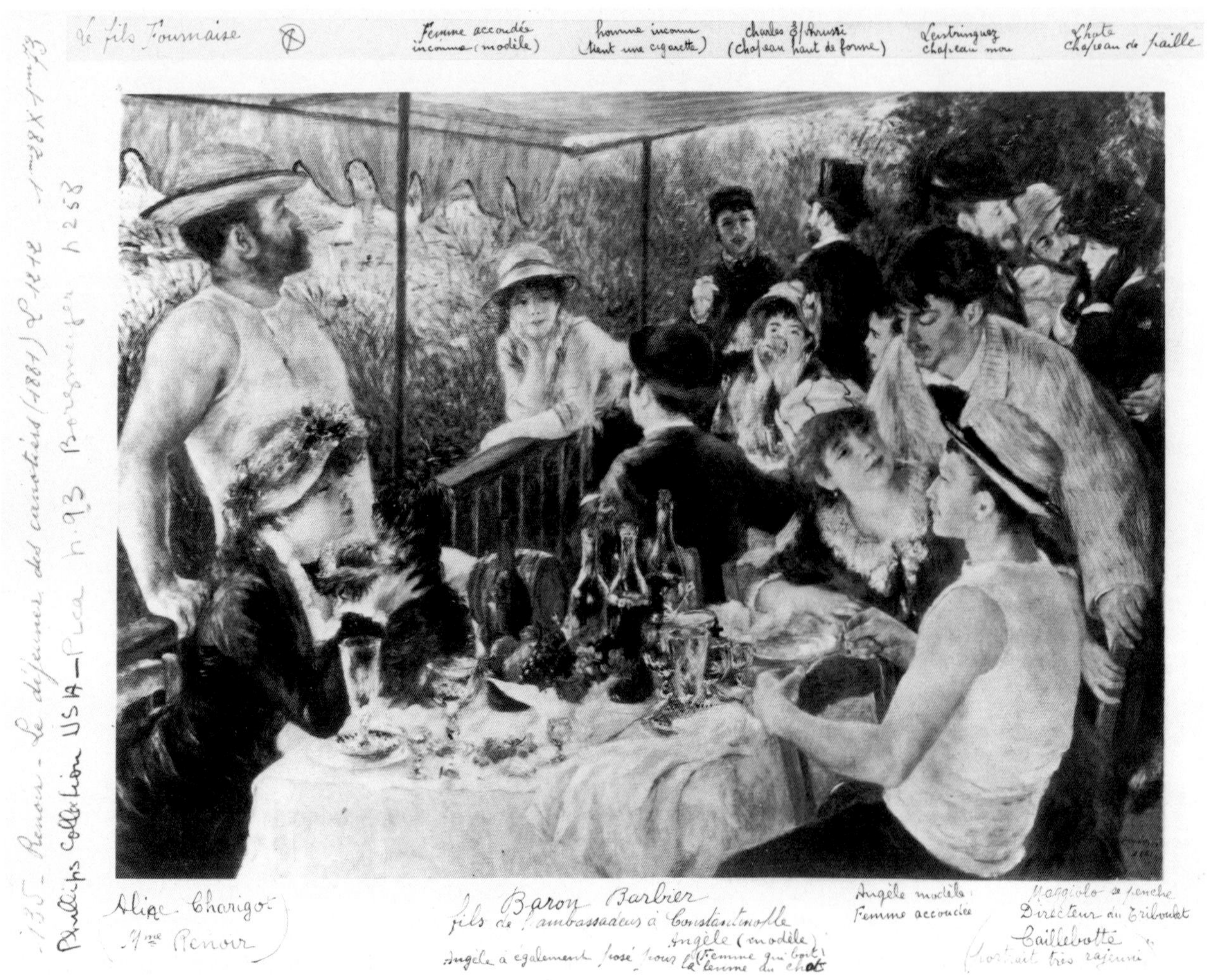

FIG. 2. Paul Durand-Ruel, photograph of Renoir's *Luncheon of the Boating Party*, c. 1891, annotated with "Phillips Collection, USA" at a later date. Archives Durand-Ruel, Paris.

Renoir personally, and Meier-Graefe, who published the earliest monograph on Renoir, well within his lifetime, appear most likely to have received these identifications from the artist himself.[22]

That names were attached to so many figures in the painting is not surprising when we consider this work in light of other genre scenes by Renoir. He often identified his models, sometimes in interviews, such as the one conducted by Ambroise Vollard (*Renoir: An Intimate Record*); specific models are mentioned consistently in the literature.[23] In some instances a painting gave away the identity of its model by the artist's truth to the subject's recognizable features. At other times Renoir would soften or generalize visual identities.[24] *Luncheon of the Boating Party* is a genre scene, not a group portrait, and the identities of the models are more complicated than might at first appear. Engaging friends for a commitment of days or weeks was no easy task, further complicated by the fact that Renoir, having made no preliminary study, rubbed out some passages and made significant changes. Fourteen individuals emerge in the final composition, but clearly more than fourteen came to Chatou, in a group or one or two at a time, to pose for hours on the terrace of the Fournaise. Renoir himself complains of one of them, "a high-class tart" whom he dismissed from the project, and a letter in the Durand-Ruel archives tells us that the Lemoine brothers (of Lemoine et Cie, a publishing house in the 8th arrondissement) posed more often than Gustave Caillebotte did.[25] Despite not being identified in the literature, they must be added to the list of those who helped Renoir achieve his grand project.

Clearly motives beyond mere convenience or availability guided Renoir's choice of models for *Luncheon of the Boating Party*. Of the fourteen figures, three create a compositional framework for the painting: Aline Charigot (in the left foreground), Gustave Caillebotte (in the right foreground), and Charles Ephrussi (in the far background). These individuals anchored this project for Renoir and, in an essential way, enabled him to achieve it. The two "physically" closest to the viewer are the people Renoir was personally closest to; Ephrussi, who was strategically most critical to him, takes his place at the apex of this triangular composition, a keystone of sorts. With his gaze turned away from us, he nonetheless stands out in his customary top hat—anomalous city attire in a country setting. That the man in the right foreground is not an unmistakable likeness of Caillebotte is less important than the fact that this figure is a lover of boating: he's dressed for it, with the hat not of an oarsman but of a gentleman sailor, and he appears to look right past all who surround him to the boats and the river beyond the balcony, as if eager to paint the view himself. That Caillebotte inspired this figure can hardly be doubted when we consider that his friendship with Renoir was at its strongest in the late 1870s and early 1880s; that the two shared the subject matter as well as the activity of boating on the Seine; and that Caillebotte at this moment was no longer spending time on the Yerres River where his boating days began, but soon

bought a property around the bend from Chatou at Petit-Gennevilliers. A close and trusting friendship between Caillebotte and Renoir is manifested by Caillebotte becoming godfather to Renoir's son Pierre and Renoir being named executor of Caillebotte's will; they painted each other's sweethearts and saw each other constantly (Cat. 5). What more could speak to the likelihood that in *Luncheon of the Boating Party* Renoir invokes the persona of his good friend, Gustave Caillebotte? Who else takes his place so naturally in a painting about a convivial lunch after boating on the river?

Virtually all the early monographs that mention *Luncheon of the Boating Party* in detail name Aline Charigot, Renoir's future wife, as a model for the painting. Charigot had already posed for him on a number of occasions in works that speak to their evolving relationship; showing her quietly sewing or reading a fashion journal (Cats. 6 and 7), these works express an intimacy between artist and sitter.[26] Most exceptional is a pastel from about 1880 (Cat. 8)—one of quite a few from this moment in Renoir's career—in which he may reference himself as the male protagonist engaged in an intimate exchange with a young woman generally assumed to be Aline Charigot. The viewer sees her over his shoulder while she gazes directly into his eyes, her hand clutching a bouquet of violets, with a ring on her third finger. Her straw hat, with a silk flower embellishing the ribbon, looks similar to the one worn by Charigot in *Luncheon of the Boating Party*, whereas he appears to be wearing the jacket donned by the writer and critic Adrien Maggiolo in that painting. Probably in the summer of 1880, not long before embarking on his large canvas, Renoir painted Charigot with her little dog (Cat. 9), seated informally on the grass, quite possibly in the environs of the Maison Fournaise, prefiguring her appearance with the dog in *Luncheon of the Boating Party*.

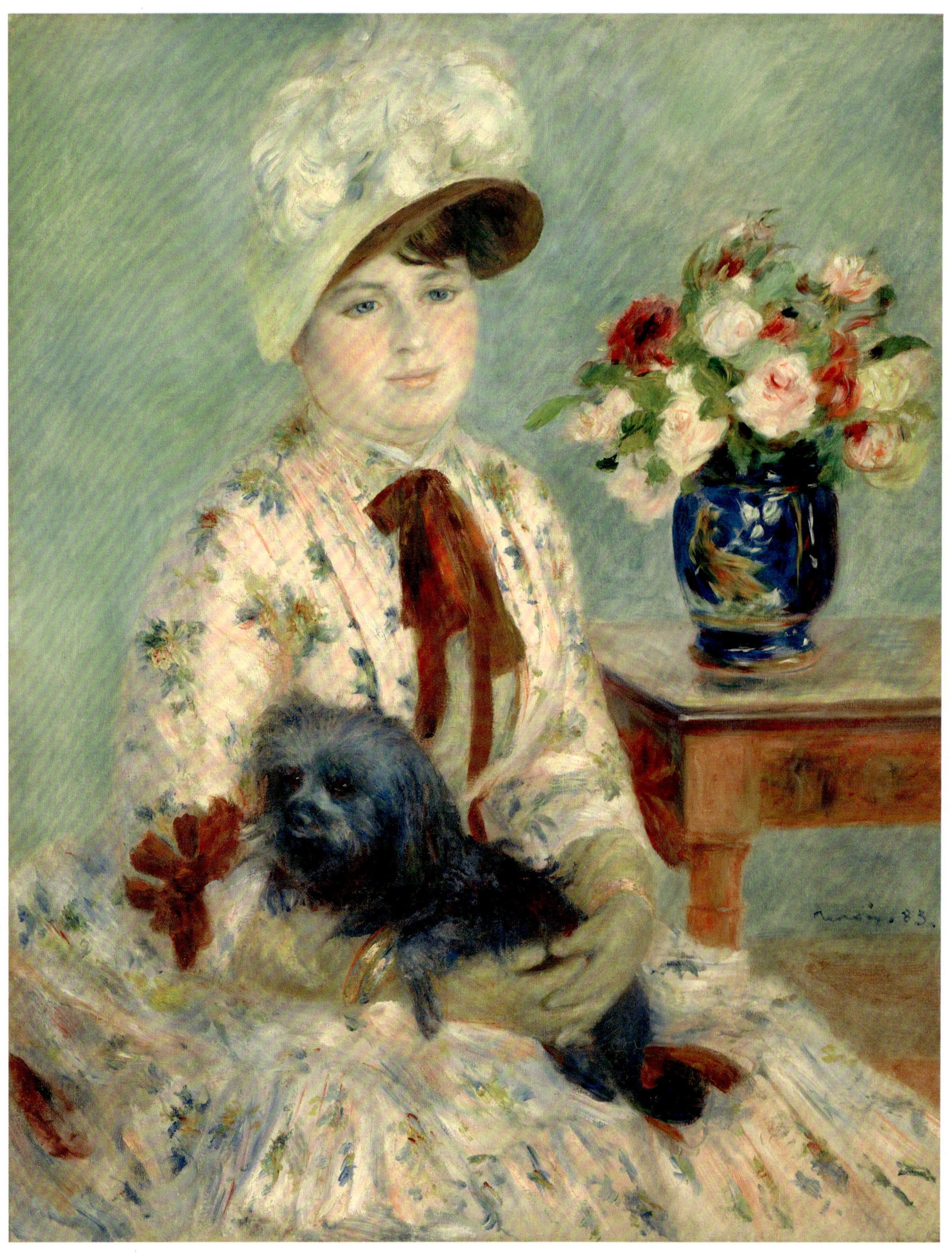

CAT. 5. Pierre-Auguste Renoir, *Mademoiselle Charlotte Berthier*, 1883, oil on canvas, 36¼ × 28¾ in.
(92.1 × 73 cm). National Gallery of Art, Washington, D.C., Gift of Angelika Wertheim Frink.

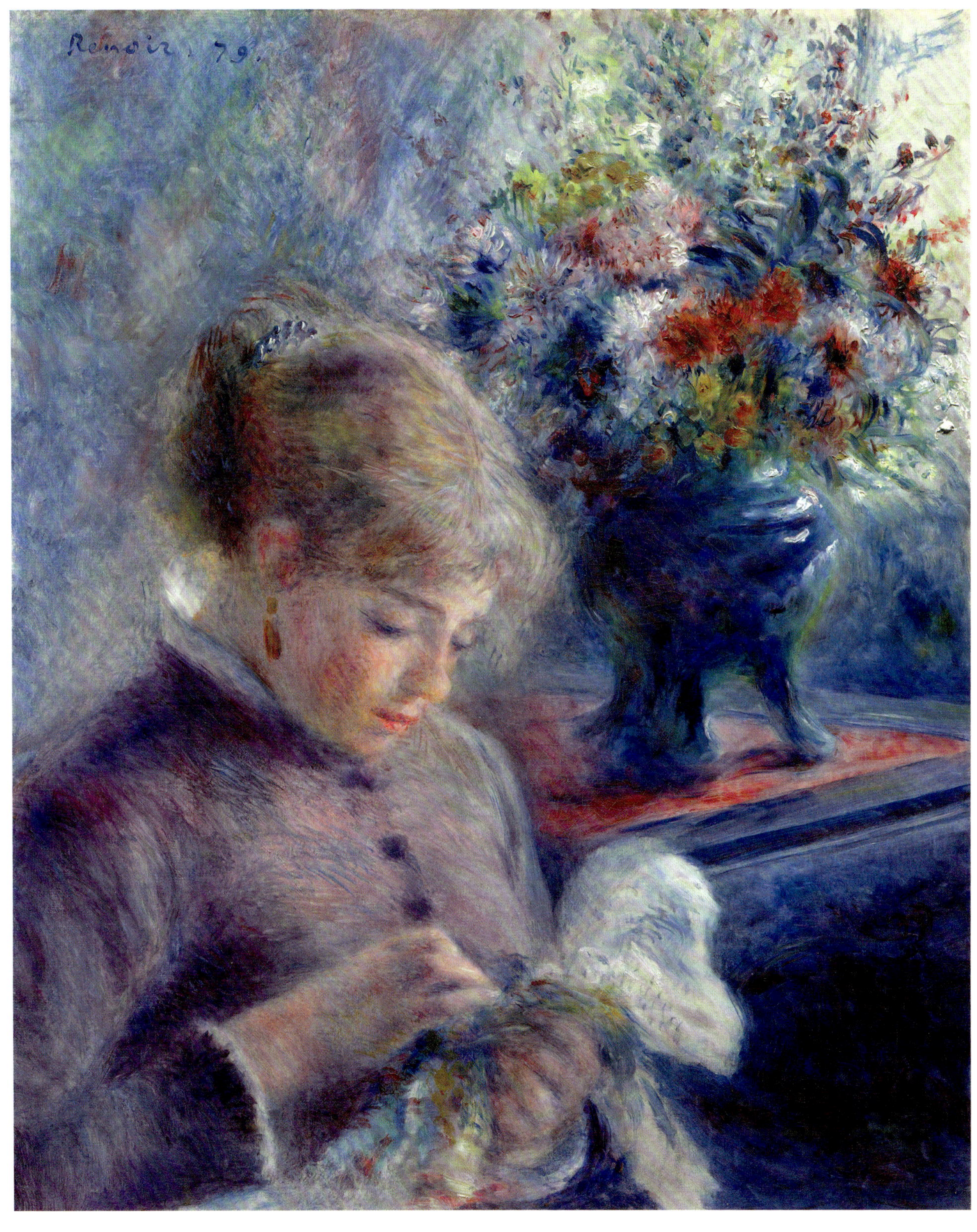

CAT. 6. Pierre-Auguste Renoir, *Young Woman Sewing* (*Jeune femme cousant*), c. 1879, oil on canvas, 24³/₁₆ × 19⅞ in. (61.4 × 50.5 cm). The Art Institute of Chicago, Mr. & Mrs. Lewis Larned Coburn Memorial Collection.

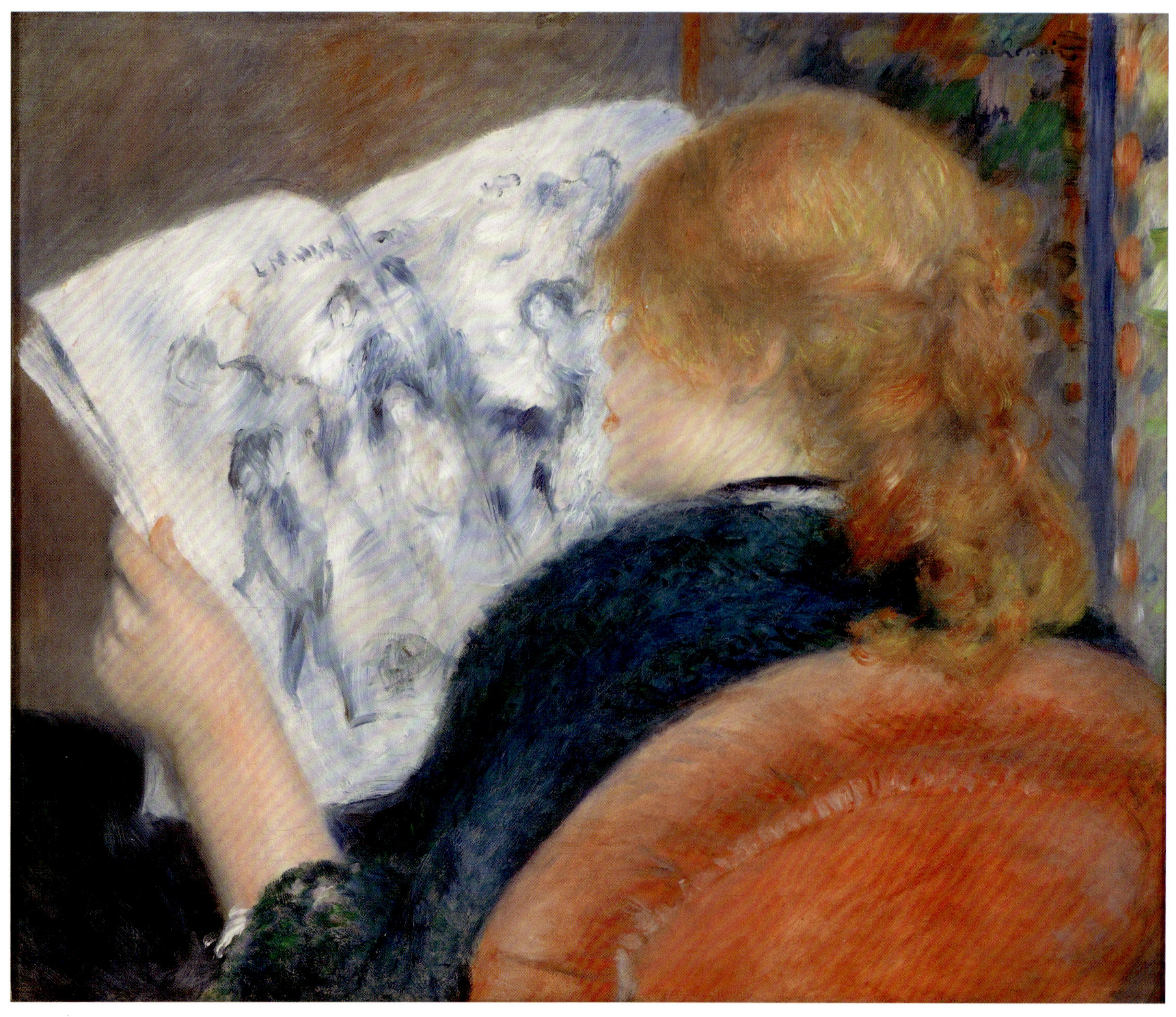

CAT. 7. Pierre-Auguste Renoir, *Young Woman Reading an Illustrated Journal* (*Jeune femme lisant un journal illustré*), c. 1880, oil on canvas, 18¼ × 22 in. (46.4 × 57.1 cm). Museum of Art, Rhode Island School of Design, Providence, RI, Museum Appropriation Fund 22.125.

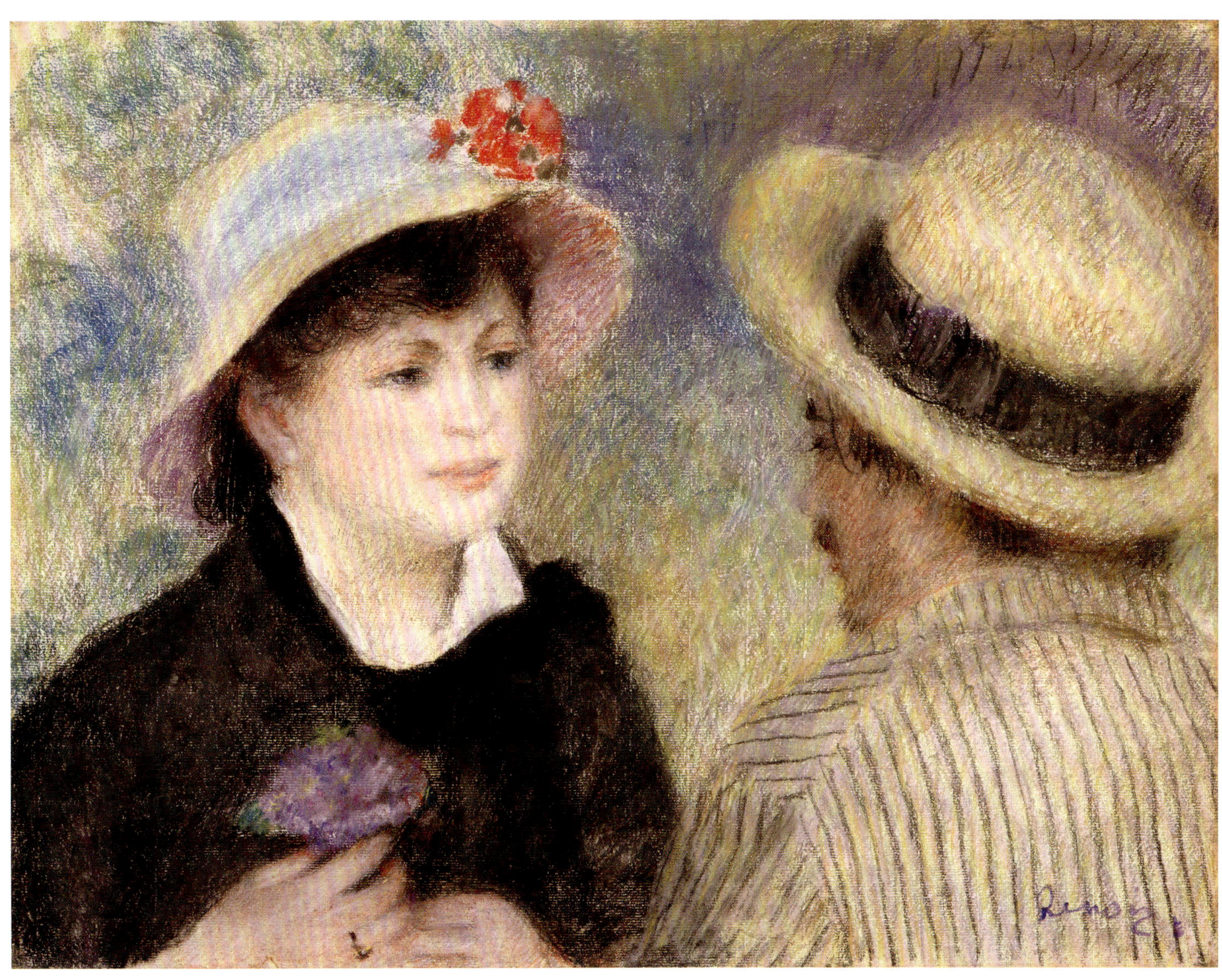

CAT. 8. Pierre-Auguste Renoir, *Boating Couple* (*Les Canotiers*), about 1881, pastel on paper, 17¾ × 23 in. (45.1 × 58.4 cm).
Museum of Fine Arts, Boston, given in memory of Governor Alvan T. Fuller by the Fuller Foundation.

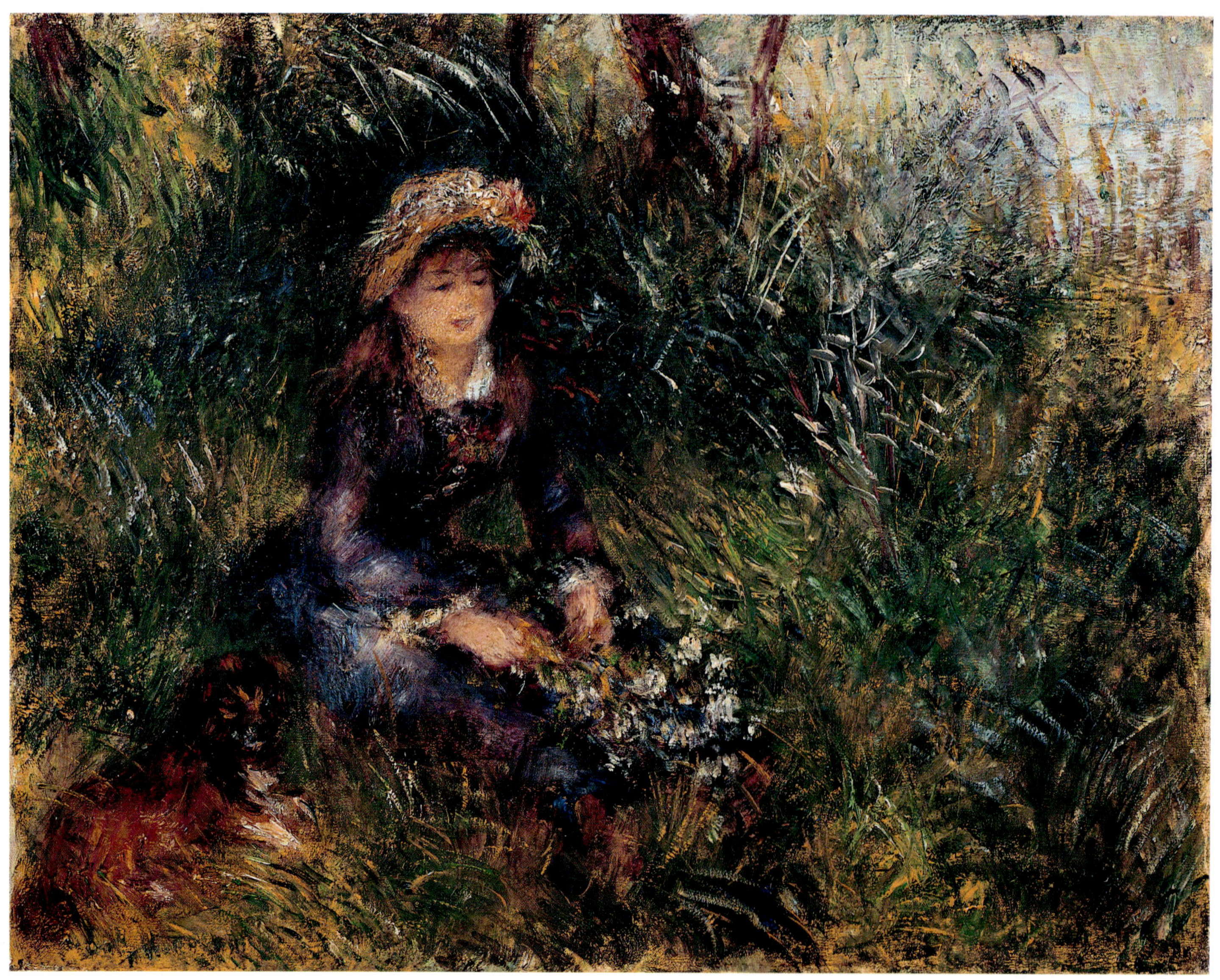

CAT. 9. Pierre-Auguste Renoir, *Madame Renoir with a Dog* (*Madame Renoir au chien*), 1880,
oil on canvas, 12¼ × 16⅛ in. (31 × 41 cm). Private collection, in cooperation with Durand-Ruel & Cie, Paris.

FIG. 3. *Chatou – Restaurant Fournaise*, digital print from an early 20th-century postcard. Via Joconde – Portail des collections des musées de France.

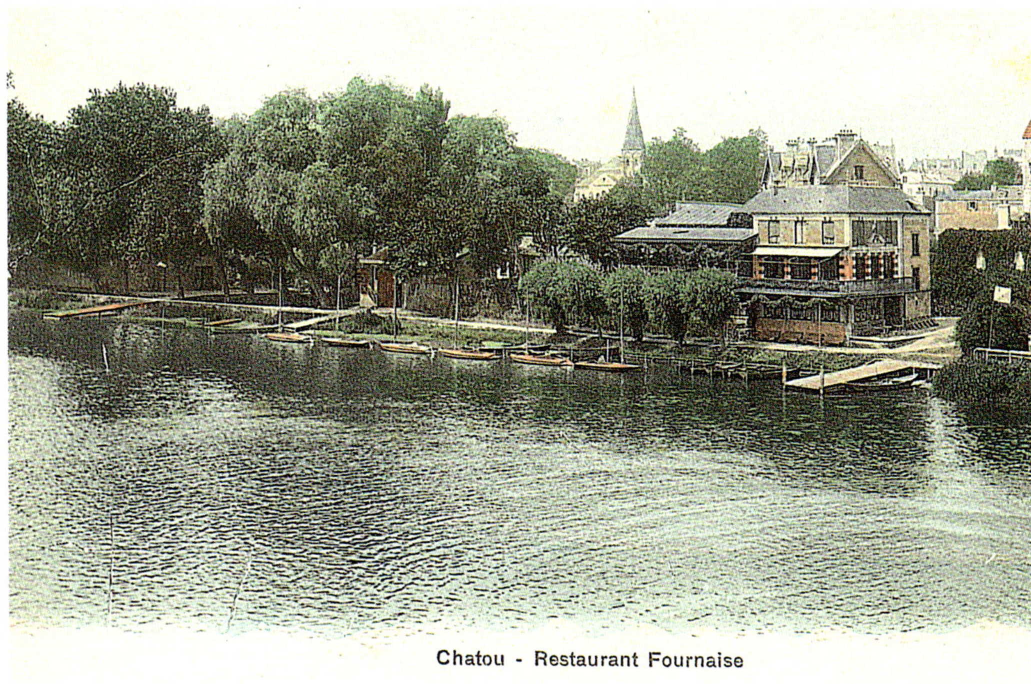

Also close in time to his larger undertaking, Renoir painted Aline and Caillebotte on the banks of the river, where an oarsman offers her a ride, though she demurely declines (see Cat. 29). A country girl at heart, Aline enjoyed activities at the Fournaise, a place Renoir knew well by the time he first brought her there. Throughout the 1870s he had frequently traveled west of Paris to visit his mother in Louveciennes and to paint along the Seine near Chatou (Cats. 2, 10–11). He became a frequent visitor to the Maison Fournaise, befriended the family, and painted a portrait of Père Fournaise and quite a few works in oil and pastel of his daughter Alphonsine (Cat. 21). Meier-Graefe names Alphonse Fournaise Jr. (Hippolyte-Alphonse Fournaise, 1848–1910) in *Luncheon of the Boating Party*, but doesn't identify the casually dressed, straw-hatted young woman also leaning on the railing as his sister Alphonsine. Standing behind Aline, opposite the Caillebotte-inspired figure, and looking towards the top-hatted man who stands out in this company, the young Alphonse epitomizes a strapping oarsman. Unlike his sister, he is thought to have modeled for only one other painting, *Dance at Bougival* (fig. 4), in which the female dancer was first modeled by Aline Charigot—in clogs and a straw hat, he looks a far cry from the male partner in *Dance in the Country* (Cat. 27) and *Dance in the City* (Musée d'Orsay, Paris) both modeled by Paul Lhote.[27]

Paul-Auguste Lhote (1851–1894) and Eugène-Pierre Lestringuez (1847–1908), who had modeled as dancers for Renoir's *Dance at Le Moulin de la Galette*, are named by both Meier-Graefe and Durand-Ruel as models for *Luncheon of the Boating Party*.[28] Though younger than Renoir by nine and six years respectively, they were among his closest friends. Lestringuez, who worked for the Ministry of the Interior, moved in literary and artistic circles, and met Renoir in the mid-1870s. Described by Rivière as "élégant, distingué, souriant dans sa barbe blonde très soignée," he traveled with Renoir and Lhote to Algeria in 1881, served as witness at Renoir's marriage to Aline Charigot in 1890, and attended the baptism of their second son, Jean, in 1894.[29]

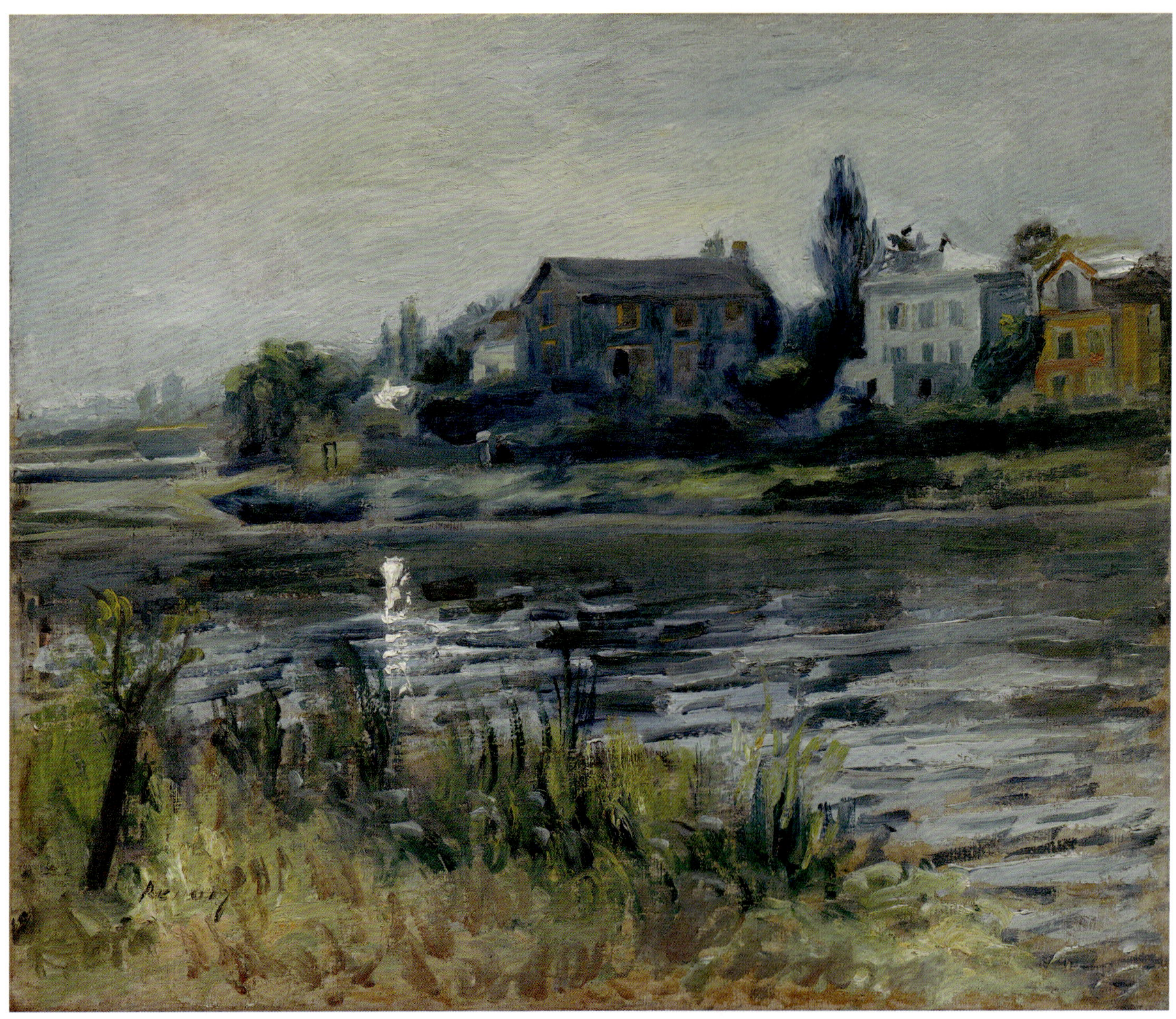

CAT. 10. Pierre-Auguste Renoir, *The Seine at Chatou* (*La Seine à Chatou*), c. 1871,
oil on canvas, 18⅜ × 22¹⁄₁₆ in. (46.7 × 56.1 cm). Art Gallery of Ontario, Toronto, Purchased 1935.

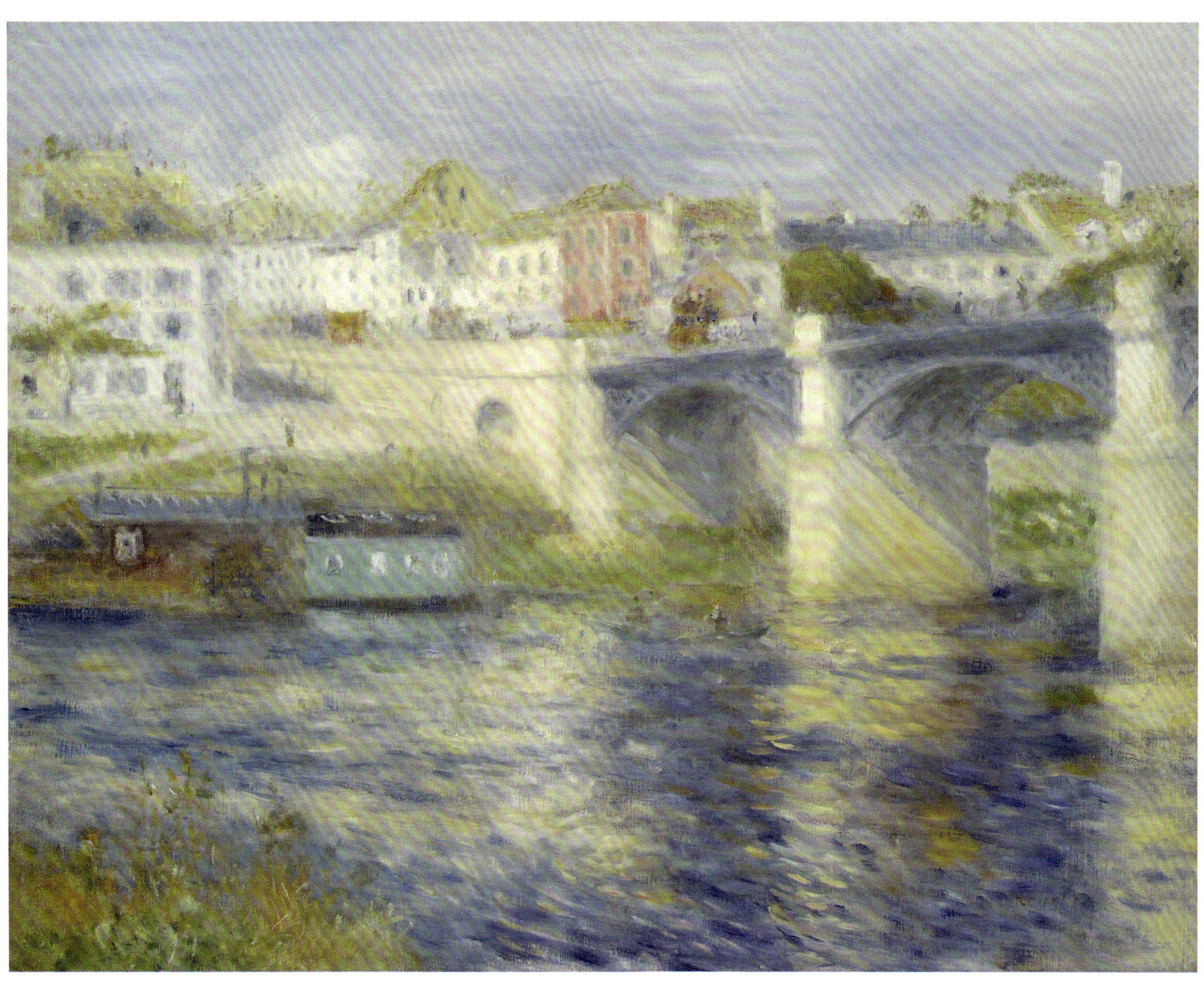

CAT. 11. Pierre-Auguste Renoir, *Bridge at Chatou* (*Pont à Chatou*), c. 1875, oil on canvas,
20⅛ × 25¾ in. (51.1 × 65.4 cm). Sterling and Francine Clark Art Institute, Williamstown, MA.

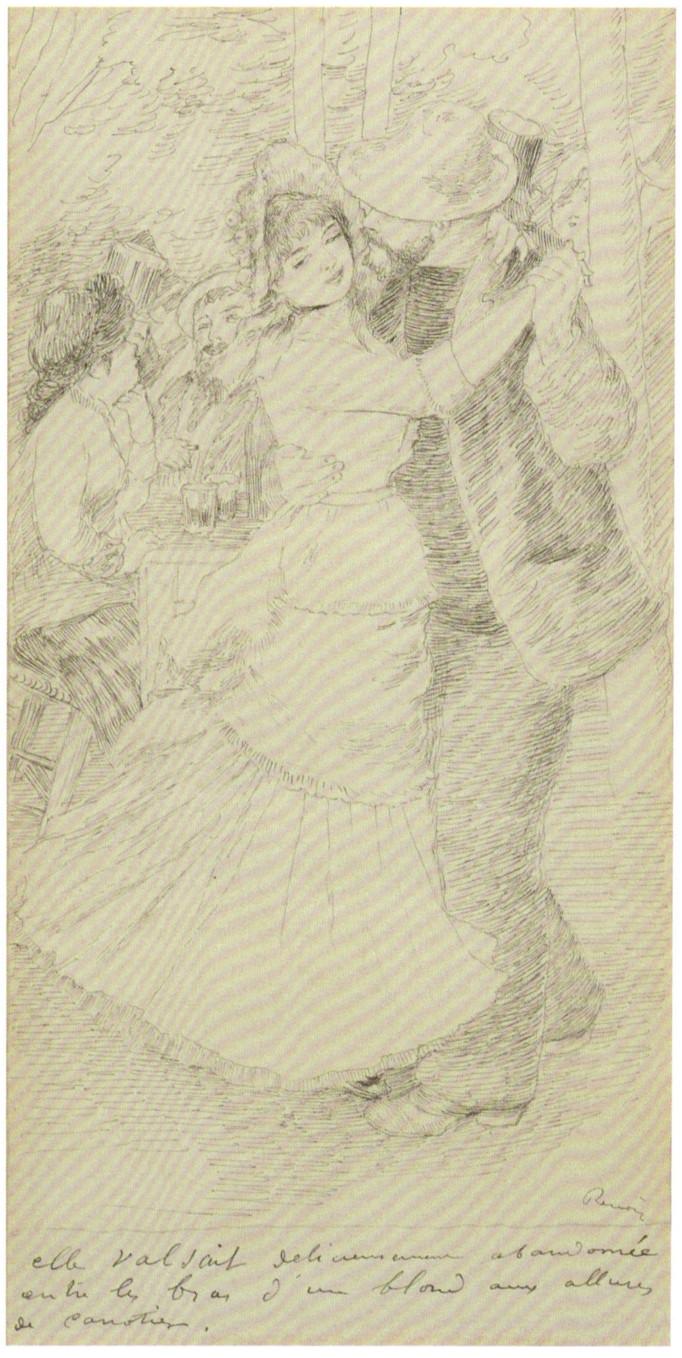

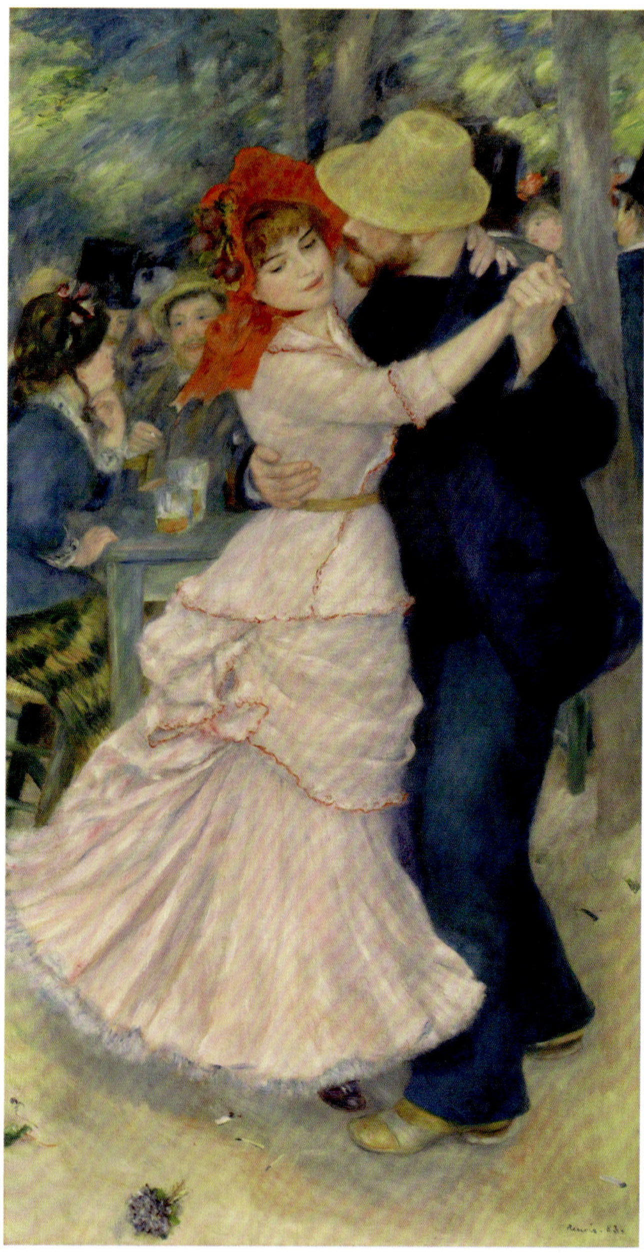

CAT. 12. Pierre-Auguste Renoir, *Dancing Couple* (study for
Dance at Bougival [*Danse à Bougival*]), 1883, pen and ink
on white wove paper, 11¹⁵⁄₁₆ × 7⁹⁄₁₆ in. (30.3 × 19.2 cm).
Philadelphia Museum of Art, The Henry P. McIlhenny
Collection in Memory of Frances P. McIlhenny, 1986.

FIG. 4. Pierre-Auguste Renoir, *Dance at Bougival* (*Danse à
Bougival*), 1883, oil on canvas, 71⅝ × 38⅝ in. (181.9 × 98.1 cm).
Museum of Fine Arts, Boston.

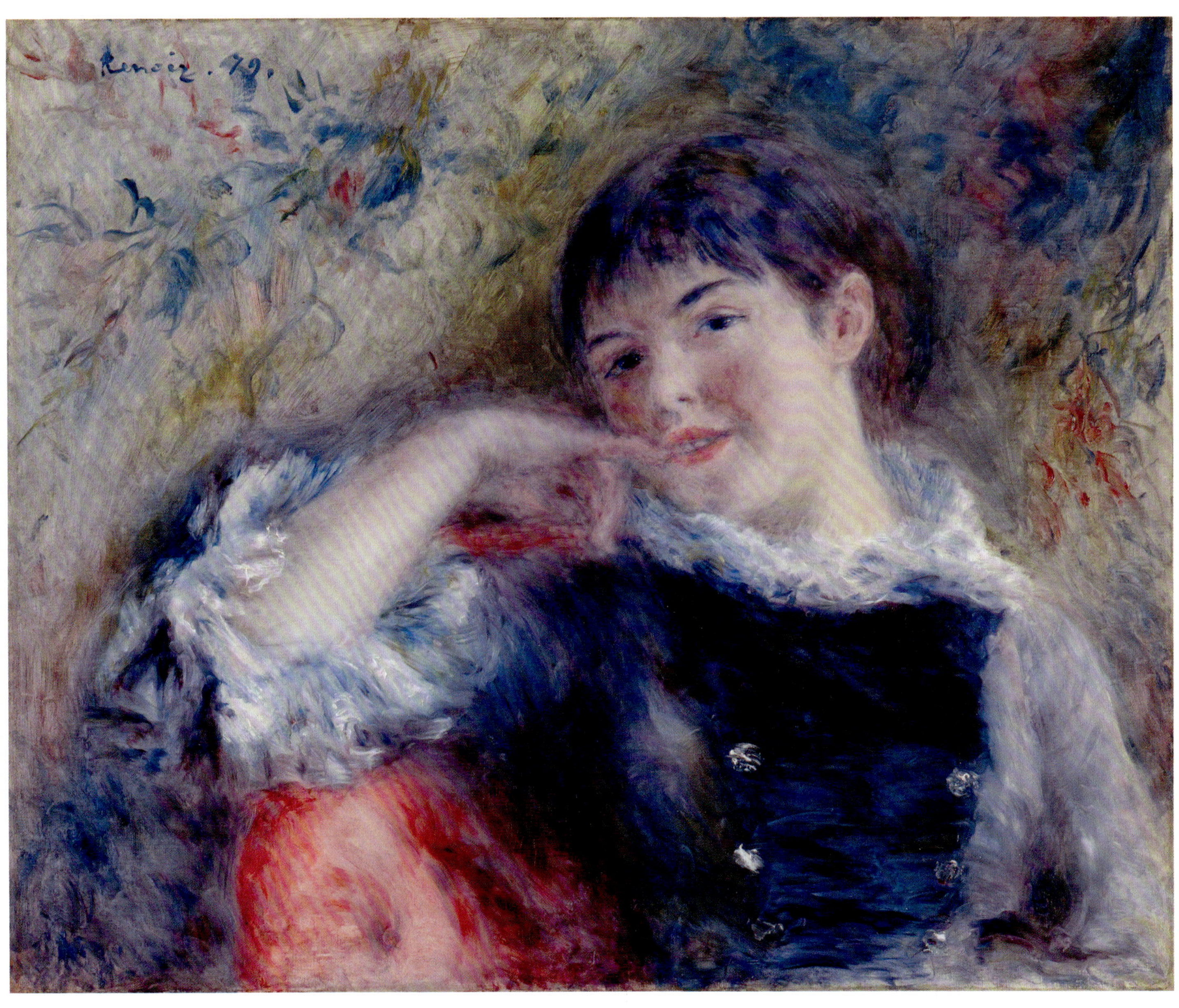

CAT. 13. Pierre-Auguste Renoir, *The Dreamer* (*La Rêveuse*), 1879, oil on canvas, 20⅛ × 24⅜ in. (51.1 × 61.9 cm). Saint Louis Art Museum, Museum purchase.

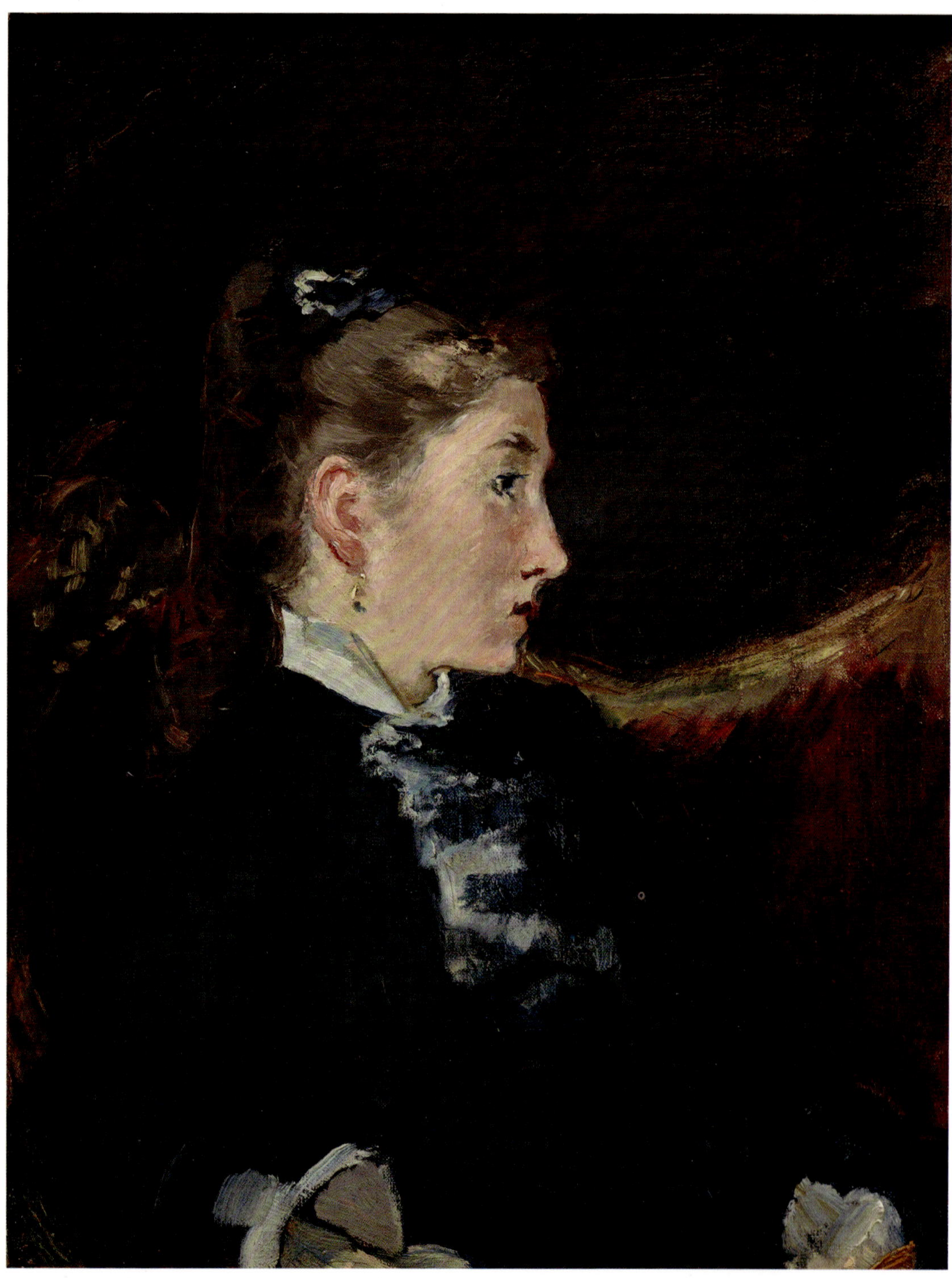

CAT. 14. Édouard Manet, *Portrait of a Young Woman – Mademoiselle Ellen Andrée* (*Portrait d'une jeune femme – mademoiselle Ellen Andrée*), c. 1880, oil on canvas, 12 × 9¼ in. (33 × 25 cm). Private collection.

In Renoir's large composition at the Fournaise, Lestringuez stands at the back of the crowd with Lhote, who wears the sailor's striped attire and hat, addressing in seemingly familiar terms a young woman who covers her ears. Lhote, "polyglotte extraordinaire" and "infatigable voyageur," per Rivière, traveled the world, including a yearlong walking trip across Germany from Strasbourg to Vienna.[30] After crossing the Atlantic as a cruise ship officer from Le Havre to New York, volunteering in a Zouave regiment, and finally settling in Paris, he worked for Agence Havas.[31] According to Jean Renoir, this risk-taking adventurer was near-sighted and had a weakness for ladies.[32] He frequently modeled for Renoir in the late 1870s and early 1880s, including as the male dancer for *Dance in the Country* (Cat. 28) and *Dance in the City* in 1882. When he died suddenly from pneumonia in 1894, at the age of forty-three, he was described as "écrivain ingénieux, esprit d'élite, et homme de cœur."[33] Lhote wrote a short story, "Mademoiselle Zélia," for Georges Charpentier's illustrated journal *La Vie moderne* in November 1883 that was illustrated by an engraving by Renoir based on his painting *Dance at Bougival*.

More speculative is the possible identity of the young woman who covers her ears. Jean Renoir first suggested that Jeanne Samary could have posed for this figure, and the same identification is made in the 1971 catalogue raisonné by François Daulte. Certainly she had been a frequent subject of portraits in oil and pastel by Renoir in the years immediately preceding *Luncheon of the Boating Party*; moreover, Michel Robida (grandnephew of the Charpentiers) tells us that she occasionally went to the Fournaise—which supports her being chosen as a model, given Renoir's desire not to invent but to depict individuals in settings they were accustomed to.[34] Indeed, he had painted her enough times that it is conceivable he

evoked a likeness of her at least partially from memory. Her gloved hands suggest she has just arrived from, or is about to leave for, the city. Her gesture of covering her ears finds plausible explanation in the fact that she was during the summer of 1880 the subject of gossip about her engagement to a banker, whose parents didn't approve despite her considerable fame on stage.

Two other young women who became actresses and modeled frequently for Renoir at the end of the 1870s appear to have modeled for the *Luncheon* as well. A young woman called Angèle is named by Meier-Graefe and Durand-Ruel as modeling for both the woman who leans on the railing and the woman with a glass raised to her lips in the center of the composition.[35] According to Rivière, Angèle was a florist and an artist's model who seemingly lived without a care in the world.[36] The other young woman whose name is associated with the painting is Ellen Andrée (born Hélène André, c. 1855/1857), who posed often for Manet, Degas (Cats. 14 and 15), and Renoir, most significantly in Renoir's *After Lunch* (*La Fin du déjeuner*) (Städel, Frankfurt, 1879).[37] A snub-nosed, lively young woman of barely twenty years of age when they met, she joined the artists' circle at the Café Nouvelle Athènes, married flower painter Henri Dumont, and joined the naturalist theater. Certainly the roles she played in paintings varied greatly, including that of a dissolute woman in Degas's *L'Absinthe* (Musée d'Orsay, Paris, 1875–1876), where she stares vacantly at the glass on the table in front of her. While the woman in the right foreground of *Luncheon of the Boating Party* resembles Ellen Andrée, she also looks like Angèle in a theater publicity photograph, raising the question of whether Renoir may on rare occasions have painted from photographs (fig. 6).[38] It's also possible Ellen and Angèle modeled interchangeably for these two young women as Renoir worked on his grand composition.[39]

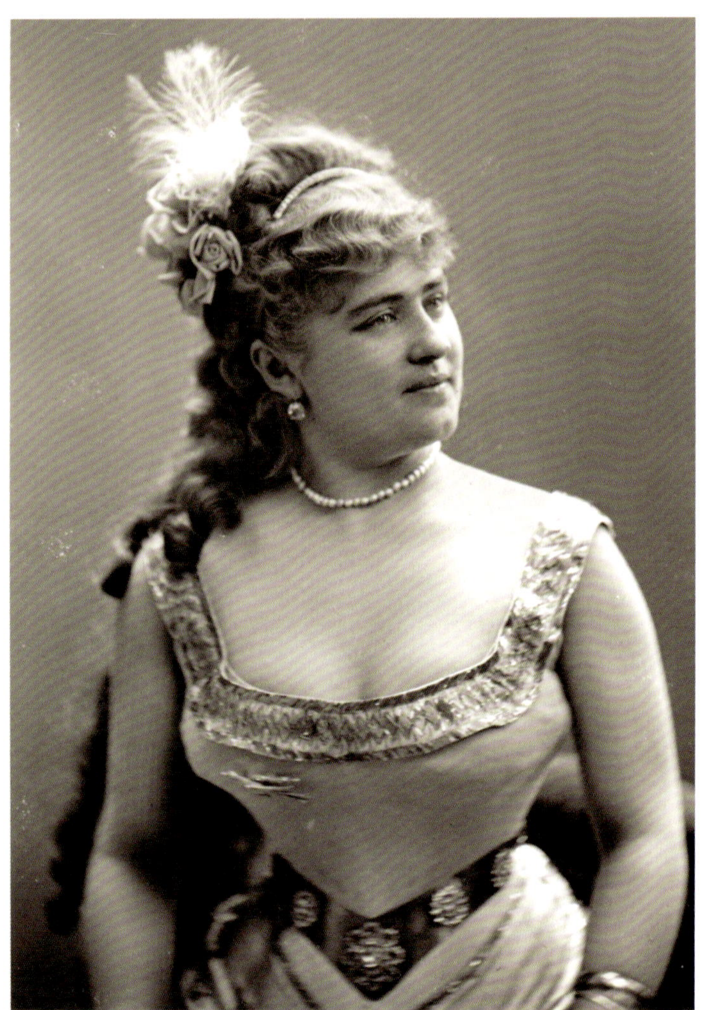

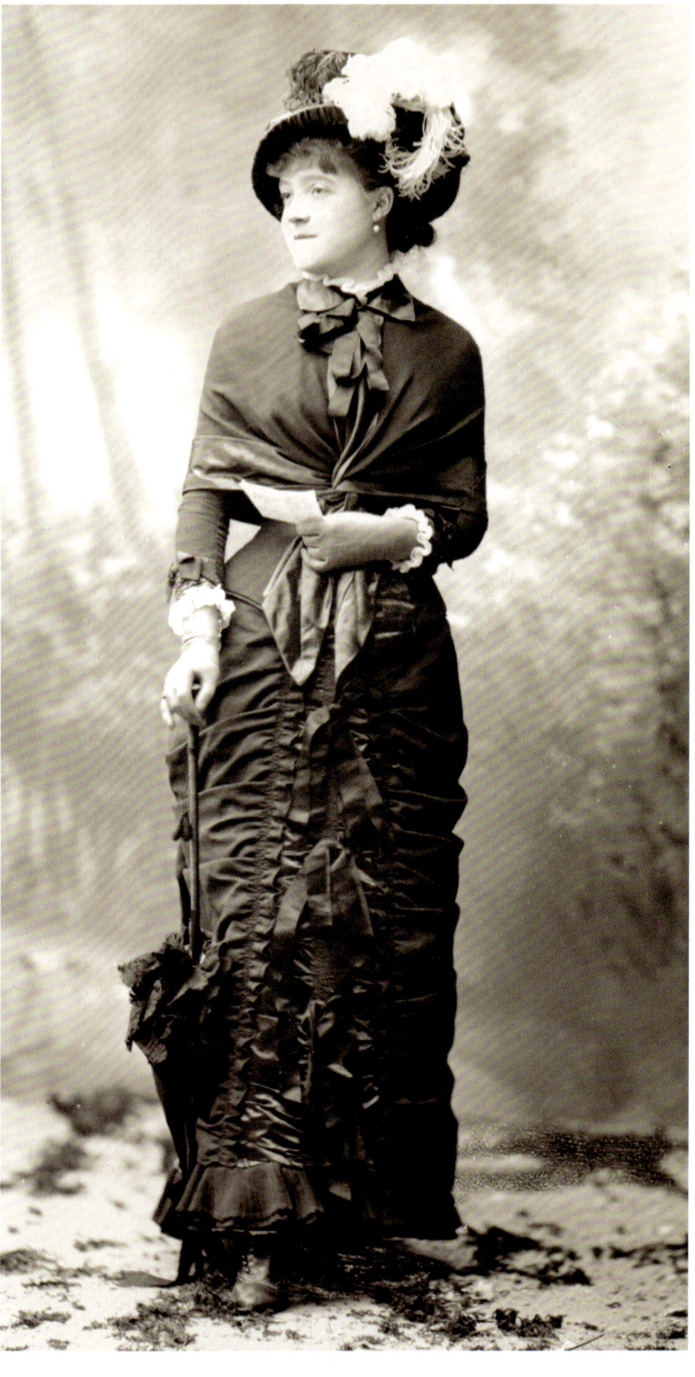

FIG. 5. Nadar (Gaspar-Félix Tournachon), *Angèle*, modern silver gelatin print from an original of c. 1878. Caisse Nationale des Monuments Historiques et des Sites, Paris.

FIG. 6. Nadar (Gaspar-Félix Tournachon), *Ellen Andrée, Actress* (*Ellen Andree, comédienne*), 1879, modern silver gelatin print from a 19th-century original. Bibliothèque Nationale de France, Paris.

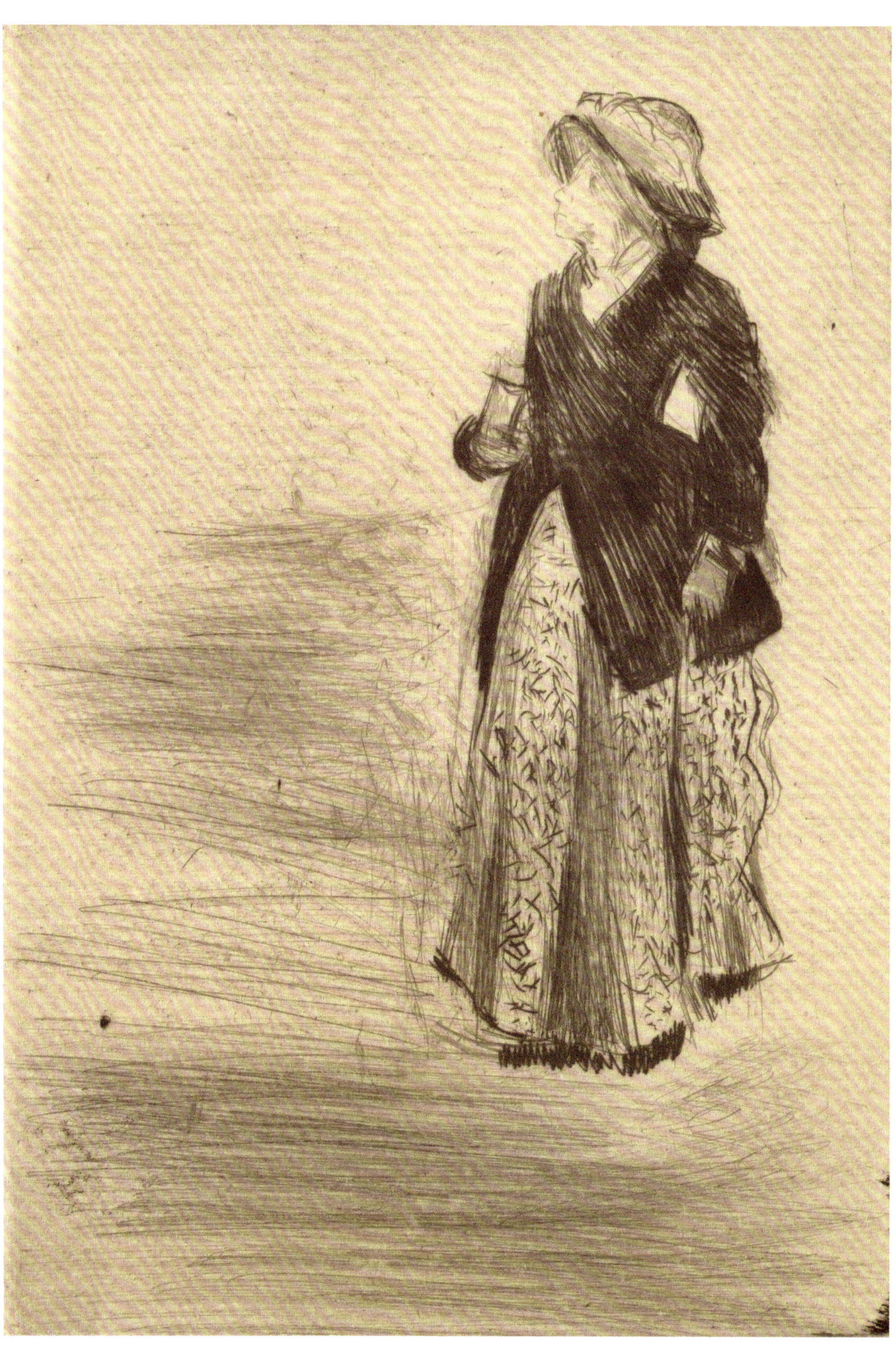

CAT. 15. Edgar Degas, *The Actress Ellen Andrée* (*L'actrice Ellen Andrée*), 1879, drypoint. Platemark: 4⁷⁄₁₆ × 3⅛ in. (11.3 × 7.9 cm), sheet: 8⅝ × 6¼ in. (21.9 × 15.8 cm). Museum of Fine Arts, Boston, Katherine E. Bullard Fund in memory of Francis Bullard, by exchange.

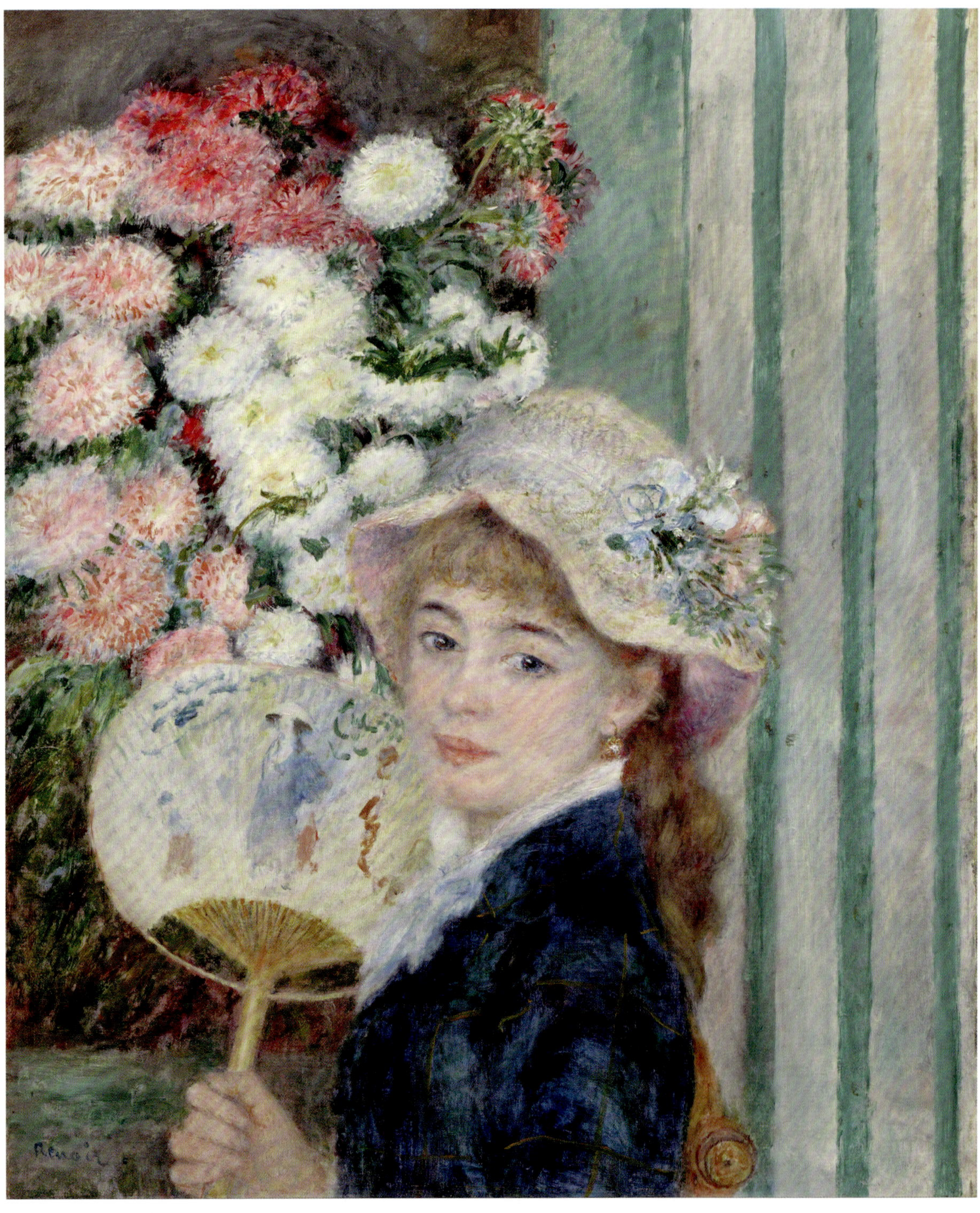

CAT. 16. Pierre-Auguste Renoir, *Woman with a Fan* (*Femme à l'éventail*), c. 1879, oil on canvas,
25¾ × 21¼ in. (65.4 × 54 cm). Sterling and Francine Clark Art Institute, Williamstown, MA.

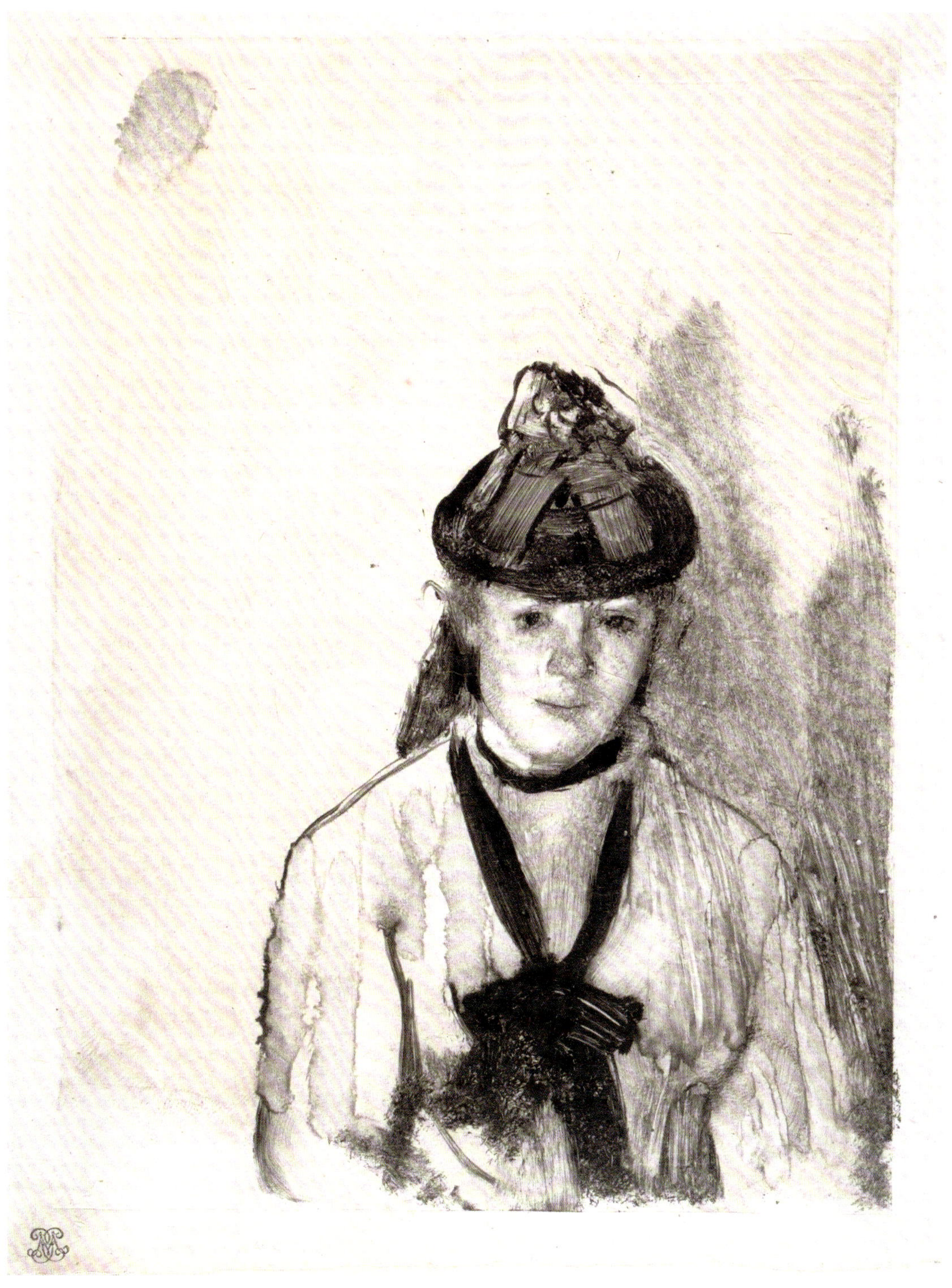

CAT. 17. Edgar Degas, *Portrait of Ellen Andrée* (*Portrait d'Ellen Andrée*), c. 1876, monotype in black and brown ink on ivory paper, perimeter mounted to a cream, laid paper, 8½ × 6¼ in. (21.6 × 16 cm). The Art Institute of Chicago, Potter Palmer Collection.

The young woman caught mid-sip gazes over the rim of her glass to observe a man in a bowler hat, whom we know from early sources as Baron Raoul Barbier (b. 1840). Renoir made two small portraits of him in 1877–1878, possibly also painted at the Fournaise since Barbier was often to be found there (Cat. 18).[40] Having returned in 1876 from years abroad—a former cavalry officer in Algeria and Crimea, he became the second mayor of Saigon (1871–1872) in the early years of French occupation[41]— he seems to have indulged his love of wine, women, and dance in establishments like the Fournaise. A bosom friend of Guy de Maupassant, Barbier was also a theater critic at *Le Chat noir*, revealing his inclination toward the company of artists and writers. Jacques-Émile Blanche tells us that Barbier occasionally stayed at the Berards', where Renoir could have been a guest at the same time. Described by Rivière as a man of inexhaustible energy and goodwill, a natural go-between, he seems fittingly located in the middle of Renoir's composition. Though Renoir depicts Barbier from the back, he is easily identifiable by his hat.

The involvement of Louise Alphonsine Fournaise (1846–1937), daughter of the proprietor, whose name has been associated with the young woman leaning on the railing, is uncertain. Is the model for this figure too young to be Alphonsine, who was born in 1846? By 1880, in her mid-thirties, she had married Louis Joseph Papillon (in 1864), been disgraced by an extramarital affair, and been widowed in 1876.[42] Nor is Alphonsine mentioned by Meier-Graefe or inscribed on the Durand-Ruel photograph. Rather, the model, who may have been Angèle, appears to pose as a working participant in the group, in a role that could in real life have been fulfilled occasionally by Alphonsine herself. Certainly she posed several times for Renoir beginning in the mid-1870s (Cat. 21). Henri Matisse met the elderly Alphonsine in Chatou; when she showed him her portrait by Renoir, he observed that "[h]er features had been changed by old age, but the expression was unaffected. Renoir had captured the essence of the person. And that's precisely Renoir's gift for capturing life."[43]

Viscount Adrien Maggiolo (1842/1843–1894), who wrote books on Robespierre and Voltaire, went into journalism, where he earned a brilliant reputation. Wearing a striped jacket and standing behind the Caillebotte-inspired figure in Renoir's painting, he leans into the conversation engagingly. He worked with *Union* and *France Nouvelle* (at one time editor-in-chief) as well as *Correspondance nationale* and the *Moniteur universel*. Described as an "écrivain, loyal, énergique, plein de verve et de talent," Maggiolo is named in association with *Luncheon of the Boating Party* by both Meier-Graefe and Durand-Ruel.[44]

Another writer-friend, Rivière, earned a living as a government employee but wrote for cultural publications in his free time. He wrote a review of the third impressionist exhibition and became one of Renoir's greatest fans. Praising Renoir's work in 1877, he remarked on "several very beautiful canvases" and said that, in the middle room, "our first glance is drawn to *Dance at Le Moulin de la Galette*," rhapsodizing about the "inspired" subject, "an essentially Parisian work."[45] Though not mentioned as a model for *Luncheon of the Boating Party*, Rivière appears in numerous smaller works from the late 1870s and early 1880s, and in retrospect we can see in many of these Renoir's preparation for the *Luncheon*, depicting as they do an encounter between a man and a woman, the leitmotif of his image of a luncheon by the Seine (Cats. 19, 23). Rivière modeled for *Moulin de la Galette* and was a constant presence in Renoir's life at the time, so an 1877 profile portrait with his strong eyebrows and pencil moustache (Cat. 20) seems to anticipate the small face in profile in the middle of *Luncheon of the Boating Party*.

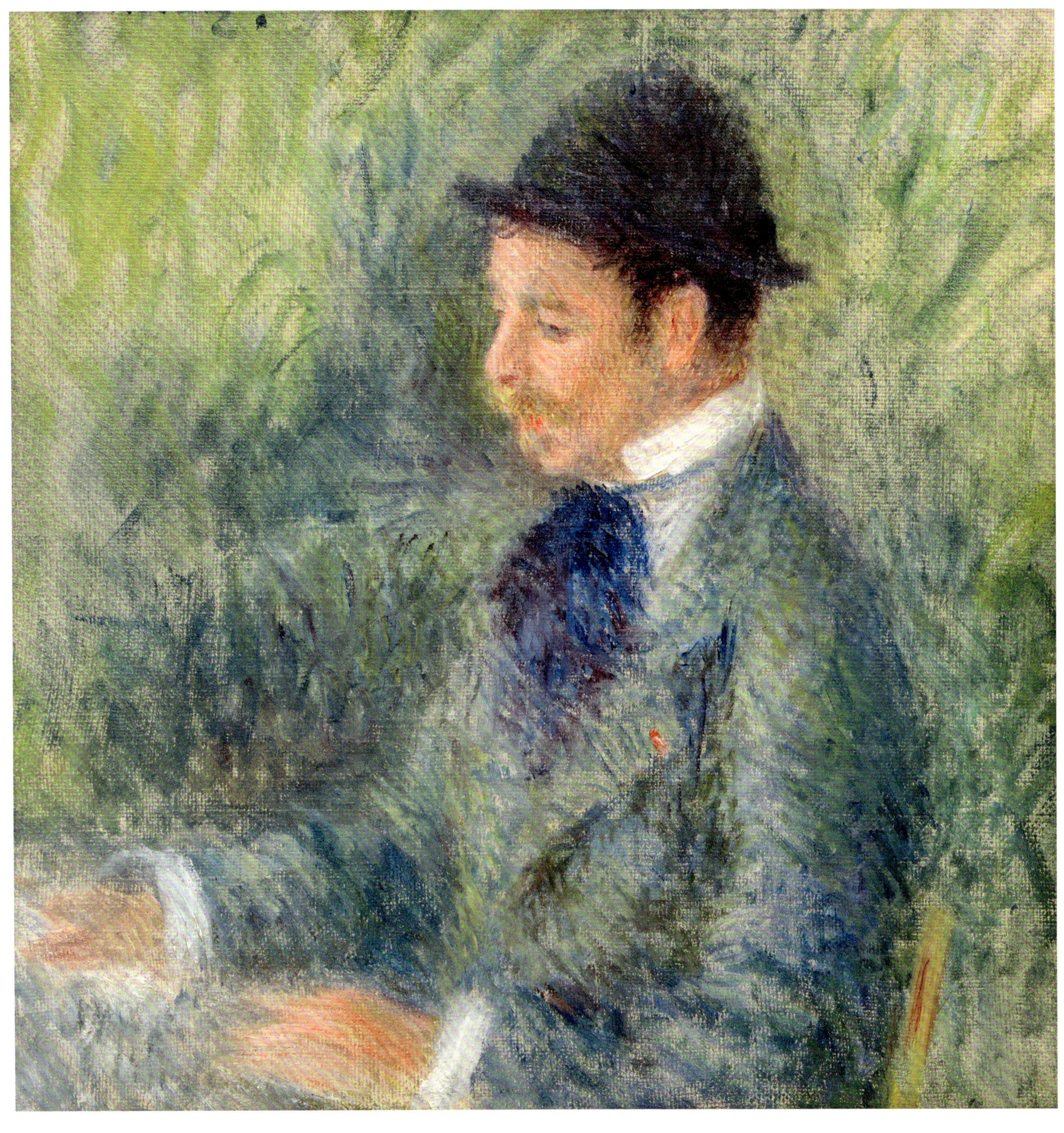

CAT. 18. Pierre-Auguste Renoir, *Man with a Little Hat* (*L'Homme au petit chapeau*), 1877, oil on canvas, 11½ × 11¼ in. (29.4 × 28.5 cm). Private collection.

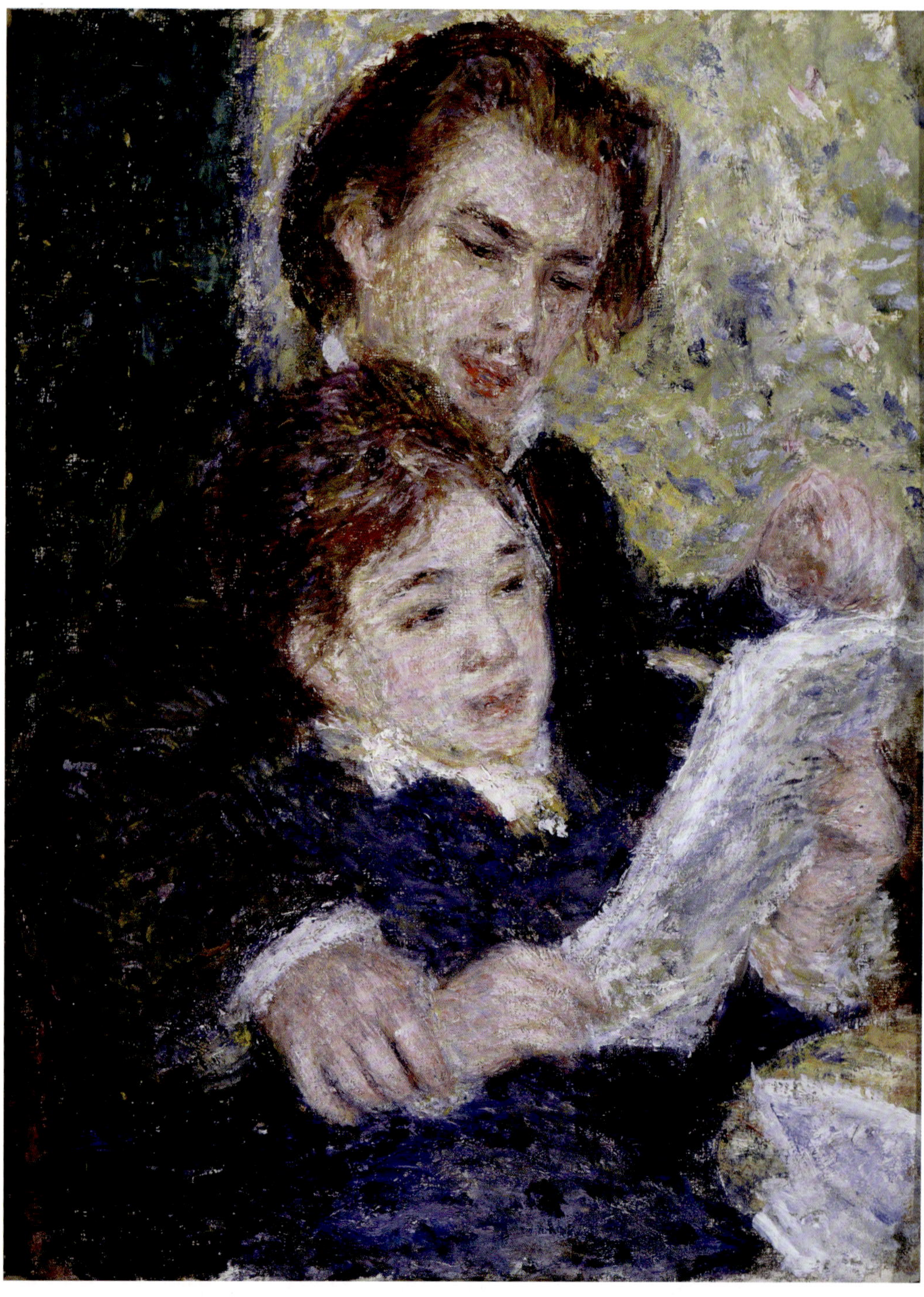

CAT. 19. Pierre-Auguste Renoir, *In the Studio* (*Dans l'atelier*) [Georges Rivière and Marguerite Legrand], 1876–1877, oil on canvas, 14¼ × 10⅝ in. (36.2 × 27 cm). Dallas Museum of Art, The Wendy and Emery Reves Collection.

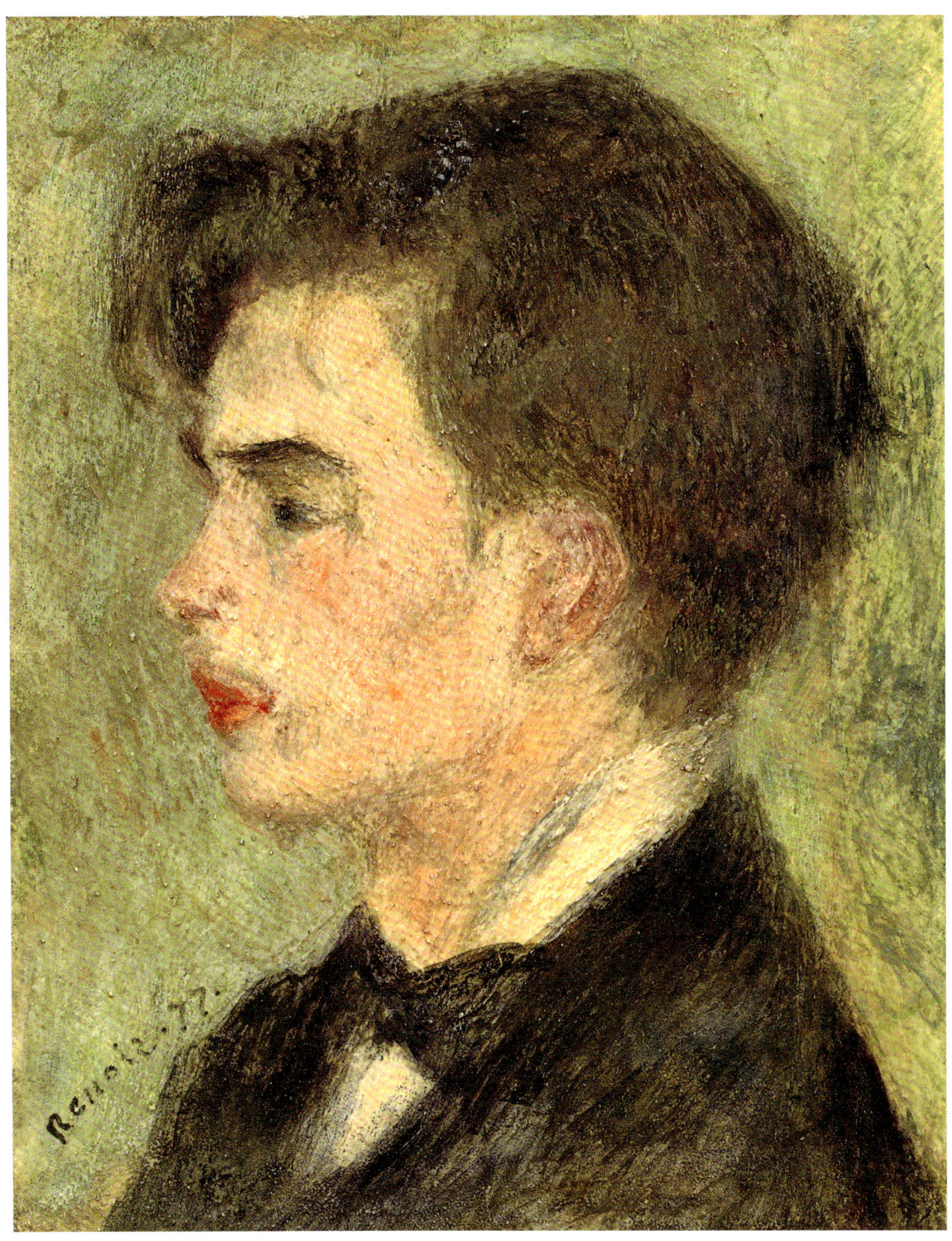

CAT. 20. Pierre-Auguste Renoir, *Georges Rivière*, 1877, oil on cement, 14½ × 11⁹⁄₁₆ in. (36.8 × 29.3 cm). National Gallery of Art, Washington, D.C., Ailsa Mellon Bruce Collection.

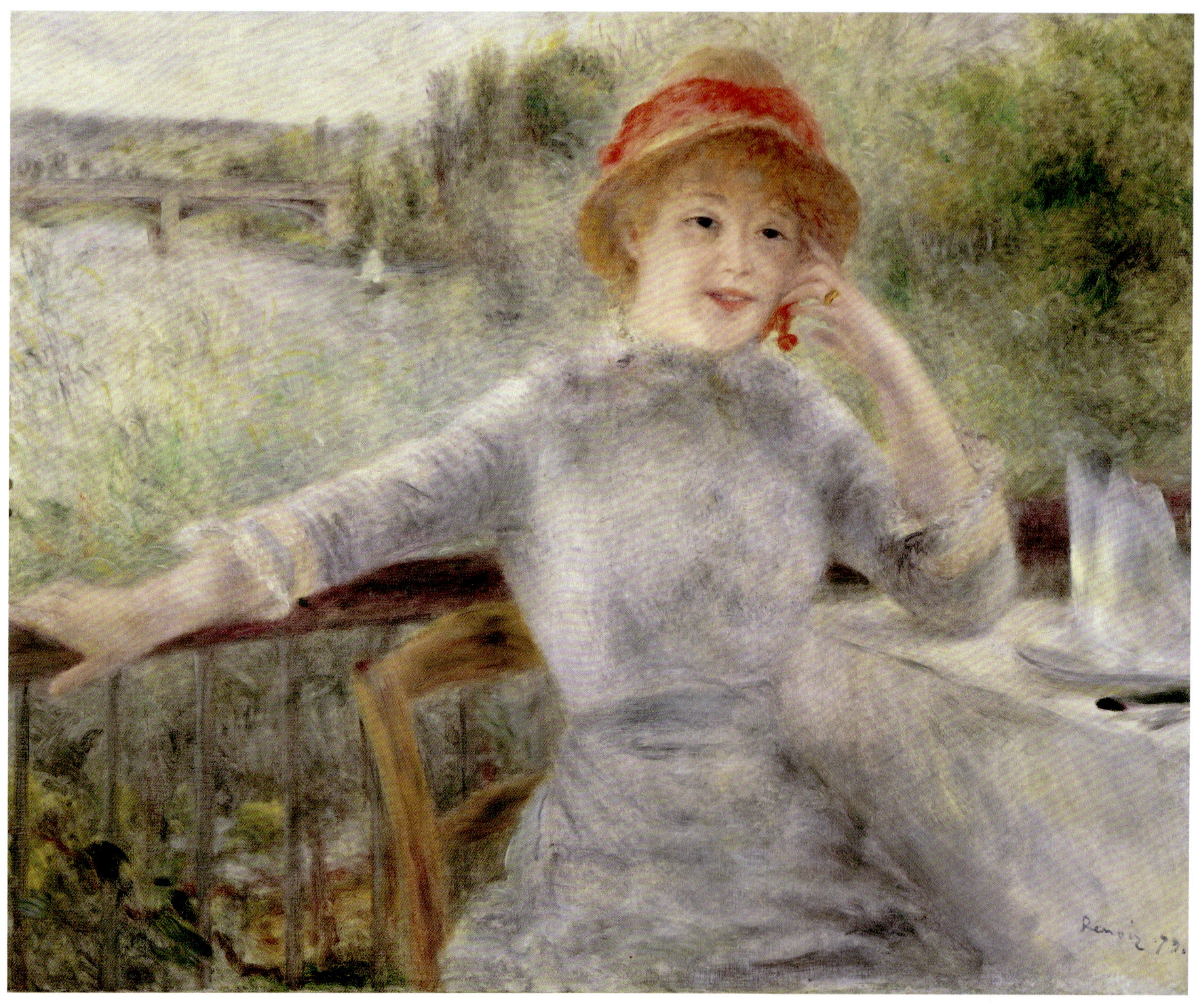

CAT. 21. Pierre-Auguste Renoir, *Alphonsine Fournaise*, 1879, oil on canvas, $28^{15}/_{16} \times 36^{5}/_{8}$ in. (73.5 × 93 cm). Musée d'Orsay, Paris, Gift of D. David-Weill, 1937.

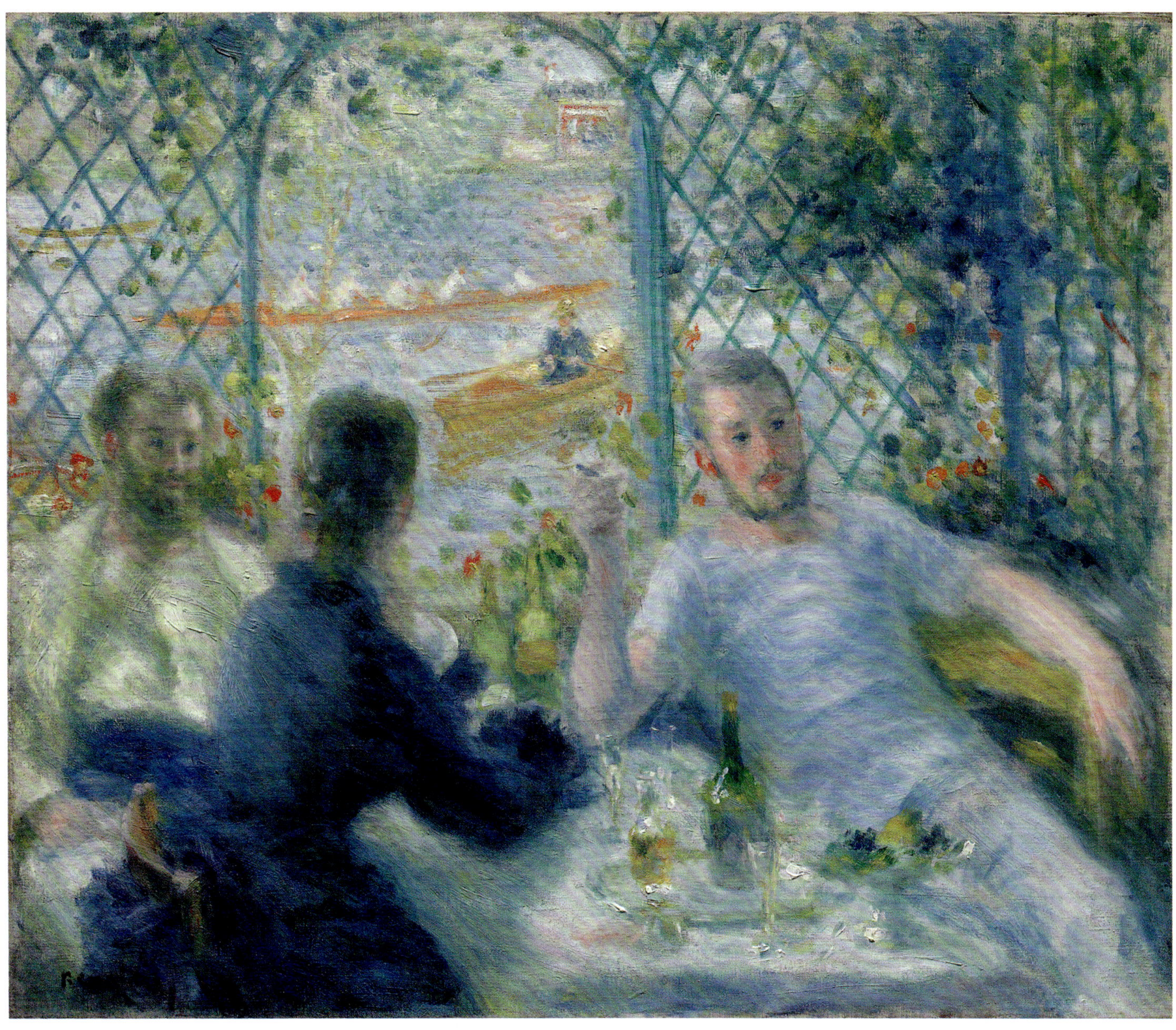

CAT. 22. Pierre-Auguste Renoir, *Lunch at the Restaurant Fournaise* or *The Rowers' Lunch* (*Déjeuner chez Fournaise* or *Déjeuner des canotiers*), 1875, oil on canvas, 21⅝ × 25¹⁵⁄₁₆ in. (55 × 65.9 cm). The Art Institute of Chicago, Potter Palmer Collection.

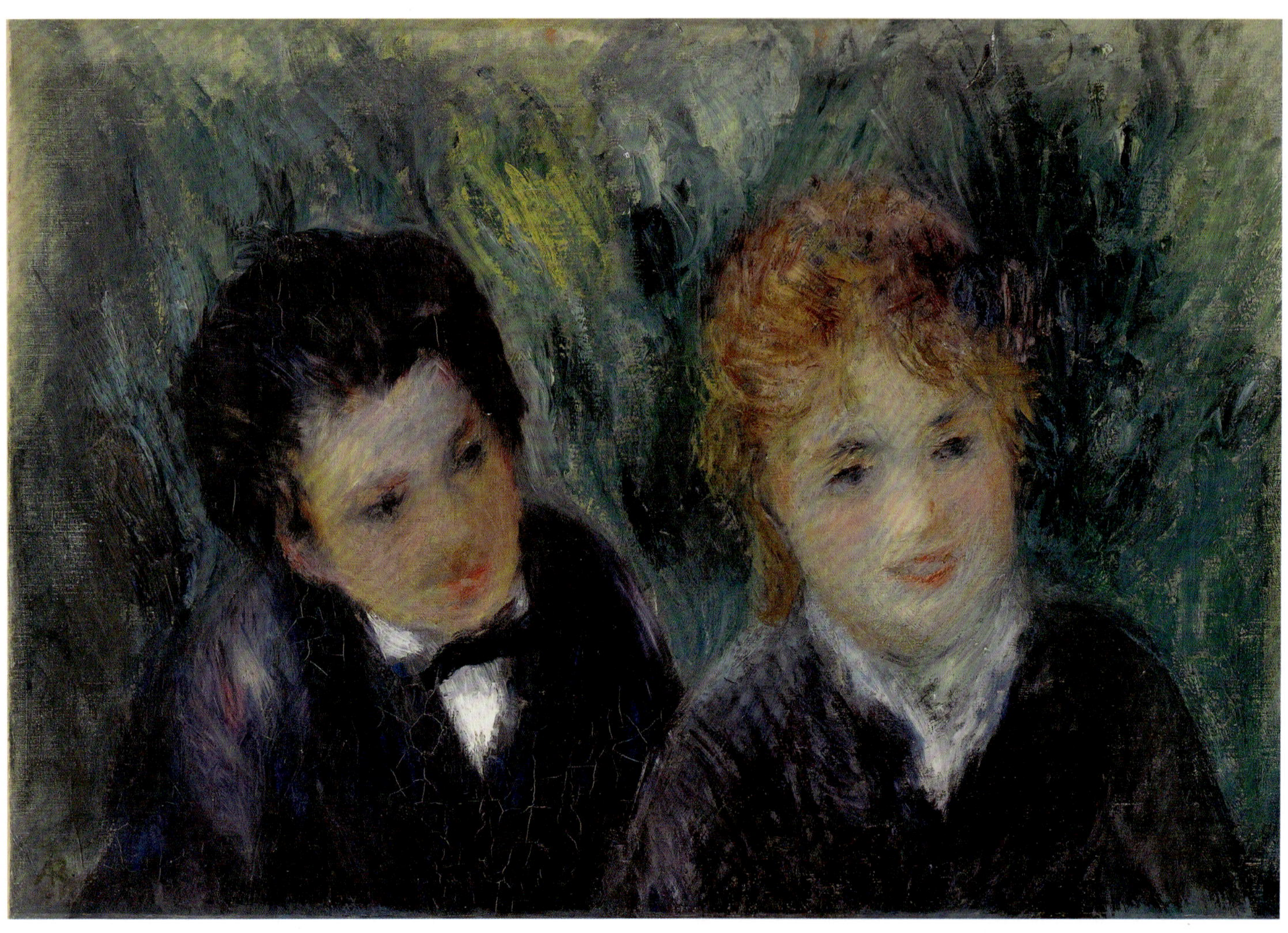

CAT. 23. Pierre-Auguste Renoir, *Portrait of a Young Man and a Young Woman* (*Portrait d'un jeune homme et d'une jeune fille*), 1876, oil on canvas, 12½ × 18⅛ in. (32 × 46 cm). Musée de l'Orangerie, Paris, Jean Walter and Paul Guillaume Collection.

The last person, significant among the individuals most consistently identified with Renoir's painting, is Charles Ephrussi. While not presented as a principal player like Aline Charigot or Alphonse Fournaise, or as a habitué of the Fournaise like Barbier, comfortably seated in the midst of the throng, or Caillebotte, as at home on the river as in his top hat in town, Ephrussi was the only person identified in the painting by a critic when the work was shown at the seventh impressionist exhibition of 1882. In describing the painting for *Le Voltaire*, Alexandre Hepp called it "full of high spirits and of propriety; we see the hero of the feast, who looks like M. Ephrussi."[46] A regular contributor to the *Gazette des beaux-arts*, Charles Ephrussi was well known to his fellow critics. As an outspoken champion of the impressionists, and especially as a friend of and advocate for Renoir, it made perfect sense that Ephrussi should appear amongst the celebratory crowd in *Luncheon of the Boating Party*. Ephrussi is one of the two individuals named in Meier-Graefe's first edition of his Renoir monograph; he describes him as the artist's "protector." Renoir himself says Ephrussi was there;[47] and in a letter to Paul Berard late in the summer of 1880, he mentions Ephrussi, apparently hoping he is back in town, and therefore not far from Chatou.[48] Could Ephrussi, "protector" of Renoir and "hero" of the feast, be not only the compositional keystone but the thematic key to the entire work? Whether intended or de facto, the relationship to Renoir of all those present appears to be their support of his work. Wearing a top hat, Ephrussi is clearly distinguished from the others, and, though we cannot be sure that the young man who engages with him was modeled by Jules Laforgue, their exchange could reflect Ephrussi's constant inclination to share his knowledge and act as a mentor to such younger men, as he would later to Marcel Proust.[49]

Ironically, *Luncheon of the Boating Party* never was shown at the Salon. Instead, its owner, Paul Durand-Ruel, sent it to exhibitions not only in Paris but in Boston, New York, London, and Zurich, allowing its fame to grow so that by the time of Renoir's death in 1919 it was internationally recognized as one of his masterpieces. In the literature the painting is often said to reflect the new social freedoms of the Third Republic, celebrating its mix of people from various backgrounds. At the same time we see a true reflection of the breadth of Renoir's acquaintance. While eschewing in this painting the narrative and anecdotal, he made each figure highly individual. The lasting resonance of Renoir's great undertaking resides in our sense of a gathering of real people, each performing in the painting very much as they would in life. By being true to the personalities of his friends and capturing, as Matisse observed, "the essence of the person," Renoir made his grand opus convincingly specific while at the same time a universal expression of the joy of living. From the artist's point of view the sentiment that binds together this group of journalists and critics, collectors and world travelers, frequent models and admirers of his work, may be the gratitude he felt to those who enabled his success. In this sense, it could also be seen as the artist's truest portrait of himself.

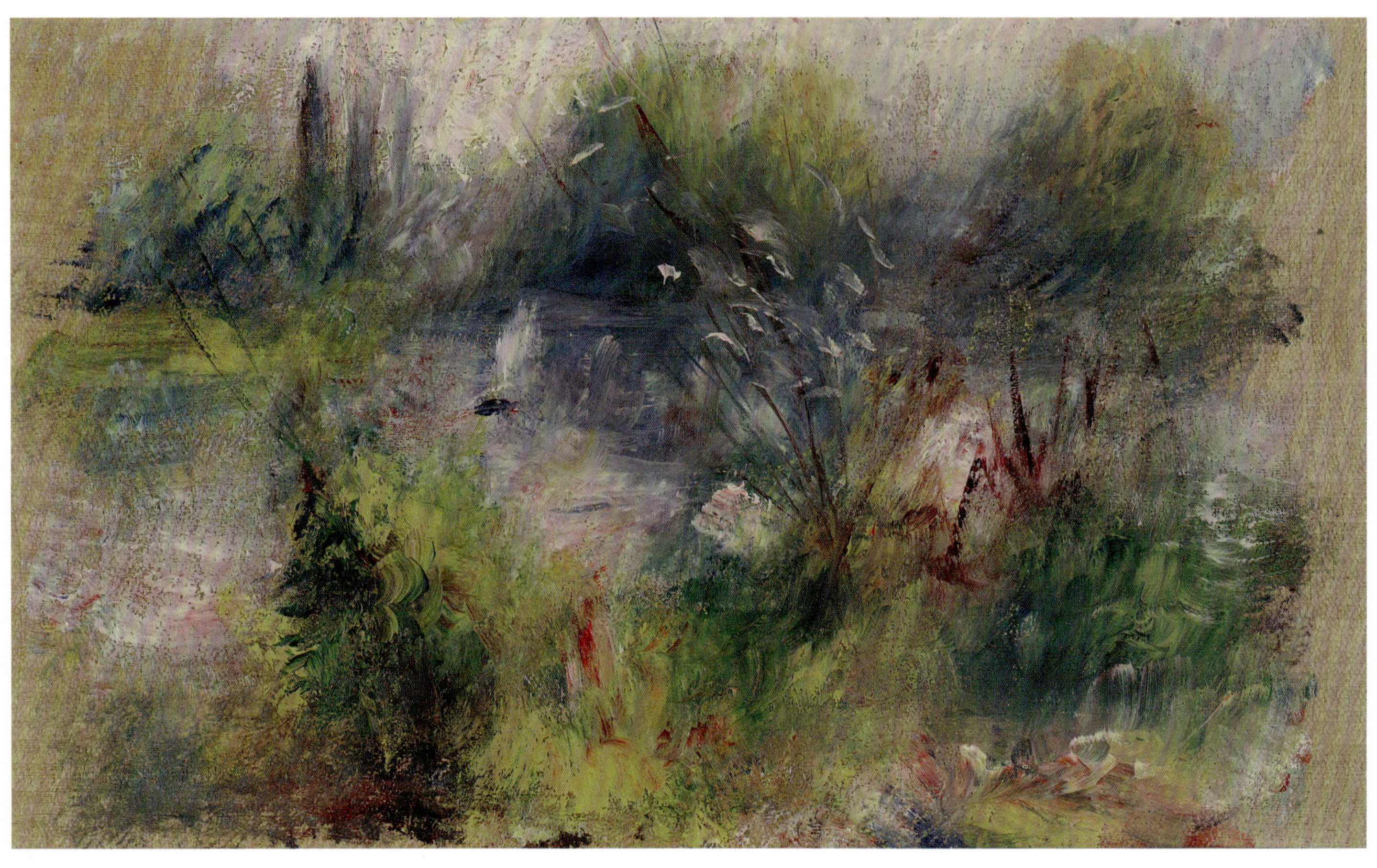

CAT. 24. Pierre-Auguste Renoir, *On the Shore of the Seine* (*Paysage bords de Seine*), c. 1879, oil on linen, 5½ × 9⅛ in. (14 × 23.2 cm). The Baltimore Museum of Art, Saidie A. May Bequest, Courtesy of the Fireman's Fund Insurance Company.

1. Berard 1968, p. 56. Renoir writes, "je vous jure que c'est le dernier grand tableau."

2. Armand Silvestre, *La Vie moderne*, March 11, 1882, in Moffett 1986.

3. Paul de Charry, *Le Pays*, March 10, 1882, in Moffett 1986.

4. See note 1.

5. Quoted in Moffett 1986, p. 234.

6. Albert Wolff, *Le Figaro*, April 3, 1876, and Louis Énault, *Le Constitutionnel*, April 10, 1876, both cited in Moffett 1986 p. 184.

7. In 1875 and 1877, in desperate need of funds, the artists had resorted to auctioning off their work, and in 1878, Ernest Hoschedé—facing bankruptcy—sold his collection of impressionist works at auction, where they went for practically nothing.

8. Pissarro to Murer, 1879, quoted in John Rewald, *The History of Impressionism*, 1946, p. 339.

9. Georges Rivière, "L'exposition des impressionnistes," *L'Impressionniste, journal d'art* (April 6 and April 14, 1877). Reprinted in *Les Archives de l'impressionnisme* (Paris and New York: Durand-Ruel, 1939), pp. 308–313.

10. Robida 1958 , p. 9.

11. Charles Ephrussi, *Gazette des beaux-arts*, May 1, 1880; *La Chronique des arts*, 1881, p. 126.

12. *Pink and Blue*, 1881 (Museu de Arte de São Paulo).

13. Georges Rivière's *Renoir et ses amis* was published in 1921 and Théodore Duret's *Renoir* in 1924.

14. See also Renoir 1958.

15. Jacques-Émile Blanche, *Portraits of a Lifetime* (New York: Coward-McCann, Inc., 1938).

16. Duret 1937, p. 81.

17. Rivière 1921, p. 176.

18. Anne Distel quoting Gustave Geffroy, in Distel 1994, p. 27.

19. Renoir quoted in Robida 1958, p. 53.

20. John House cites Martha Carey (1981) and notes correspondence between Meier-Graefe's identifications and those on the photograph in the Durand-Ruel archives; he also proposes Ellen Andrée as the model for the woman lower right. House and Dayez-Distel 1985, p. 223.

21. See Rathbone 1996, p. 40.

22. My deepest gratitude to Flavie Durand-Ruel and her uncle, Paul-Louis Durand-Ruel, for so generously sharing with me these photographs and other key documents in their archives. They note that the hand that inscribed the later photograph is that of Charles Durand-Ruel, son of Joseph, who was the eldest son of Paul. Perhaps he annotated the photograph based on

information from his father and grandfather (who died in 1922) in an attempt to capture this information before it was lost, or perhaps it came from the earlier photograph or a conversation with Meier-Graefe.

23. The veracity of Vollard's account seems confirmed by the phonetic spelling of Lhote's name (as Lauth), suggesting a secretary took notes during the interview from which the dialogue was transcribed for the book (see Vollard 1925).

24. Bailey 2012, p. 203.

25. Berard 1968, p. 55. A letter in the Durand-Ruel archives addressed to Messieurs Durand-Ruel, New York, from Joseph Durand-Ruel, dated December 26, 1923, states: "J'ai parlé à André Aude [brother-in-law of Joseph and George Durand-Ruel] du *Déjeuner à Bougival*; il m'a dit que Lemoin [sic], éditeur de musique, prétend avoir posé beaucoup plus que Caillebotte pour le soi-disant portrait de Caillebotte qui est dans le tableau. Son frère a également posé pour Renoir et a dû servir pour une des petites figures qui sont en haut."

26. The possibility that Renoir had Aline join him at Wargemont, or nearby, in the summer of 1880, is given credence by two things: he brought a model with him in 1879 (Margot, as described in Blanche, *Portraits of a Lifetime*, p. 38, and wrote a letter to Aline—presumably in 1880—about coming to meet him in Normandy in words that suggest he himself was not yet overly familiar with the place.

27. Bailey 2012, p. 203. The female dancer was subsequently modeled by Suzanne Valadon.

28. Lestringuez's full name appears on his marriage certificate of April 1887, and in the publication of his marriage in *Le Gaulois*, April 4, 1887.

29. Rivière 1921, p. 62.

30. Ibid., p. 63.

31. Agence Havas was an international news agency where Lhote presumably was valuable for his extensive travel.

32. Hélène Adhémar, "La danse à la ville de Renoir," *La Revue du Louvre et des musées de France* 3 (1978), p. 201. Also see Renoir 1958, p. 185.

33. *Journal des débats du samedi matin*, March 10, 1894. Also *Le Gaulois*, March 9, 1894.

34. Robida 1958, p. 42. Renoir may allude to Samary's suitor in the hand at her waist of a figure outside the painting. See Rathbone 1996, pp. 46–47.

35. Angèle Legault who posed for *La Dormeuse* (private collection, 1880) and *Sleeping Girl* (*Jeune

Fille au chat*, Clark Art Institute, 1880).

36. Rivière 1921, p. 138.

37. The fullest account of Ellen Andrée is given by John Collins in Jiminez 2001.

38. This possibility is also raised in White 1984, p. 92.

39. Ellen Andrée modeled for many artists in major compositions, including Manet's *The Parisienne*, Henri Gervex's *Rolla*, and numerous works by Degas. She joined the Théâtre Libre, "the temple of Naturalist theater," in 1887 (*Degas*, exh. cat., Metropolitan Museum of Art, New York, 1988, p. 285).

40. Barbier himself was the first owner of both small portraits by Renoir. I am grateful to Isabelle Gaetan, Musée d'Orsay, for her assistance, and to Teresa Ciapparoni La Rocca, referred by Sylvie Patry, for sharing her work on Barbier.

41. Barbier, a businessman, succeeded M. Turc, who was first mayor of Saigon.

42. René de Pont-Jest, "Gazette des Tribunaux, L'adultère de Chatou," *Le Figaro*, March 11, 1870.

43. Matisse, quoted in *Chatting with Matisse: The Lost 1941 Interview* (Los Angeles: Getty Research Institute, 2013), p. 90.

44. *La Nouvelle Revue*, Paris, November–December 1897, p. 258.

45. Rivière, *L'Impressionniste, journal d'art*, reprinted in Venturi 1939.

46. Alexandre Hepp, *Le Voltaire*, March 3, 1882, in Moffett 1986, p. 413.

47. Vollard 1925, p. 76. Renoir says of *Boatmen at Bougival* (i.e. *Luncheon of the Boating Party*), "Lauth [sic] appears with Lestringuez and Ephrussi." Renoir mentions Caillebotte as "the first 'protector' of the impressionists," p. 62.

48. Berard 1968, p. 55.

49. Laforgue was proposed as a possible identity for the young man in Rathbone 1996, p. 39. Though he did not yet work for Charles Ephrussi, he could have known him by the summer of 1880. Not only was he a friend of Paul Bourget, editor of *La Vie moderne*, founded in 1879, but also "at the age of 20 [he turned 20 in August 1880] Laforgue became an art critic for the *Gazette des Beaux Arts*." In Linda Nochlin, *Impressionism and Post-Impressionism, 1874–1904* (Englewood Cliffs, NJ: Prentice Hall, 1966). Ephrussi introduced Laforgue to Charpentier and *La Vie moderne* at some point prior to Laforgue's poems being published (they were turned down on the first attempt) in a December 1880 issue. See Laforgue 1903, p. 241.

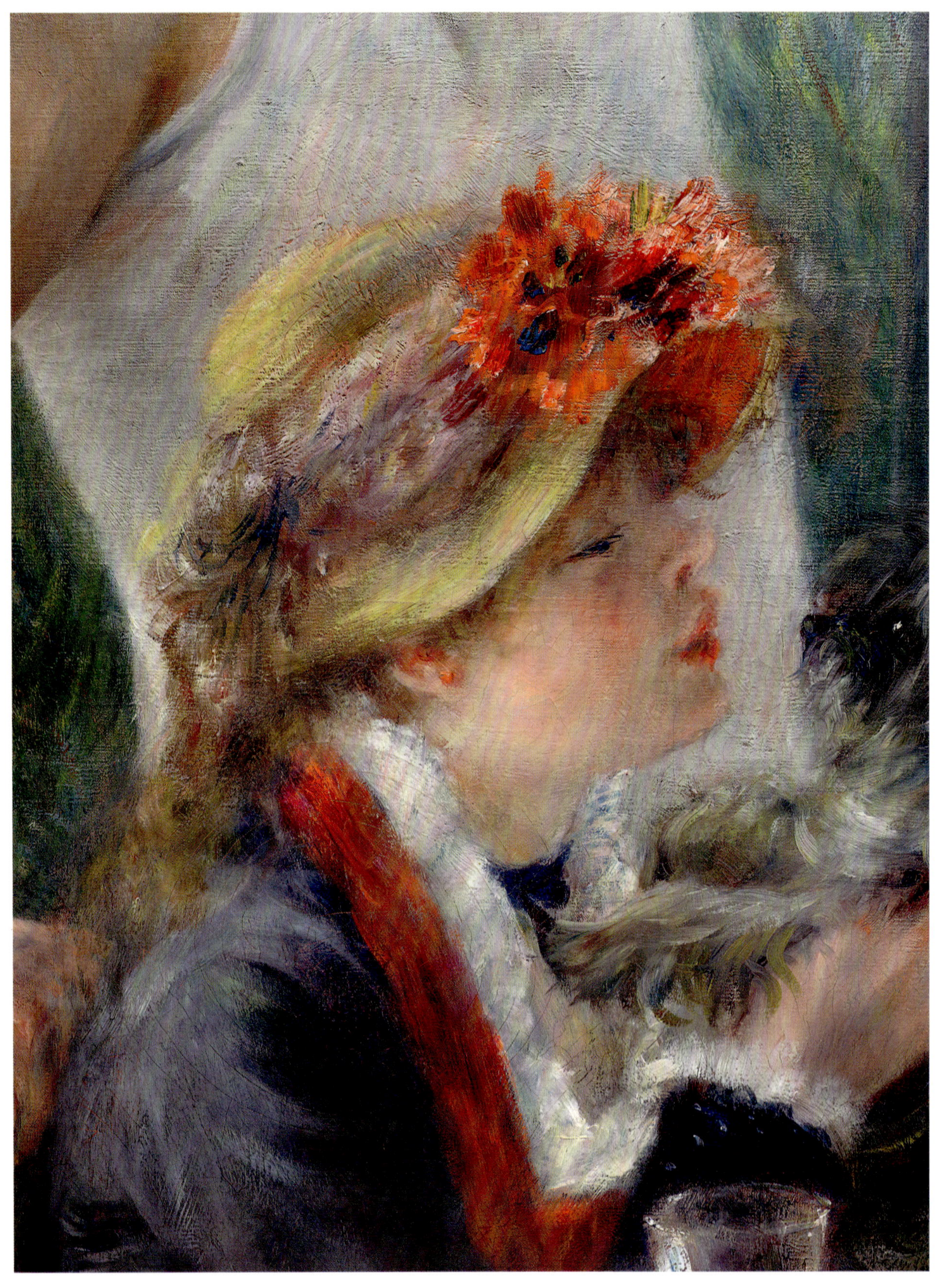

Aline Charigot:
Model, Wife, and Muse

SYLVIE PATRY

N 2004, WHEN INTERVIEWED ON her recently published book *Chers disparus* ("Dearly Departed"), about the companions of the writers Jules Michelet, Robert Louis Stevenson, Marcel Schwob, and Jules Renard—Renoir's contemporaries—the novelist Claude Pujade-Renaud justified her approach by explaining that "all of them played a key role."[1] More recently, Ruth Butler devoted a study to the wives "hidden in the shadow" of three artist friends of Renoir's: Camille Monet, née Doncieux; Hortense Cézanne, née Fiquet; and Rose Rodin, née Beuret.[2] Camille and Hortense have both been the subject of exhibitions bringing together works they inspired.[3] The twenty-seven portraits of Hortense done by Cézanne between 1877 and 1894 were examined in depth by Susan Sidlauskas in 2009.[4] Countering the prevailing idea of "depersonalization" in these portraits, which are often seen as detached and abstract, she highlighted instead the emotional, pictorial, and theoretical aspects of what she considered an active and reciprocal exchange between the painter and his favorite model.

There has been no such interest in Aline Renoir . The woman who was Renoir's companion from the late 1870s and his wife from 1890 until her death in 1915 has attracted very little attention beyond the biographical basics. Stripped of any artistic role, her biographers often describe her in such unflattering terms as a "plump peasant woman,"[5] authoritarian,[6] possessive and cantankerous,[7] or indeed as a social climber eager for bourgeois respectability, her husband's career finally reaching a peak after 1900—features that are in every respect the opposite of the women who fill Renoir's canvases: Berthe Morisot said of her, "I will never manage to convey my astonishment at the sight of such a hefty woman who, I don't know why, I had imagined to be just like her husband's paintings."[8] While Aline is credited with a role in Renoir's painting, it is, according to Tamar Garb, as the embodiment *par excellence* of the "natural woman."[9] We are a long way from the (often emotionally charged) image conjured by her son Jean. His mother was such a central and inspirational figure that in his eyes all women painted by Renoir are subsumed into the figure of Aline. A long way too from the astute, sharp-tongued woman described by Degas. Between all these differences of opinion and the fact that she was often overshadowed by other

51

models—like the famous Gabrielle, a distant cousin who inspired no fewer than two hundred of Renoir's paintings between 1894 and 1913—it is surely worth reconsidering Aline's role. The purpose of this essay is therefore to review Aline's career and importance to Renoir's work, examining how she featured in and allowed him to explore different styles of painting and to walk a line between a fictional utopia and concrete reality, particularly at that key moment when the painter was working on *Luncheon of the Boating Party*.

The Parisian peasant woman?

Aline was born on May 23, 1859 in Essoyes, a village on the borders of the Aube and Champagne regions. The most accurate account to date of her childhood is that given by Chartrand and Pharisien.[10] Like Renoir, she came from a humble background: her father, Victor, a baker from a family of winemakers, married her mother, Emélie, a girl from the village who became a seamstress, in 1859. Very soon afterwards, in August 1860, Victor, then in debt, abandoned his wife and daughter. Emélie resurfaces in Paris seven years later while Aline was growing up in Essoyes in the care of an aunt and then, until the age of fifteen, in a religious boarding school. In 1874, she joined her mother in Paris. If the image of Aline as a provincial peasant has endured, it is because historians have attached great importance to this village childhood and adolescence. And yet, between 1874 and her death in 1915, Aline essentially lived in the heart of Paris. She may have retained certain country ways or cultivated her Burgundian origins (in much the same way as the novelist Colette, who made them her trademark from 1900[11]), especially since her most eloquent portraitists—her husband, in his paintings, and her son Jean, in *Pierre-Auguste Renoir, mon*

père and in his films—idealized the simple woman in contrast to the Parisian "deadly and decadent beauties."[12] But when Aline met Renoir in the late 1870s, four or five years after she had first gone up to Paris, she was one of those typical *grisettes* of what is now the 9th arrondissement, at the foot of Montmartre, and that's precisely how she is depicted in Renoir's works of the period.

It was around 1879–1880 that Aline saw Renoir for the first time, "with Messrs. Monet and Sisley; all three wore their hair long and caused a stir in the rue Saint-Georges where she lived."[13] In fact, it was Renoir who lived on rue Saint-Georges; Aline and her mother lived in a modest one-room apartment on nearby rue Breda,[14] a street at that time synonymous with prostitution. Renoir apparently met the young woman— nineteen, according to Jean Renoir—at the home of Madame Camille, a fellow Burgundian who owned a *crèmerie*, a kind of small tearoom or restaurant, on place Saint-Georges.[15] It was right in the thick of what might be termed the "Nouvelle-Athènes" years—a reference to the neighborhood where Aline and Auguste lived and worked—that their relationship began. Aline, like her mother, found employment as a seamstress. Renoir, who avoided using professional models out of both choice and economic necessity, was in the habit of recruiting models from among the "common people" of Paris, a world with which artistic bohemia so readily mingled, as typified by *Dance at Le Moulin de la Galette*. Aline is thought to have started posing for the painter almost right away. She would have found herself thrust into an artistic and literary milieu, an avant garde abuzz with ideas, in thrall to the "New Painting" and to literary realism; an environment and a circle of people that were no doubt totally new to her. Renoir lived with his brother Edmond, a journalist and critic, most notably for *La Vie moderne*.

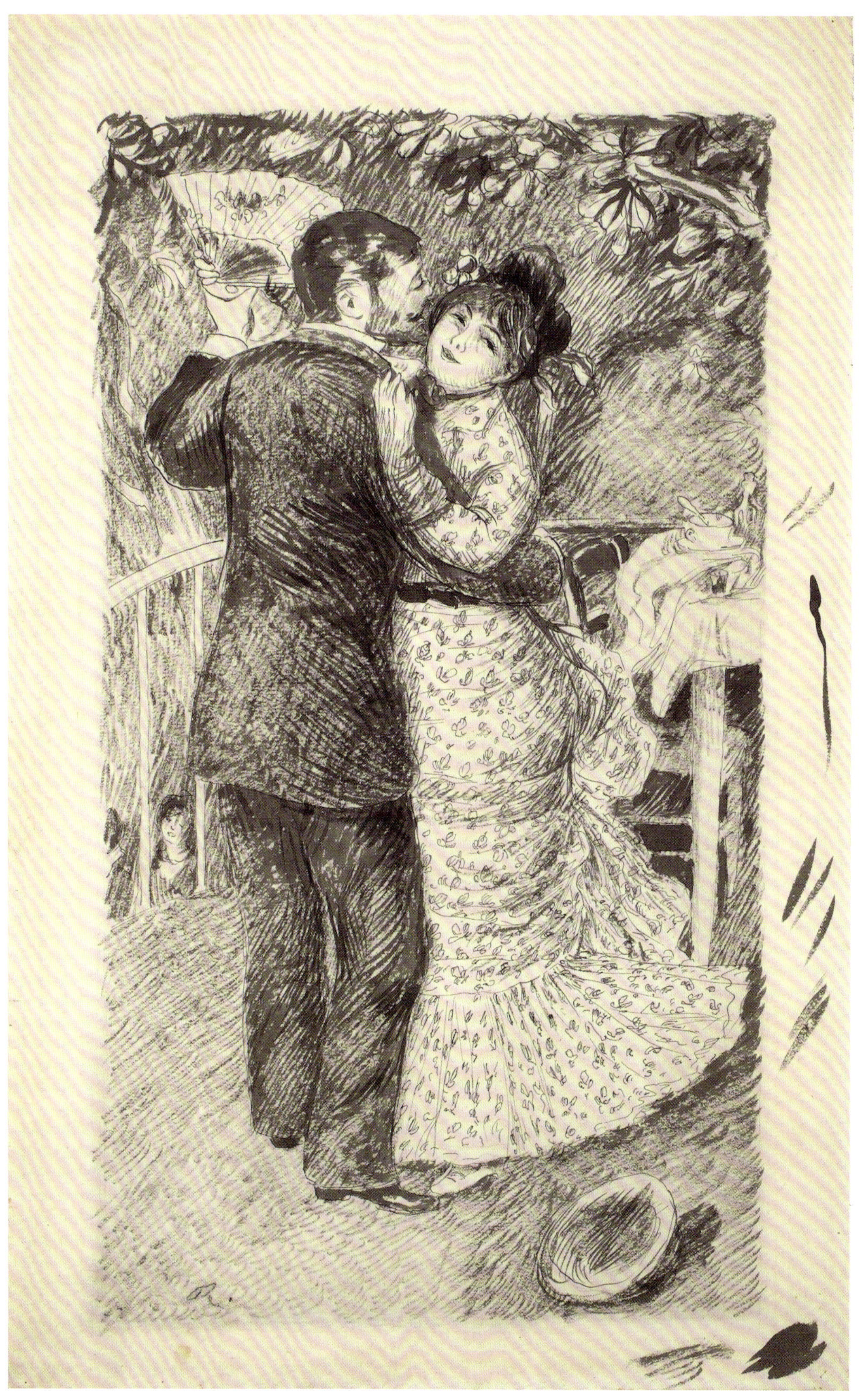

CAT. 25. Pierre-Auguste Renoir, *Dance in the Country* (*Danse à la campagne*), 1883, pen, brush, and gray ink on wove paper, 18¾ × 11⅞ in. (47.6 × 30.2 cm). National Gallery of Art, Washington, D.C., Collection of Mr. & Mrs. Paul Mellon, 1995.

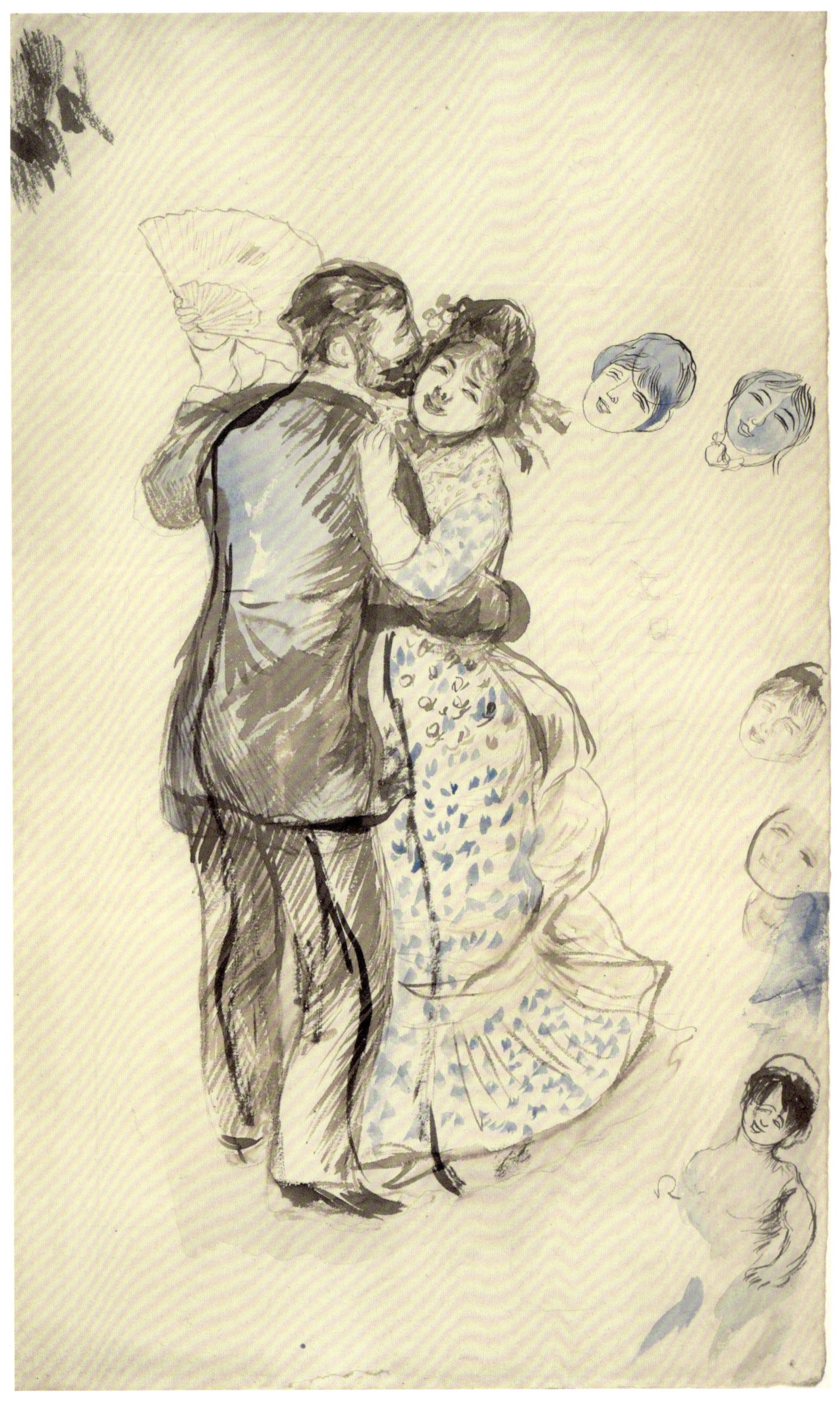

CAT. 26. Pierre-Auguste Renoir, *Dance in the Country* (*Danse à la campagne*), 1883 or later, brush and brown, blue, and black wash over black chalk or graphite, 19½ × 12 in. (49.5 × 30.5 cm). Yale University Art Gallery, New Haven, CT, Bequest of Edith Malvina K. Wetmore.

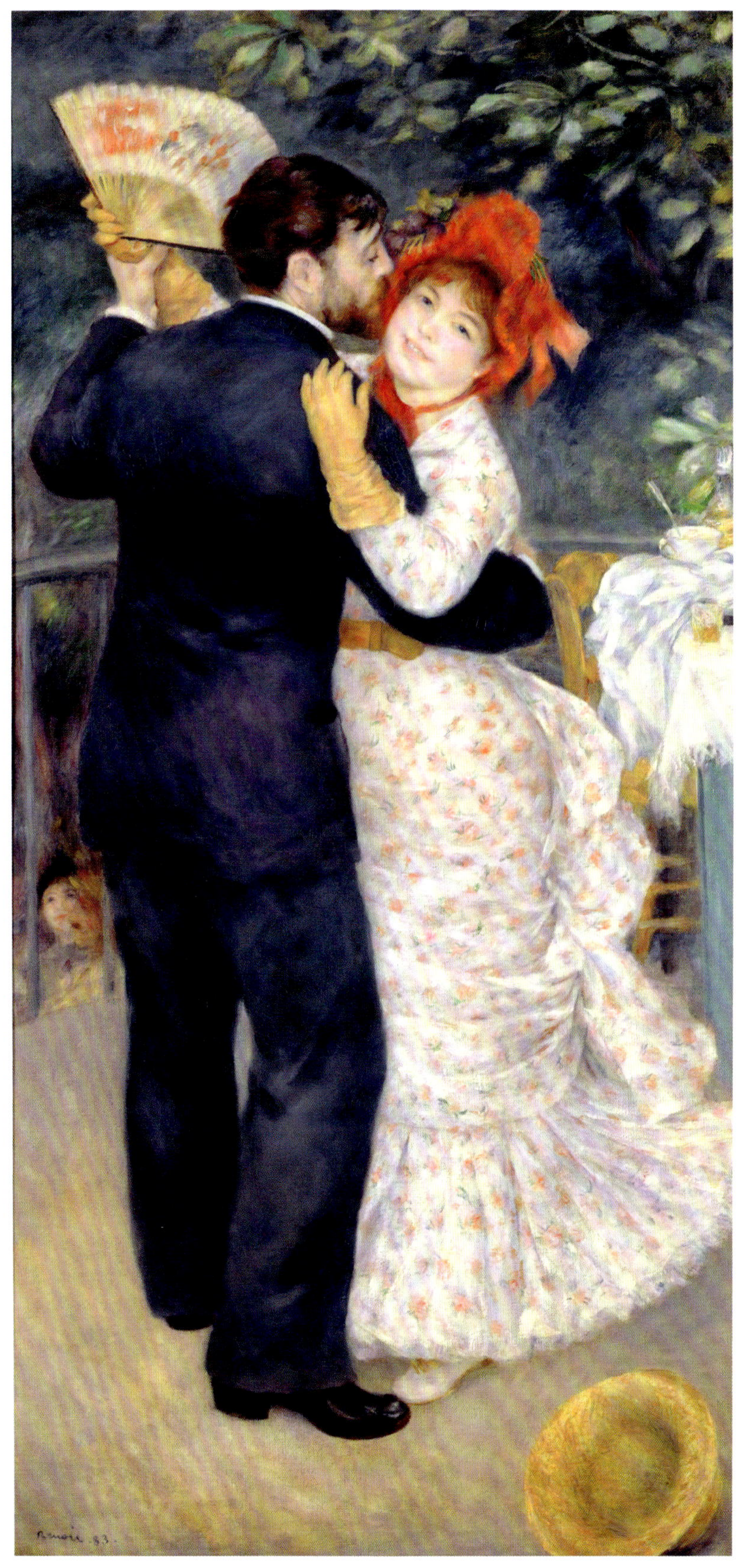

CAT. 27. Pierre-Auguste Renoir,
Dance in the Country (*Danse à la
campagne*), 1883, oil on canvas,
70⅞ × 35⁷⁄₁₆ in. (180 × 90 cm).
Musée d'Orsay, Paris.

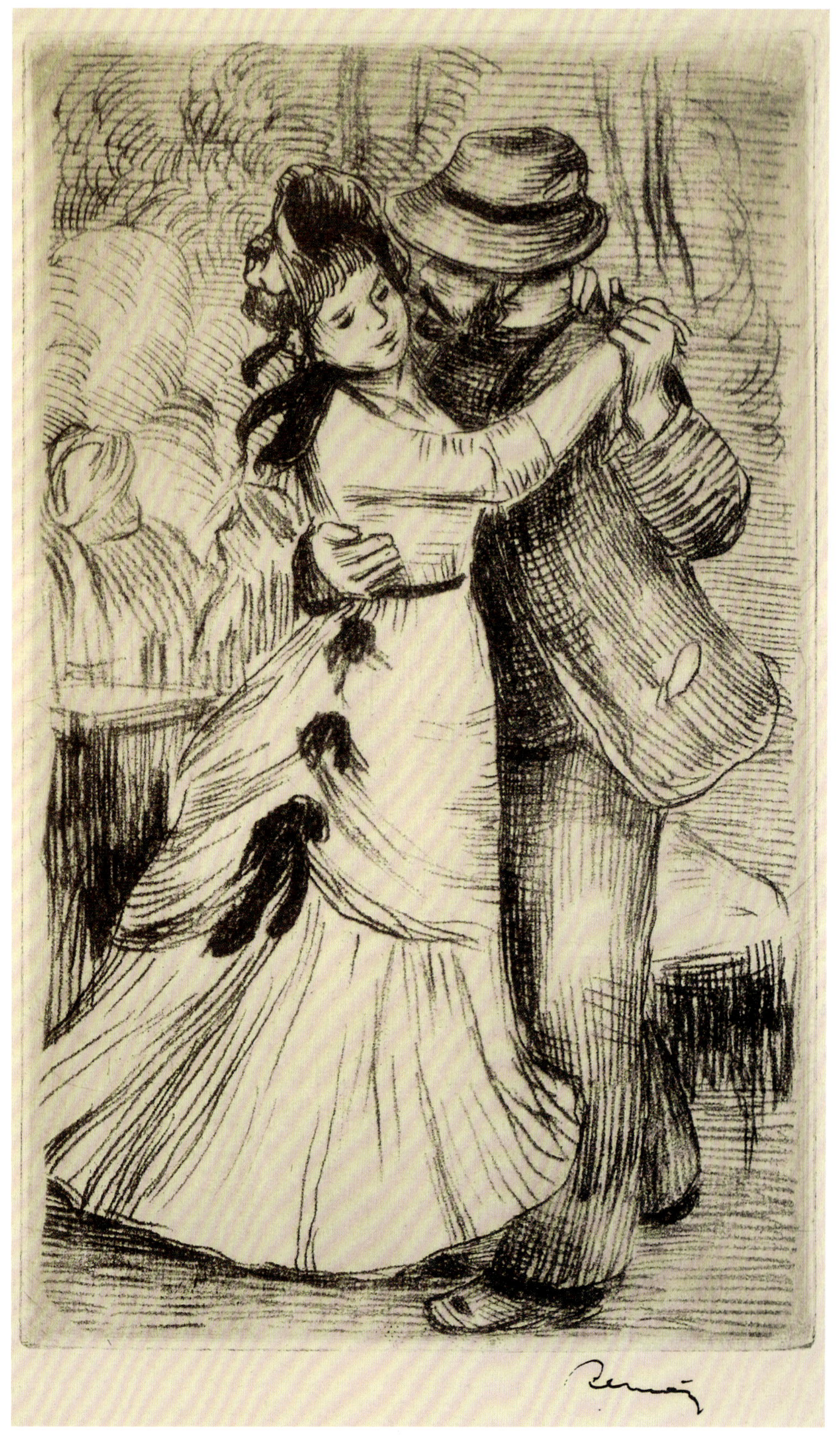

CAT. 28. Pierre-Auguste Renoir, *Dance in the Country* (*Danse à la campagne*), c. 1890, soft-ground etching on paper, 12¾ × 9¾ in. (32.4 × 24.8 cm). The Phillips Collection, Washington, D.C., Acquired 1949.

Pierre-Auguste was close to Georges Rivière, who has left us such a good description of those years, and to the painter Franc-Lamy, the bureaucrat Eugène-Pierre Lestringuez, and the writer Paul Lhote. All of them posed for *Dance at Le Moulin de la Galette*, and, except Rivière, for *Luncheon of the Boating Party*; the latter three, along with Italian painter Federico Zandomeneghi, were witnesses at Aline and Auguste's wedding in 1890 at the town hall of the 9th arrondissement.[16] And it was in Paul Lhote's arms that a radiant Aline was depicted in *Dance in the Country* in 1883 (Cat. 27).

The age of bohemia and freedom?

Unpublished letters[17] give us an idea of the early days of Aline and Pierre-Auguste's romance, probably between 1880 and 1882, coinciding with the great enterprise of the *Luncheon*. Renoir left Paris and Chatou to do portrait commissions, for example at the Berards' in Wargemont (summer of 1879, 1880, and 1881), or to travel to London and Algiers (early 1881 and early 1882). These commissions were a reliable source of income, allowing him to send money to Aline.[18] Sometimes lasting several months, Renoir's absences seem to have weighed heavily on her; in one letter, he responds, "My dear little thing, I'll be back at the end of the month. I beg you to stop fretting because you make me very proud knowing how much I'm loved. I'm not enjoying myself at all and as soon as I'm entitled to return with something proper I won't hesitate."[19] The converse also seems true; when Aline's father urged her to join him in the United States, where he had gone to seek his fortune and had remarried (despite still being legally married to Aline's mother), Renoir wrote from Algiers in early 1881 that "[i]f you go to America, which I don't find funny, but you must so I don't want to put you off, I'll return to Algiers because I've too little

time to do anything good. We must make arrangements so we don't waste time and we need some time beforehand to get ourselves organized. Tell your father that there's a fortune to be made from wine-growing here."[20] The informal tone betrays a close bond and, as in his (spring?) 1881 letter to his "dear little friend," Renoir expresses himself with his usual humor:

> I have just read your letter full of anger and despair. So you're fishing for compliments, are you? Of course you're not ugly, you're quite the prettiest thing. Just to infuriate you, I'm not going to say it. Since I'm such a rogue and I've behaved so badly etc. etc. I must play my role. I don't know if you're pretty or ugly. But I know I have a dreadful desire to continue misbehaving. And it's not so far off. You know what we've agreed once you're back. So try to prepare yourself for that. We'll go as far away as possible. Choose a place and write to me. Tomorrow I'll take a look at the railway timetable. I have to be in Paris in eight or ten days unless I get instructions to go back to the Château de Ninville [sic]. I don't know where it is but it's near [?] Paris [?]. If you want I can get very close to Essoyes, if you don't want to come back [to Paris]. I'll spend the day with you. So get ready because even though you're so ugly, I have a wild desire to kiss you in all the best spots.[21]

The Château de Nainville, in the Essonnes region, was then owned by Meyer Joseph Cahen d'Anvers (d. September 1881). In September 1881, his younger son Albert posed for Renoir at Wargemont—another son, Louis Raphaël, had asked him to do portraits of his daughters,[22] which were exhibited at the Salon in the spring of 1881. Renoir was introduced to these prestigious patrons by his friend Charles Ephrussi, who, like Aline, modeled for *Luncheon of the Boating Party*. Though Aline was not invited to the Berard family estate at Wargemont or to the country home of the Cahen d'Anvers family ("I'm trying to find a day for you to come to the countryside without setting tongues wagging"),[23] and met Renoir in secret, she did mingle with the bohemian crowd that congregated at the Restaurant Fournaise, the epicenter of Renoir's painting and his love life in 1880–1881.

Some letters seem to support Jean Renoir's claim that this restaurant was where Aline and Pierre-Auguste used to meet.[24] Jean identifies a boating scene of 1879 as Aline's first appearance in his father's work (Cat. 29).[25] Seen in profile, she's graceful, slender-waisted, and wearing a blue, white, and red dress, and, as in the *Luncheon*, she's about to get on a boat. She is accompanied by a dapper man whose white summer jacket recalls that of the journalist Adrien Maggiolo in the *Luncheon*. The two paintings, following on from *Dance at Le Moulin de la Galette*, offer a friendlier and more relaxed vision of the relationship between social classes and between the sexes. The presence of Aline, magnified in the foreground of the *Luncheon*—a later addition, since she was painted over another figure—is a reminder of how such scenes contributed to Renoir's creation of a utopia and to his very personal conception of realism, which was then the subject of vigorous debate. In Aline's case, the details of her biography, without making too much of anecdotal and psychological considerations, reveal the tensions of a "family romance," a concept at the heart of Nancy Locke's study of Manet,[26] who was active at the same time. As was the case with many of his impressionist friends and their companions, Aline entered Renoir's painting (and life) under a veil of secrecy. Although they were not an unsuitable match—as Caillebotte's, Cézanne's, and Monet's partnerships were—the young woman's existence was carefully concealed from some of Renoir's circle. He deliberately placed Baron Barbier (fig. 49)

at the heart of the action of the *Luncheon*,[27] which is interesting in light of the fact that he sometimes used Barbier (or Alphonsine) as an intermediary between himself and Aline when he was traveling. He often urged Aline to be cautious; in one letter, he asked her to "[t]ell Madame Alphonsine I'm thinking of going to Chatou September 8 or thereabouts, unless the weather's bad. I would like to finish my boat, which is at Baron [Barbier]'s. I'm not stopping you from going to spend a few days at Chatou; quite the contrary. Just be careful not to get involved in any gossip so you can keep in with everyone, as it's likely that nothing has changed in that respect on the island of Chatou."[28] For fifteen years, discretion was the order of the day; Aline's existence was only really made public after their marriage in 1890. As with Caillebotte, Cézanne, Manet, Monet, Pissarro, and Sisley, affairs and illegitimate children, sometimes long-hidden even from those closest to them, made for an unspoken "family romance." As Émile Zola noted in 1868 with insightful clarity, these artists depict "our mistresses," a recognizable social type easily understood by audiences of the time. Zola's remark was inspired by *Lise with a Parasol*, Lise Tréhot being Renoir's former companion and mother of his first two children, whose existence, revealed in 2007, may always have been hidden from Aline.[29] These complex—though common in the nineteenth century—situations, implying a subtle social stratification of friendships and relationships, find their counterpoint in the harmonious and cohesive community of Renoir's *Luncheon*. Dance halls, open-air cafés (*guinguettes*), and leisure spots outside Paris are the favored settings—perhaps the only ones, in Renoir's eyes—of this social utopia, as is still evident two years later in the happy vision of the couple modeled by Lhote and Aline in *Dance in the Country* (Cat. 27).

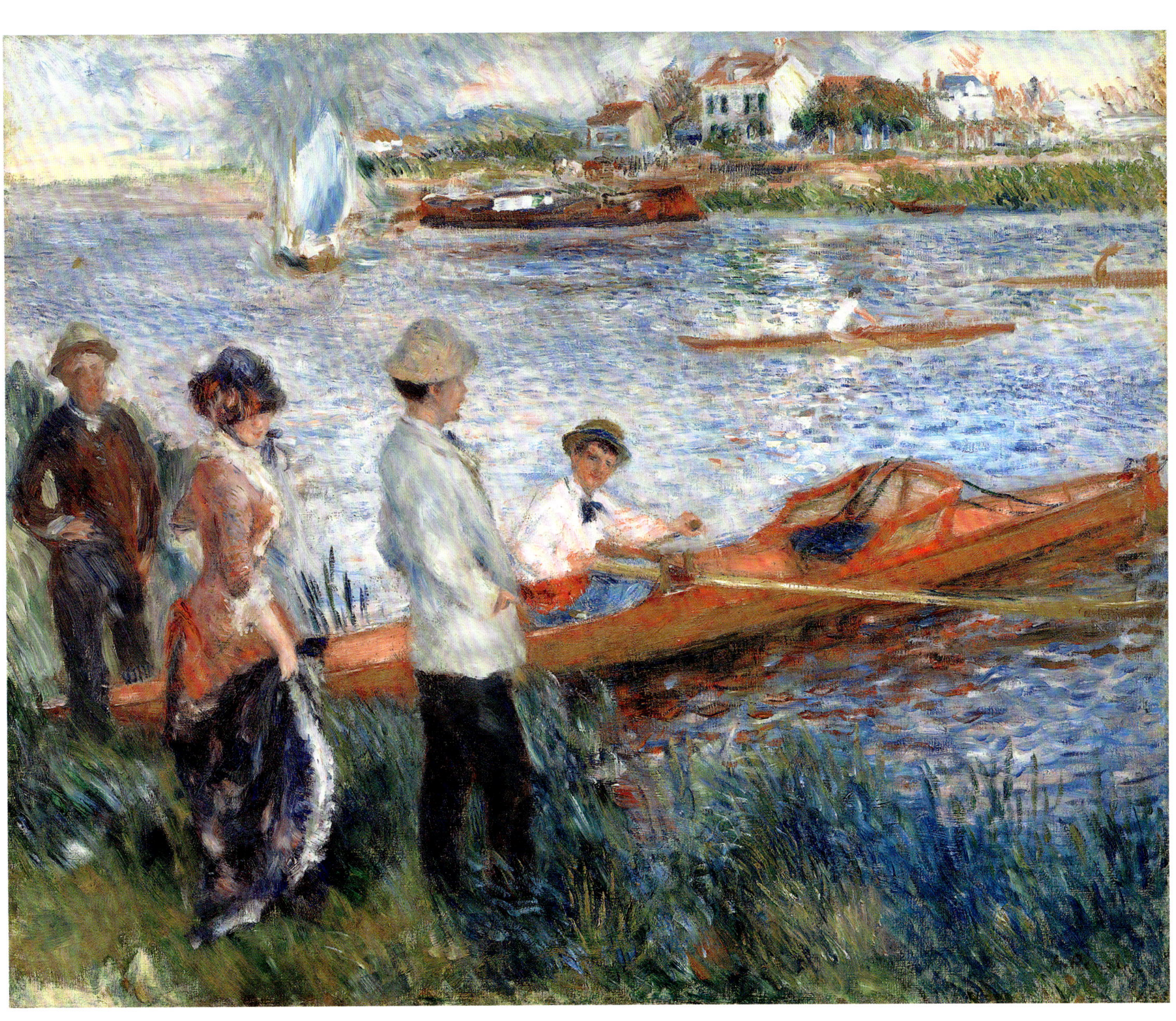

CAT. 29. Pierre-Auguste Renoir, *Oarsmen at Chatou* (*Les Canotiers à Chatou*), 1879, oil on canvas,
31¹⁵⁄₁₆ × 39⁷⁄₁₆ in. (81.2 × 100.2 cm). National Gallery of Art, Washington, D.C., Gift of Sam A. Lewisohn.

Presence/absence

Dance in the Country also marks a temporary shift toward portraits of Aline. Until then she had been not easily recognizable in genre scenes, sometimes lost amid the greenery, and similar to other female figures in Renoir's work. With *Dance in the Country*, a painting that later hung in the well-appointed apartment of the very conservative Paul Durand-Ruel, Renoir produces a dazzling and besotted portrait of his lover. Her partner, reduced to little more than a body, acts as a foil, while the young woman directs her bright and confident gaze straight at the viewer. The dialogue between Renoir and Aline is further developed in a series of nudes, such as *Blonde Bather* (fig. 7), inspired by what Aline billed as her honeymoon[30] in Italy, but Aline's blonde hair and facial features do not match her appearance in the other works she inspired in those same years. In the spring or summer of 1885 Renoir produced a masterful portrait of her (Cat. 30), which has interesting parallels with Cézanne's work: the brushstroke, the framing, the effects of decentering and instability relate to devices used in Cézanne's portraits (fig. 8), but the openness and confidence of the model

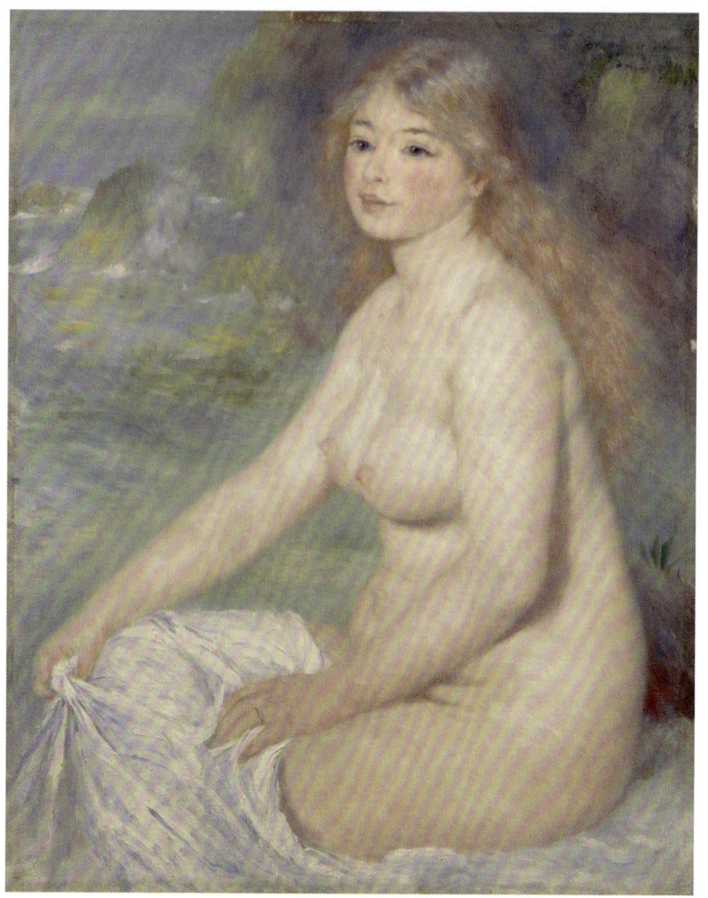

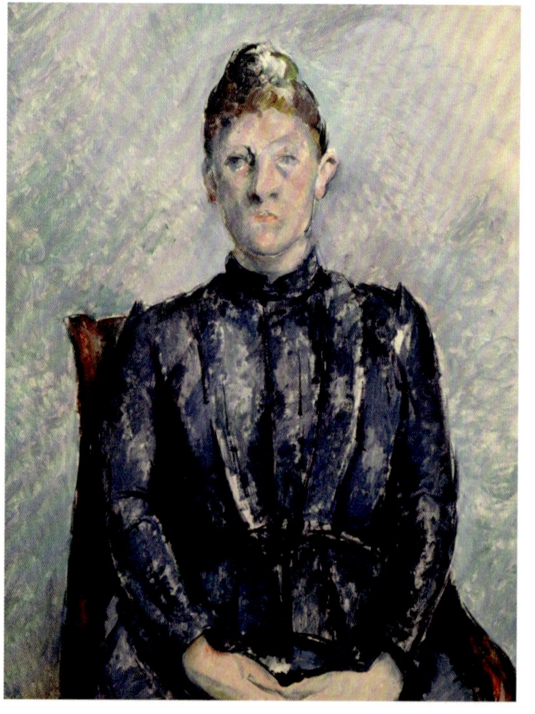

ABOVE

FIG. 7. Pierre-Auguste Renoir, *Blonde Bather* (*Baigneuse blonde*), 1881, oil on canvas, 32⅛ × 25¾ in. (81.6 × 65.4 cm). Sterling and Francine Clark Art Institute, Williamstown, MA.

LEFT

FIG. 8. Paul Cézanne, *Portrait of Madame Cezanne* (*Portrait de madame Cézanne*), c. 1890, oil on canvas, 31⅞ × 24 in. (81 × 61 cm). Musée de l'Orangerie, Paris, Jean Walter and Paul Guillaume Collection.

OPPOSITE PAGE

CAT. 30. Pierre-Auguste Renoir, *Portrait of Madame Renoir* (*Portrait de madame Renoir*), c. 1885, oil on canvas, 25¾ × 21¼ in. (65.4 × 54 cm). Philadelphia Museum of Art, Purchased with the W.P. Wilstach Fund.

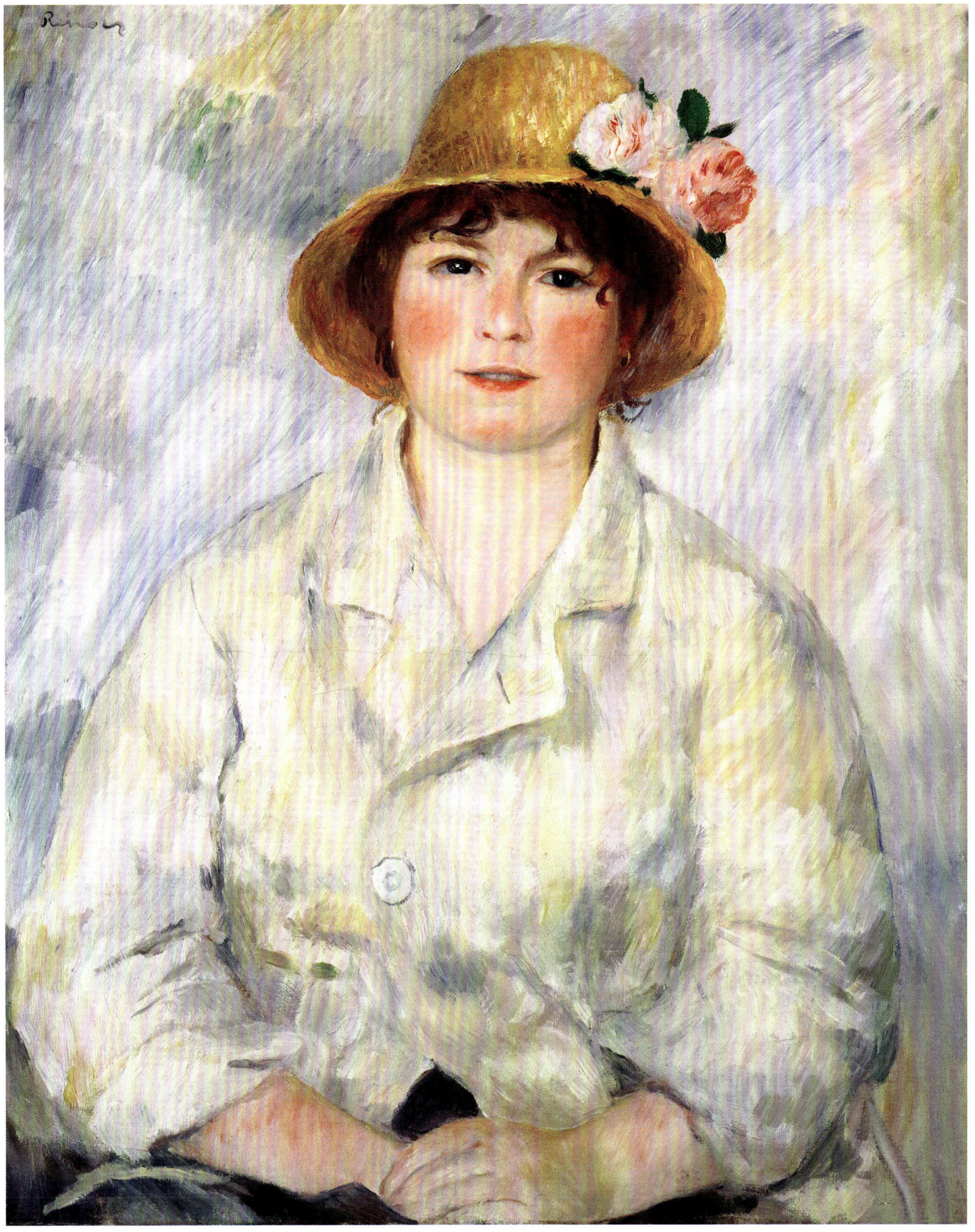

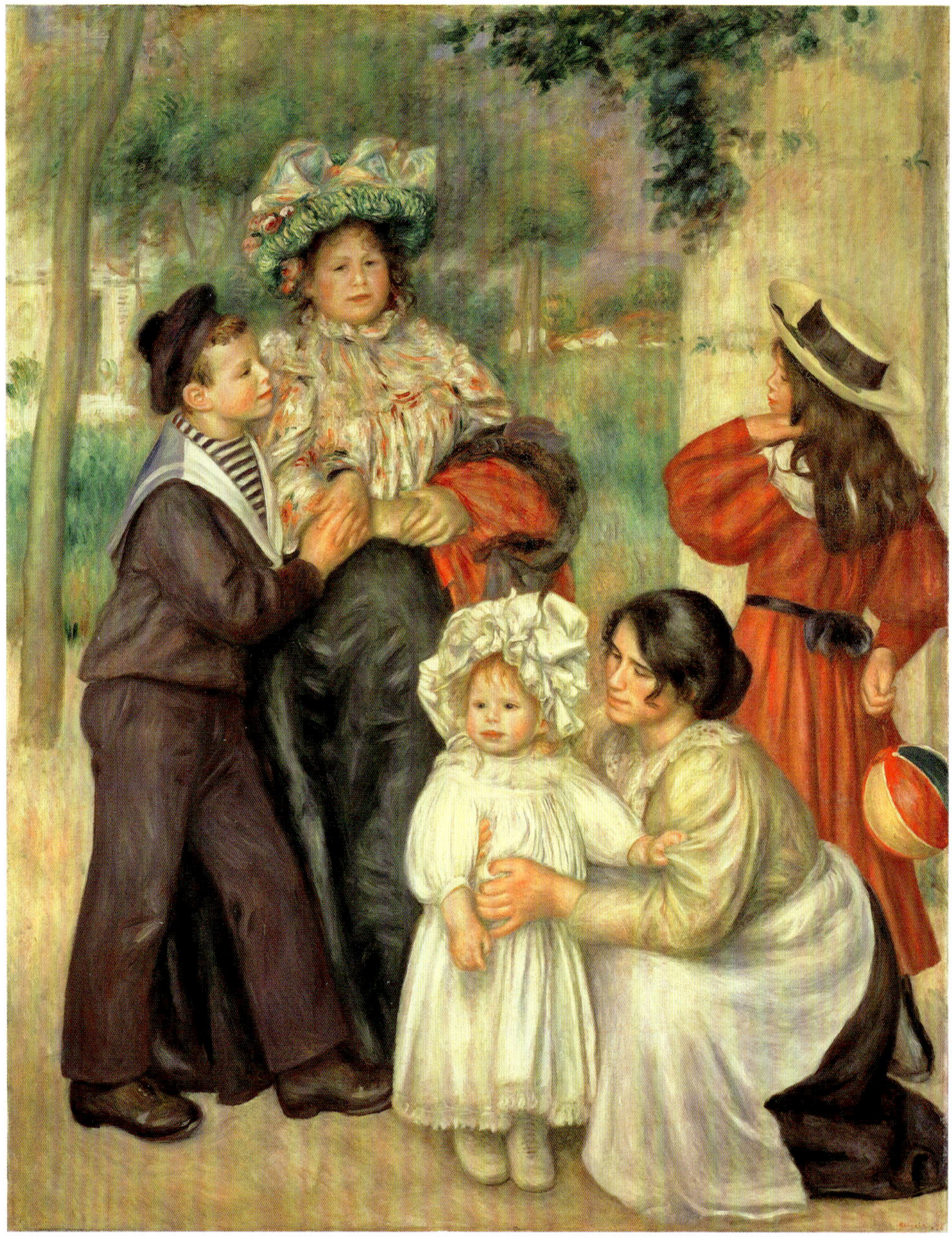

FIG. 9. Pierre-Auguste Renoir, *The Artist's Family* (*La Famille de l'artiste*), 1896, oil on canvas, 68⅛ × 54 in. (173 × 137.2 cm). The Barnes Foundation, Philadelphia.

and the closeness created between Aline and the viewer are unique to Renoir—and also visible in the informal portrait he did of Caillebotte's mistress in the same period. This portrait was followed by a series of three works depicting mother and child (fig. 10), painted at La Roche Guyon in 1885 and 1886,[31] which are midway between portraits and genre paintings. It was as if, in the mid-1880s, Aline was the lucky beneficiary of Renoir's shift toward drawing. The features of the young woman, wearing the same *timbale* hat, are recognizable, even if the artist was seeking to achieve a kind of simplicity and purity

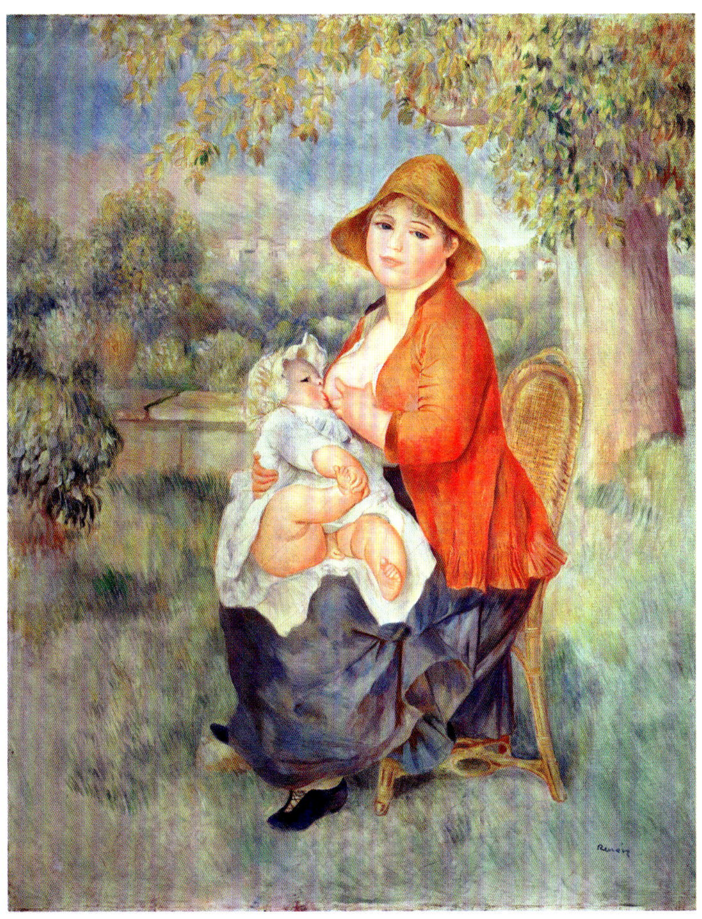

FIG. 10. Pierre-Auguste Renoir, *Motherhood* or *Child at the Breast* (*Maternité* or *L'Enfant au sein*), 1885, oil on canvas, 36 × 28⅜ in. (91.5 × 72 cm). Private collection.

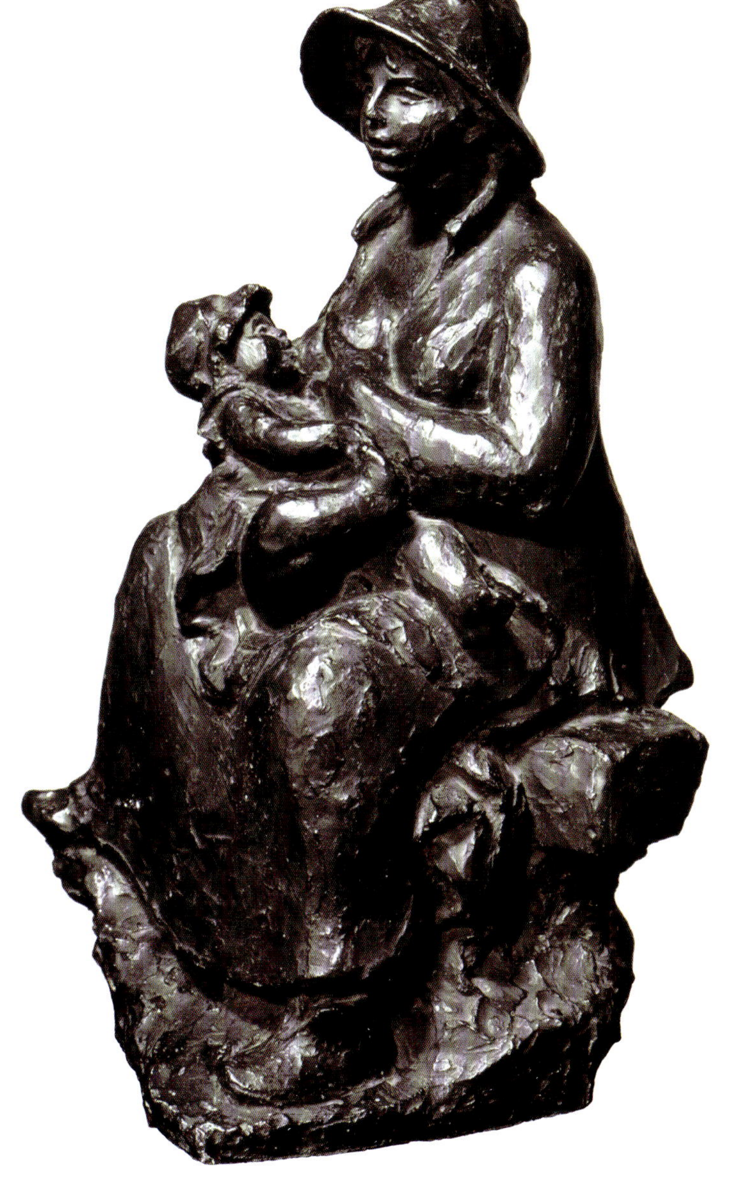

CAT. 31. Pierre-Auguste Renoir and Richard Guino, *Mother and Child* (*Mère et enfant*), 1916, bronze, 21½ × 8 × 8½ in. (54.6 × 20.3 × 21.5 cm), The Phillips Collection, Washington, D.C., Acquired 1940.

that run counter to the individuality of portraiture. With Aline as his constant companion and regular model, Renoir was able to achieve this back-and-forth between observation and imagination that increasingly came to characterize his work from the live model. The mother-and-child series was also a pivotal point in terms of marking Aline's gradual withdrawal from her companion's work, as though, having been "invented" on canvas, she joined the throngs of models who continued to fuel Renoir's work, both present and absent, simultaneously individualized and generalized. Aline was portrayed by her husband on three later occasions (figs. 9 and 10);[32] *Motherhood*, in particular, a version of which she had in her room at her death in 1915,[33] would inspire a posthumous representation,[34] just as the glowing portrait of 1885 was the basis for her funerary bust, the ultimate symbol of Aline's perpetual reinvention in the art of Renoir.

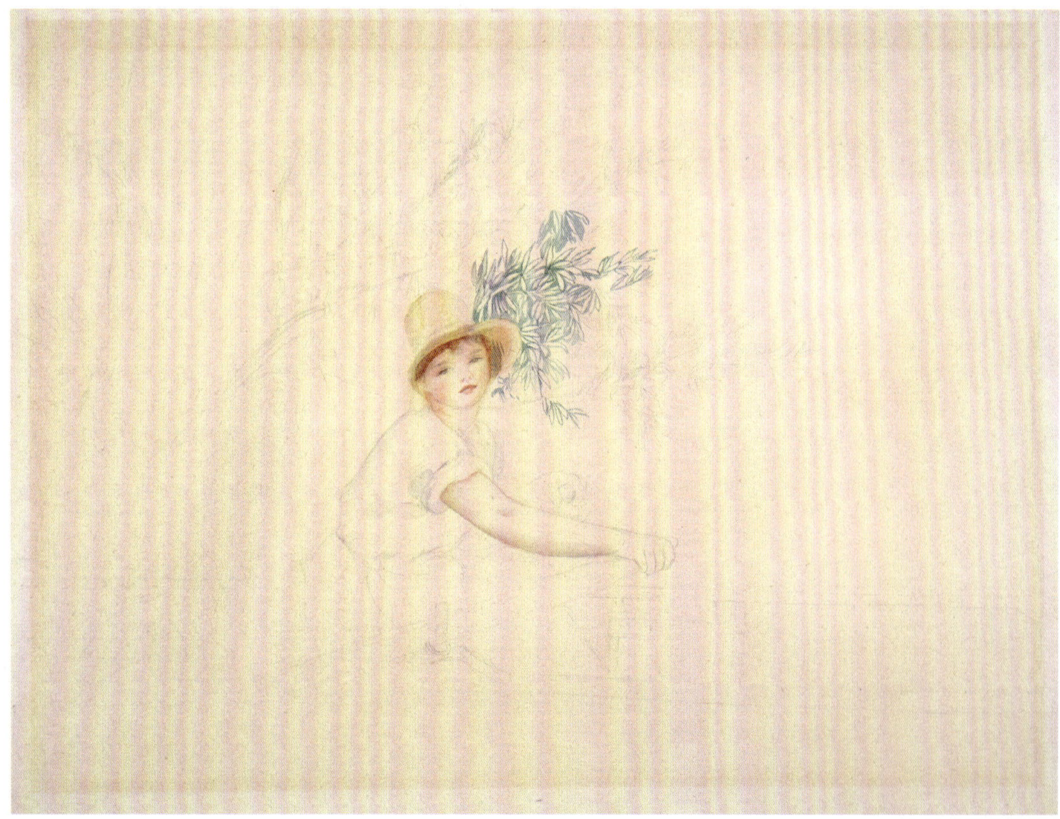

FIG. 11. Pierre-Auguste Renoir, *Madame Renoir in a Boat* (*Madame Renoir dans un bateau*), mid 1880s, graphite pencil and watercolor on paper, 8¼ × 11¼ in. (21 × 28.6 cm). Allen Memorial Art Museum, Oberlin College, Gift of the Adele R. Levy Fund, with life interest retained by David M. Levy.

1. *Chers Disparus* (Arles: Actes Sud, 2004). Interview with Claude Pujade-Renaud published on Lelittéraire.com, http://www.lelitteraire.com/?p=1778, consulted April 4, 2016.

2. Ruth Butler, *Hidden in the Shadow of the Master: The Model-Wives of Cézanne, Monet, and Rodin* (New Haven and London: Yale University Press), 2008.

3. See Dorothee Hansen, *Monet und Camille: Frauenporträts im Impressionismus*, exh. cat., Kunsthalle Bremen (Bremen and Munich, 2005) and Dita Amory, *Madame Cézanne*, exh. cat., The Metropolitan Museum of Art, New York (New York, 2015).

4. Susan Sidlauskas, *Cézanne's Other: The Portraits of Hortense* (University of California Press, 2009).

5. See Bailey 1997, in which Aline is referred to as a "grosse paysanne." p. 212.

6. "'I should have had,' he told us, 'a woman who leads me by the nose.' 'But isn't that what already happens?' we ventured. . . . M. Renoir seemed very surprised and, some time later, said that we had taught him something he hadn't suspected." Manet 1987, p. 129, Saturday, February 5, 1898.

7. Mary Cassatt, letter to Mrs. H.O. Havemeyer, December 28, 1913. The Metropolitan Museum of Art Archives, New York.

8. Berthe Morisot, letter to Stéphane Mallarmé from Mézy, in Denis Rouart, *Correspondance de Berthe Morisot avec sa famille et ses amis* (Paris: Quatre Chemins-Editart, 1950), p. 163.

9. For Garb (1992), the "natural woman" is a social and political construct implying a harmonious continuity between women and nature, especially through the exaltation of motherhood.

10. Pierre Chartrand and Bernard Pharisien, *Victor Charigot, son grand-père* (Bar-sur-Aube: Némont, 2007), p. 35ff.

11. Michel Del Castillo, *Colette: une certaine France* (Paris: Stock, 1999).

12. See Jean Renoir on Ingrid Bergman, cited in *Renoir/Renoir*, exh. cat., Musée d'Orsay (Paris: Éditions de la Martinière, 2005), p. 75.

13. Manet 1987, p. 67, September 19, 1895.

14. See Archives de Paris, register 1876, DIP4/545: "dame Charugo, appartement d'une pièce au 1er étage." Bailey 1997, note 18, p. 320.

15. Jean Renoir, *Pierre Auguste Renoir, mon père* (Paris: Gallimard, 1981), p. 229ff. Jean cannot be fully relied upon either for the date (in this case 1878) or for the circumstances of Aline and Pierre-Auguste's meeting, since he often strays from the facts when it comes to Aline's childhood/youth and family background (as Chartrand and Pharisien have shown).

16. According to records kept at the town hall of the 9th arrondissement, Paris (AD/FF 275), Renoir was living at 11 boulevard de Clichy; Alice Victorine, seamstress, resided at 15 rue Breda.

17. See *The Unknown Renoir: The Man, The Husband, The Father, The Artist* auction at Heritage, New York, September 19, 2013 (hereafter New York Auction 2013; individual letters are referred to by their lot number).

18. New York Auction 2013, lot 89029, from Dieppe: "I am sending you a hundred francs, it's all I can manage for the time being and I'll take that [?] out of next month's allowance, I'm letting you know in advance. It's up to you to work things out." See also lots 89030 and 89032.

19. New York Auction 2013, lot 89028.

20. Ibid., lot 89053.

21. "Je viens de lire ta lettre grosse de désespoir et pleine de malice. Car tu veux que je te réponde des compliments, tu veux que je te dise ? Mais non tu n'es pas laide, tu es tout ce qu'il y a de plus joli. Eh bien pour te faire enrager je ne te le dirai pas. Puisque je suis si canaille que je me suis si mal conduit etc. etc. Il faut que je reste dans mon rôle. Je ne sais pas si tu es jolie ou laide. Mais je sais que j'ai une sale envie de me mal conduire encore. Et si ce n'était pas si loin. Tu sais ce que nous avons convenu à ton retour. Tâche de t'arranger pour ça. J'irai aussi loin que possible. Choisis un pays et écris moi. Demain je regarderai sur l'indicateur. Je dois être à Paris dans huit ou dix jours à moins de contrordre pour repartir au château de Ninville [sic]. Je ne sais pas où c'est mais c'est près [?] Paris [?]. Si tu veux je peux aller tout près d'Essoyes si tu ne veux pas revenir. J'irai passer une journée avec toi. Enfin arrange-toi car quoique tu sois si laide j'ai envie de t'embrasser dans les bons coins mas une envie folle." New York Auction 2013, lot 89024.

22. On these portraits, see Bailey 1997, nos. 37 and 38. See also Cat. 3 and figs. 34 and 35 in this volume.

23. New York Auction 2013, lot 89032.

24. J. Renoir, *Pierre Auguste Renoir*, p. 232.

25. Ibid., p. 230.

26. Nancy Locke, *Manet and the Family Romance* (Princeton University Press, 2001).

27. See J. Renoir, *Pierre Auguste Renoir*, p. 226.

28. New York Auction 2013, lot 89035.

29. See Jean-Claude Gélineau, *Jeanne Tréhot: la fille cachée de Pierre-Auguste Renoir* (Essoyes: Éditions du Cadratin, 2007), especially p. 81.

30. "Mme Renoir spoke of her trip to Italy after her wedding; we found it funny when we heard her telling us all this, since we had so often heard M. Renoir talking about it as if he had done the trip on his own, at a time when we didn't know his wife." Manet 1987, p. 67.

31. And not at Essoyes, as stated in Distel 2009, p. 234.

32. The third portrait is *Madame Renoir and Bob*, Wadsworth Atheneum, Hartford, CT, c. 1910.

33. See unpublished estate inventory.

34. *Aline Renoir Nursing Her Baby*, Kunstmuseum, Bern, Gottfried F. Keller bequest, 1918.

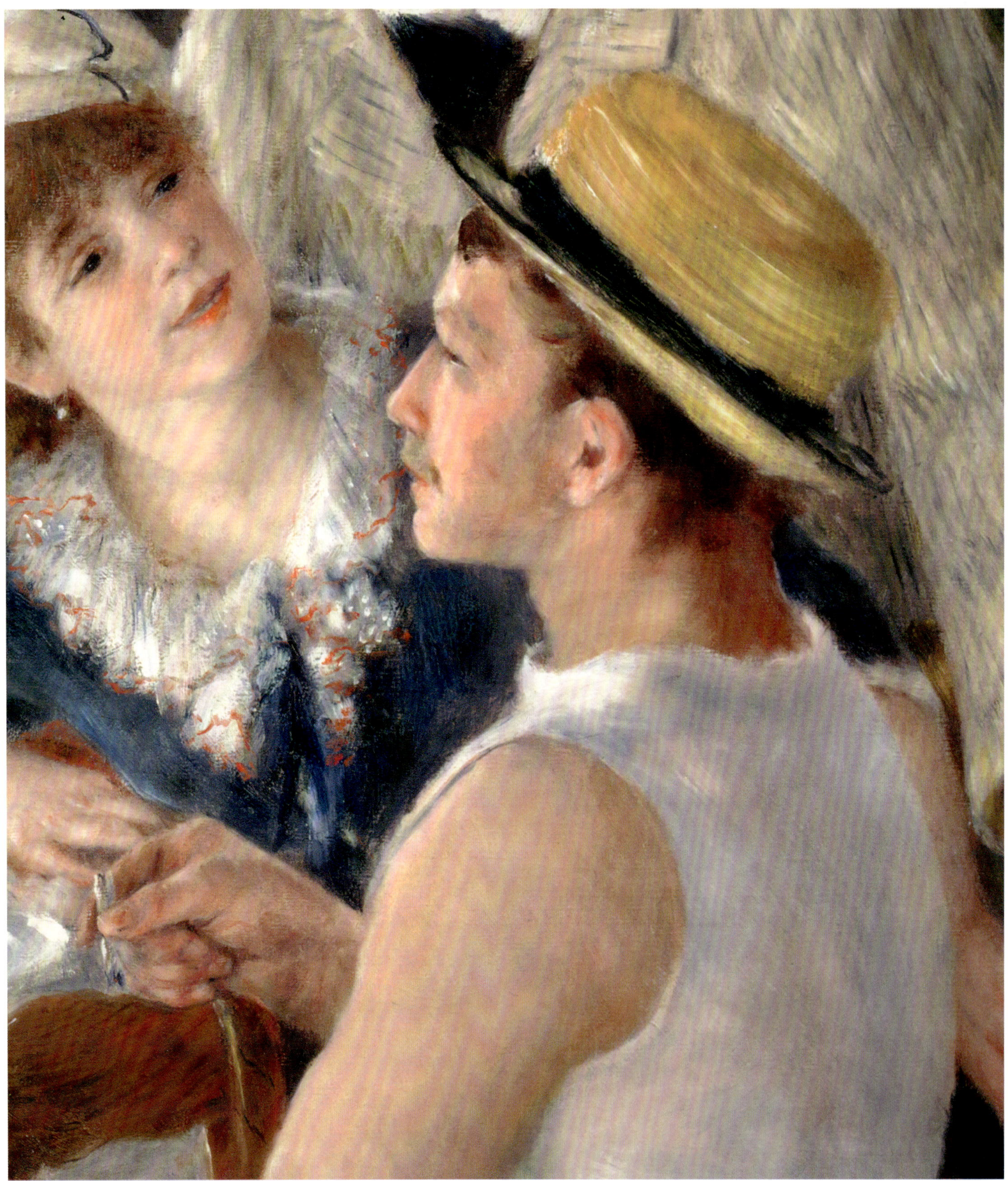

Renoir/Caillebotte: Realist Relations

MARY MORTON

I N RENOIR'S *LUNCHEON OF THE BOATING PARTY*, the athletic young man in a straw "boater" and sleeveless shirt straddling a chair at the edge of the table, a cigarette smoldering between his fingers, has traditionally been identified as Gustave Caillebotte, the least-known member of the "core" impressionists. Although not universally accepted by scholars, the identification is bolstered by the fact that Caillebotte was an avid sailor and a good friend of Renoir's. Indeed, during the late 1870s and early 1880s, the two were closely connected artistic comrades at the center of a dramatic revolution in French painting.

Caillebotte came somewhat late to the impressionist movement. He was almost a decade younger than the others, and missed the group's early development in the 1860s and early 1870s, starting his career as an artist in the first years of the Third Republic. On the heels of a Salon rejection in 1875, he was recruited by Renoir to join the second impressionist exhibition in 1876. Despite the dearth of primary documents related to Caillebotte's life, his friendship with Renoir is well established: following the 1876 exhibition, and several days after the death of his younger brother René, the exceedingly wealthy Caillebotte wrote a will in which he named Renoir executor of his estate, a designation confirmed in a new will in November 1883, and again when he reviewed his will in 1889. In 1885, Renoir reciprocated the honor, naming Caillebotte godfather to his son Pierre. Renoir was a frequent guest at Caillebotte's estate at Petit-Gennevilliers, often bringing his family (Cat. 32).[1] And it was Caillebotte who lobbied for national recognition of Renoir's contribution to the arts, despite the latter's ambivalence.[2]

The artists' bond was forged during an art historical moment of high excitement and heady ideals: the launching of a movement that aimed to revive the great French tradition of painting, a two-century-old tradition claimed by critics in the 1860s to be foundering. Caillebotte's commitment to impressionism famously extended to his collecting practice. Having inherited a fortune from his father, a successful textile merchant and real estate investor and developer who died in 1874, Caillebotte had the means to advance the cause by buying works from his confrères. He built the finest collection

OPPOSITE PAGE
Detail of Cat. 1, *Luncheon of the Boating Party*:
Gustave Caillebotte.

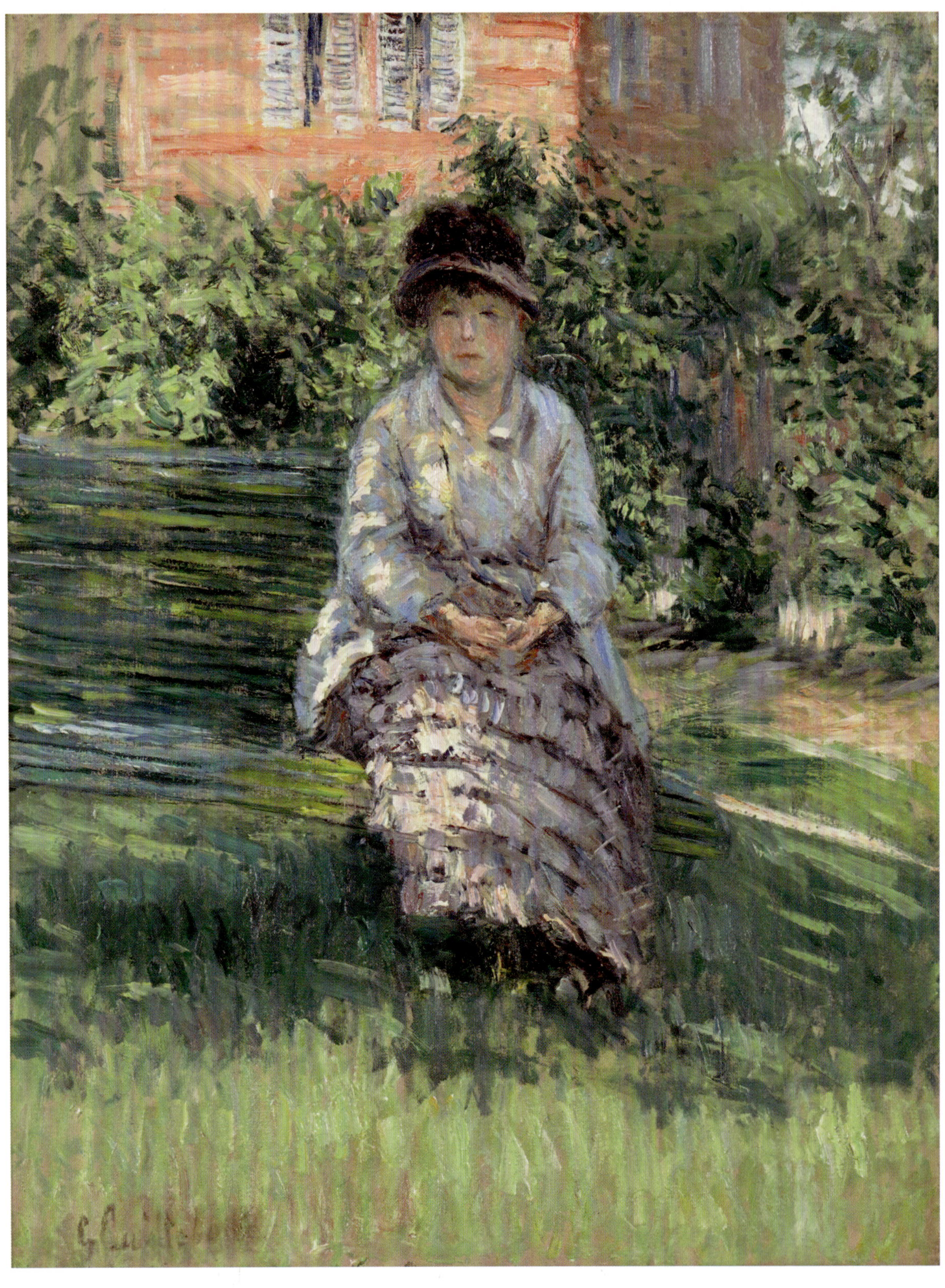

CAT. 32. Gustave Caillebotte, *Madame Renoir in the Garden at Petit-Gennevilliers* (*Madame Renoir dans le jardin du Petit-Gennevilliers*), 1891, oil on canvas, 25¼ × 19¾ in. (64.1 × 50.2 cm). Collection of Bruce Toll.

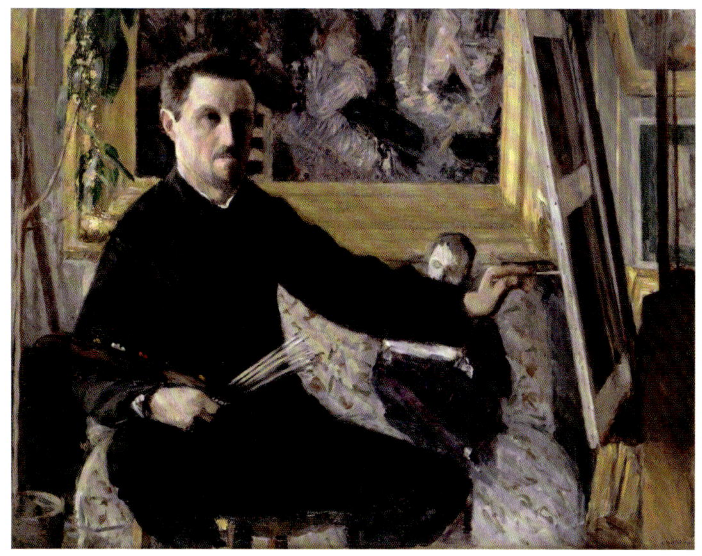

FIG. 12. Gustave Caillebotte, *Self-Portrait at the Easel* (*Autoportrait au chevalet*), 1879–1880, oil on canvas, 36 × 46 in. (90 × 115 cm). Private collection.

of impressionist paintings in existence, bequeathing it to the French state. Several years after his untimely death in 1894, when most of it was formally accepted, it formed the core of the national impressionist holdings. With major works by Cézanne, Degas, Manet, Monet, Pissarro, and Sisley, the collection was perhaps strongest in works by the artist's closest friend, Renoir (fig. 12). Indeed, when the collection hung at the Palais du Luxembourg and then in 1929 was transferred to the Louvre, Renoir looked better than anyone else. One artist wrote that year, "I waited in line to see the new rooms at the Louvre. Remarkable group . . . the Caillebotte collection. It's an enchantment. Sisley, Monet, Pissarro. Voilà the masters. Renoir is beyond unequalled. Manet is strong, but one feels a bit much of the museum about him."[3]

Beyond issues of patronage and emotional affinity, however, was the artistic exchange between them, particularly between 1876 and 1884. During these years, Renoir and Caillebotte were committed to painting urban and suburban life and society, representing classic Parisian types inhabiting the boulevards, cafés, and apartments of the city and its surrounding countryside. Their quest to make modern paintings involved stylistic strategies of cropping, fragmentation, and the close-up. Unexpected views of mundane contemporary scenes were intended to elicit a sense of immediacy and the "real." But where Renoir focused on images of women and amorous conviviality, Caillebotte insistently registered a more masculine milieu, expanding the iconography of impressionism.

At the first independent exhibition, Renoir had exhibited only three works, all large-scale images of women perceived in the criticism as "Parisiennes": a young ballerina wearing makeup and a black ribbon around her neck; a woman dressed up in street couture, and indeed titled *La Parisienne* (1874, National Museum of Wales, Cardiff); and a well-dressed visitor to the Opéra preening in her box, positioning herself to be seen.[4] In the second impressionist show, aside from portraits of his friends (Frédéric Bazille, Victor Chocquet, and Claude Monet) Renoir exhibited a voluptuous female nude in dappled sunlight, two compositions of women in front of a window, women at the piano, and the marvelous fête galante *La Promenade* (J. Paul Getty Museum, Los Angeles, 1870). The latter, portraying an ardent suitor guiding his reluctant conquest along a riverbank, underlined the neo-rococo strain running through Renoir's oeuvre that modernized the sensual odes to romantic love found in the work of Boucher, Fragonard, and Watteau.

Producing a masculine counterpart to Renoir's Parisian panoply, Caillebotte sidestepped the landscapes of the city and countryside that Monet, Pissarro, and Sisley were exhibiting to develop the figural vein of impressionism. At the second impressionist exhibition, he debuted with an image of three men stripped to the waist planing the floors of a Haussmannian apartment, *The Floor Scrapers* (Musée d'Orsay, Paris, 1875). In later shows, he exhibited portraits of his friends Paul Hugot,

"Monsieur R.," and Richard Gallo; and genre scenes of men in urban interiors: *Young Man at his Window* (private collection, 1876), *Man at the Piano* (Bridgestone Museum, Tokyo, 1876), *Portrait of a Man* (Cleveland Museum of Art, 1880), *Man on Balcony, Boulevard Haussmann* (private collection, 1880), and *In a Café* (Musée des Beaux-Arts, Rouen, 1880).

In 1877, Renoir and Caillebotte joined forces to organize arguably the most unified and consistently high-quality impressionist exhibition. Caillebotte found the space on rue Le Peletier and paid the rent, and he and Renoir orchestrated the hang. Their own work dominated the show: Caillebotte's *Paris Street, Rainy Day* (Art Institute of Chicago, 1877) and *Le Pont de l'Europe* (fig. 13), and Renoir's *Dance at Le Moulin de la Galette* (fig. 15) and *The Swing* (Musée d'Orsay, Paris, 1876), both of which Caillebotte owned or would soon acquire. These multi-figured, large-scale paintings announced a level of ambition on par with history painting, and established the two men as the movement's leaders.[5] They show scenes of quintessential Parisian sociability, young urbanites interacting in recognizable city spaces. Renoir's *Moulin de la Galette* celebrated a festive milieu, "this open-air dance hall, perhaps the last that exists still in Paris," that critics perceived with a tinge of nostalgia. Critic Charles Flor O'Squarr continued, "one dances in the little skinny garden next to the windmill . . . there is a great light . . . that illuminates the depths of the canvas like a joyous flame, like a rainbow." And Georges Rivière wrote that "[i]t is an essentially Parisian work . . . it is a page of history, a precious monument to Parisian life, done with rigorous exactitude. No one before him had thought of portraying an event in ordinary life on a canvas of such big dimensions."[6]

Caillebotte's *Le Pont de l'Europe* was only slightly larger, and also represented a mixture of Parisian types in a familiar Parisian venue: the newly constructed cast-iron bridge that spanned the railroad tracks near the gare Saint-Lazare. While the epically scaled *Paris Street, Rainy Day* also portrayed pedestrians on a brand new Haussmannian *carrefour*, *Le Pont de l'Europe* had an anecdotal flavor that enticed the critics. A well-dressed man, often identified as a self-portrait, has just passed a female streetwalker and trains his attention on the young worker leaning against the railing. The explosion of prostitution, female and male, in Paris in the early Third Republic having been newly deemed an urgent social problem, critics picked up on the aura of sexual commerce.[7] The critic Jacques described the sly ambiguity of the scene as "the young idler in front of *une élégante*, exquisite under her transparent birdcage veil: a small common comedy that we've all observed with a discreet and benevolent smile. The figure of the worker leaning on the balustrade is audacious: it stops the action. However, it is a necessity. The painter could not leave the whole foreground of his canvas completely empty. It was tactful for him to have understood that."[8]

Renoir's *Leaving the Conservatory* (fig. 14), also painted in 1876–1877, is similarly anecdotal. Like *Le Pont de l'Europe*, the scene takes place on the street in the 9th arrondissement, presented as if glimpsed by a passerby. Here the viewer observes a flirtatious engagement between fashionable young girls and well-to-do young men, a scene full of portent but unrealized by the temporal limitations of the painting. Although sexual commerce could also be suggested in this scene, it has a more romantic tone. Where *Le Pont de l'Europe* records the urban practice of sexual cruising, Renoir's protagonists interact through gaze and touch in a more familiar mode.

Inspired by Manet, Caillebotte and Renoir addressed another archetypically modern urban motif, the café. The focus

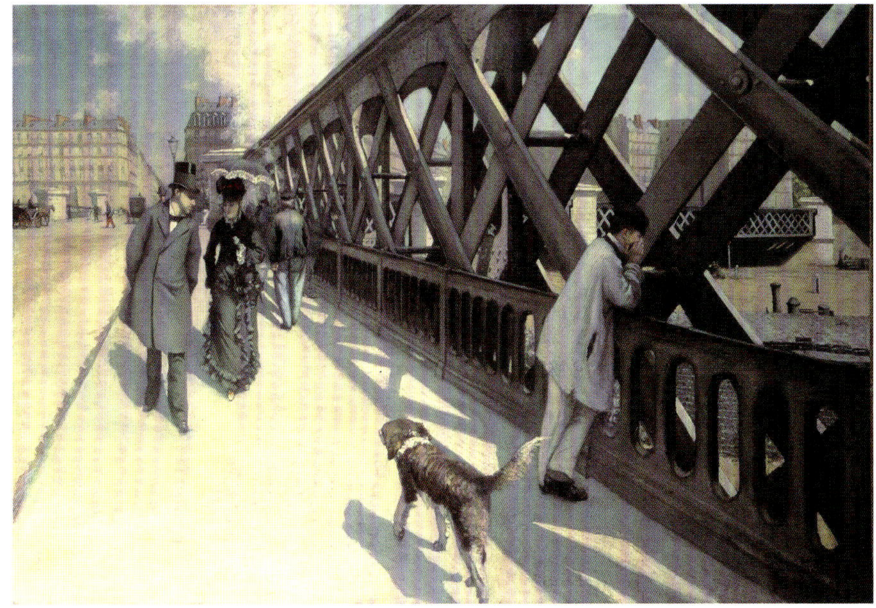

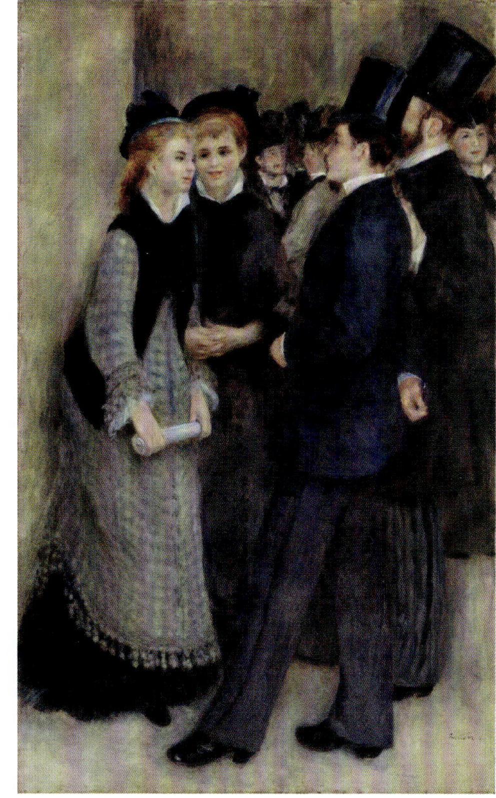

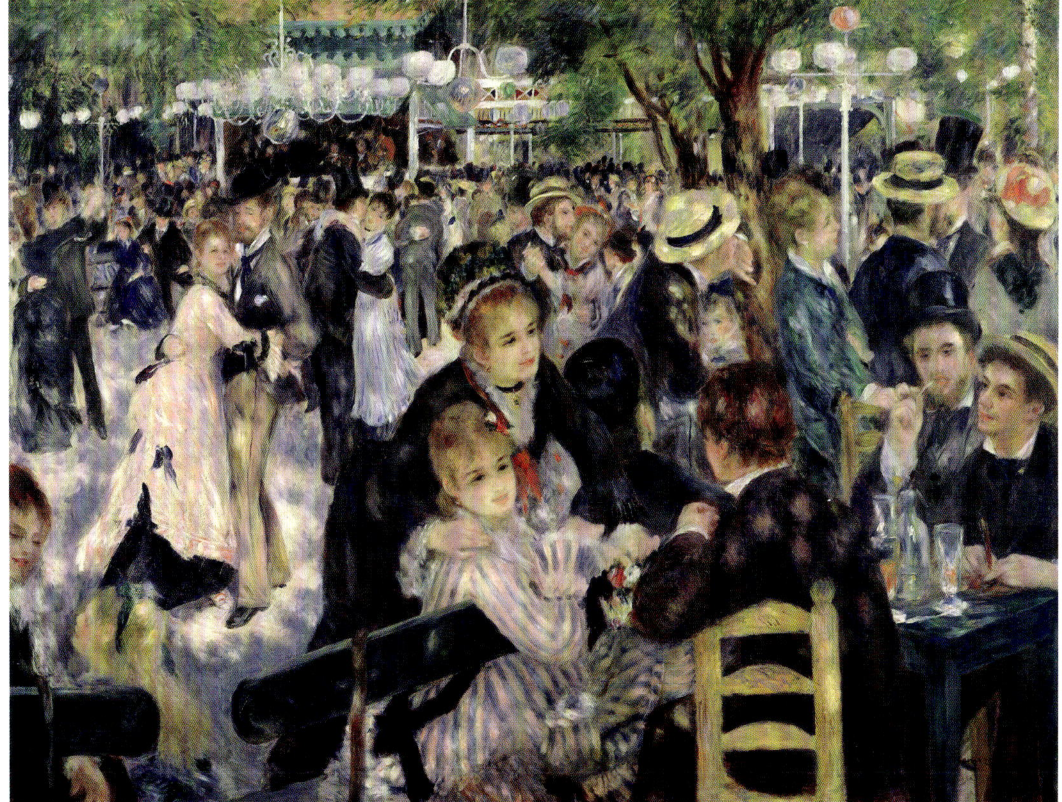

FIG. 13. Gustave Caillebotte, *Le Pont de l'Europe*, 1876, oil on canvas, 49¼ × 70⅞ in. (125 × 180 cm). Petit Palais, Geneva.

FIG. 14. Pierre-Auguste Renoir, *Leaving the Conservatory* (*La Sortie du conservatoire*), 1876–1877, oil on canvas, 73⅞ × 46¼ in. (187.5 × 117.5 cm). The Barnes Foundation, Philadelphia.

FIG. 15. Pierre-Auguste Renoir, *Dance at Le Moulin de la Galette*, (*Bal du Moulin de la Galette*) 1876, oil on canvas, 51¾ × 69½ in. (131.5 × 176.5 cm). Musée d'Orsay, Paris.

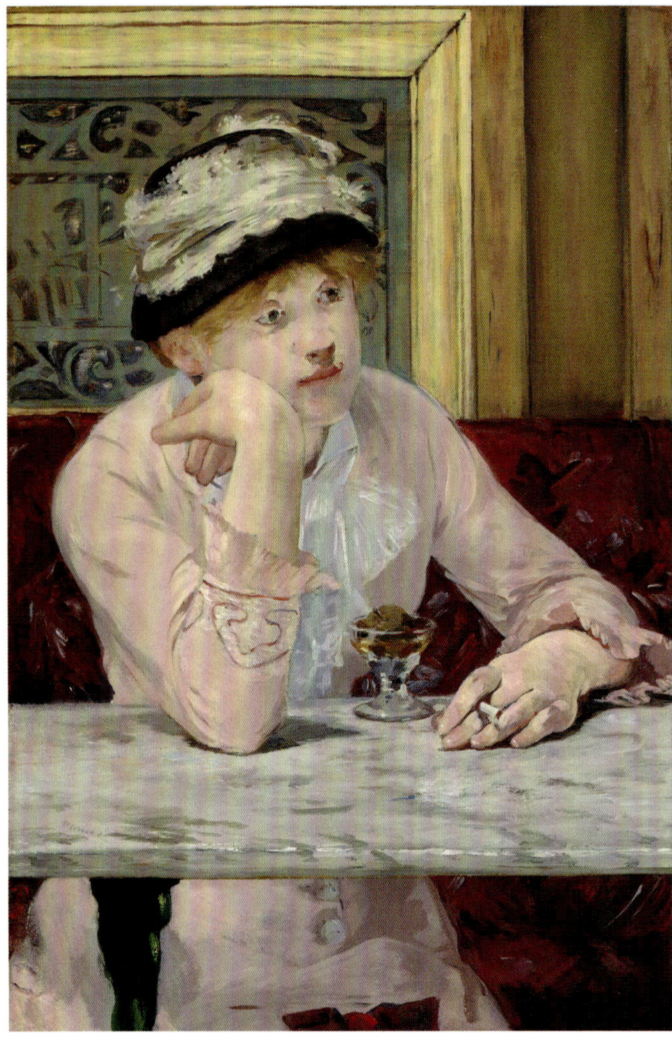

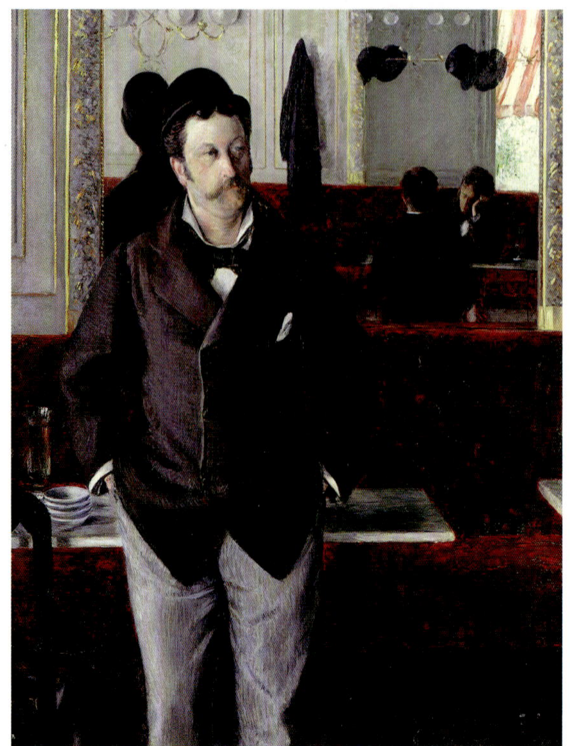

FIG. 17. Gustave Caillebotte, *At the Café, Rouen* (*Au Café, Rouen*), 1880, oil on canvas, 60¼ × 44⅞ in. (153 × 114 cm). Musée des Beaux-Arts, Rouen.

FIG. 16. Édouard Manet, *Plum Brandy* (*La Prune*), 1877, oil on canvas, 29 × 19¾ in. (73.6 × 50.2 cm). National Gallery of Art, Washington, D.C., Collection of Mr. & Mrs. Paul Mellon.

of Manet's compositions is generally the female table server, client (fig. 16), or most notoriously, and not until 1881–1882, a barmaid.[9] Renoir followed suit, depicting women participating in Parisian nightlife made freshly spectacular by the proliferation of cafés with technologically advanced artificial lighting (fig. 18). In Caillebotte's *At the Café*, his only foray into this genre, he replaced the female subject with a male barfly, who stands slightly rumpled and outmoded before the marble table, velvet banquette, and gilt-edged mirror waiting for the evening's events to begin (fig. 17).

Turning to leisure culture on the river just outside the capital, Manet became intrigued with the possibilities of boating compositions while working with Monet and Renoir in Argenteuil in 1874. *Argenteuil* (fig. 19) and *Boating* (Metropolitan Museum of Art, New York, 1874) feature couples along the Seine engaged in an activity culturally codified as romantic by advertisers, caricaturists, and contemporary writers like Maupassant and Zola.[10] In a vessel made for two, a boater, dressed in a tight cotton shirt that exposes his arms, guides his precious cargo across the river's surface with no real aim other than the pleasure of her company. She wears a brightly colored patterned dress and a hat with ribbons that will stream in the breeze, an appealing sunlit spectacle. It is a genre characterized by sensuality and seduction, promising fleeting "Sunday" pleasures despite the rather distracted tone of Manet's boaters.

Both Renoir and Caillebotte seized on the boating genre, an ideally impressionist motif in its combination of a fashionable,

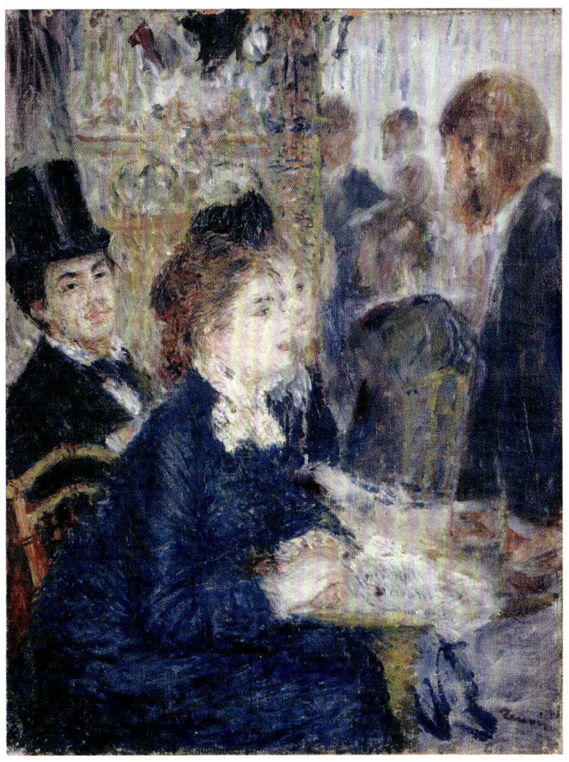

FIG. 18. Pierre-Auguste Renoir, *In the Café* (*Au Café*), c. 1877, oil on canvas, 14 × 10¾ in. (35.7 × 27.5 cm), Kröller Müller Museum, Otterlo.

FIG. 19. Édouard Manet, *Argenteuil*, 1874, oil on canvas, 58⅝ × 45¼ in. (149 × 115 cm). Musée des Beaux-Arts, Tournai.

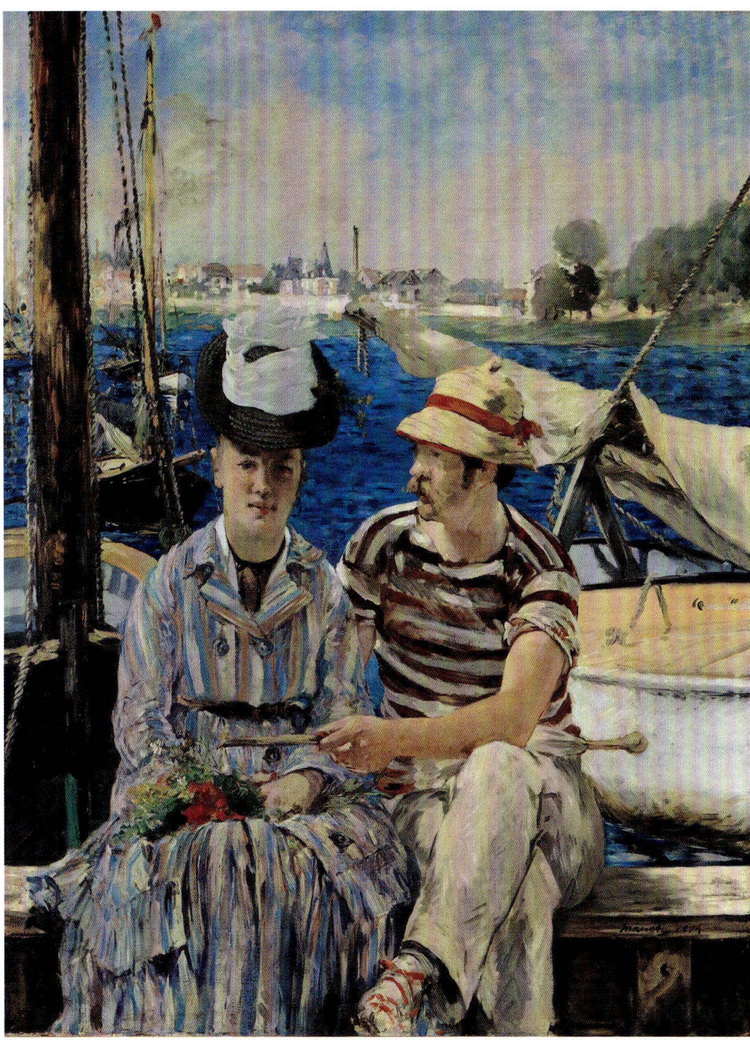

contemporary subject with the painterly challenge of sunlit figures and the river's reflective surface. Like Manet's *Boating*, Renoir's *Girl in a Boat* (private collection, 1877) places the viewer in the hull with a young woman, who gazes directly at her beholder while loosely holding a rigging rope. Behind her in another boat, a *canotier* avidly paddles after her.

In 1877 and into 1878, Caillebotte painted a series of boating pictures devoid of female presence, their focus on athletic *canotiers* expertly paddling and rowing from a range of angles, or handling their boats, as in *A Man Docking His Skiff* (Cat. 33). These were activities with which Caillebotte was intimately familiar, himself a passionate boater, an award-winning sailboat racer and designer, and president of the Paris Sailing Club.[11] His most accomplished painting in

the genre, surely inspired by Manet, is *Rower in a Top Hat* (fig. 20). Again, the artist places the viewpoint inside the boat, in this case opposite a handsome dandy in a striped shirt and top hat. Two men in boating-club attire—white cotton jersey and straw hat—hover over his shoulder in their own craft.

The "erotics of boating" underlie the emotional charge of these paintings, as they do earlier works like *Lunch at the Restaurant Fournaise* (Cat. 22) and, perhaps most amusingly, Renoir's later *Oarsmen at Chatou* (Cat. 29), in which a boater impatiently awaits his passenger; but is it the gentleman standing on the bank in the white jacket or the curvaceous, colorfully attired woman who averts her gaze—or both? The rest of the hastily brushed-in painting seems an afterthought to the detail of this small drama.

73

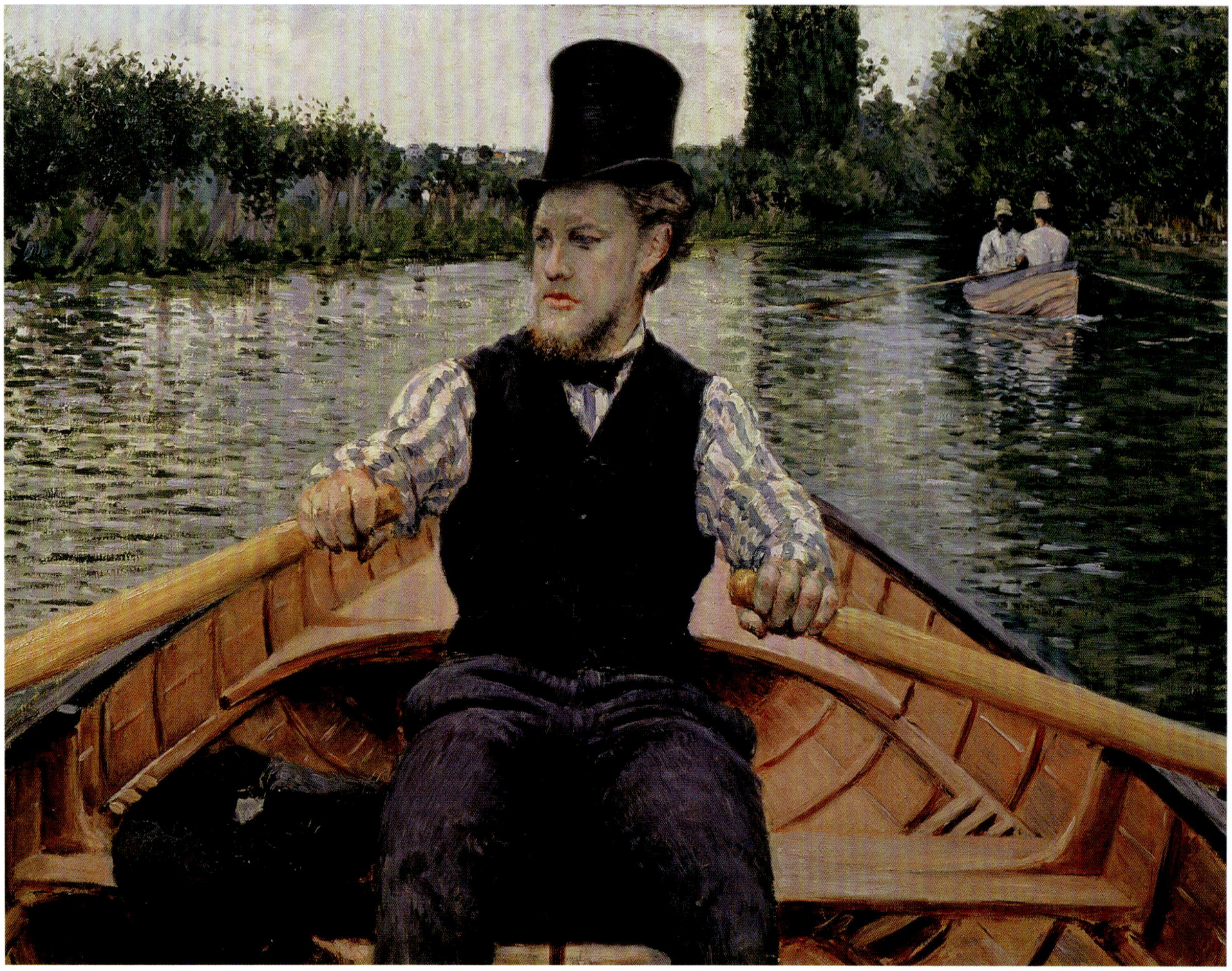

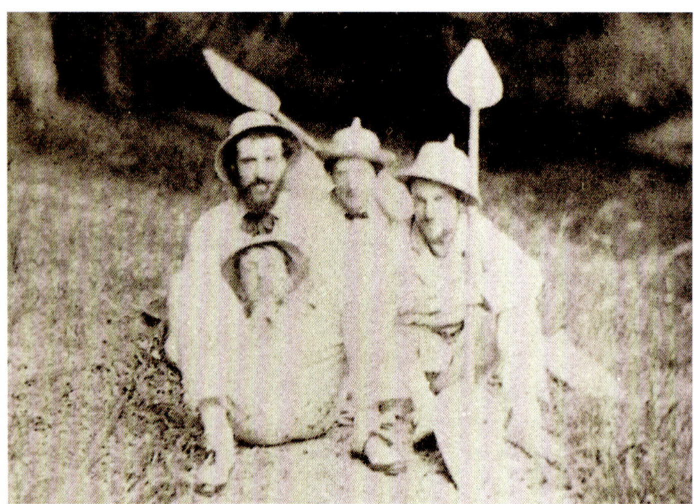

FIG. 20. Gustave Caillebotte, *Rower in a Top Hat* (*Canotier au chapeau haut de forme*), c. 1877–1878, oil on canvas, 35⅜ × 46 in. (90 × 117 cm). Private collection.

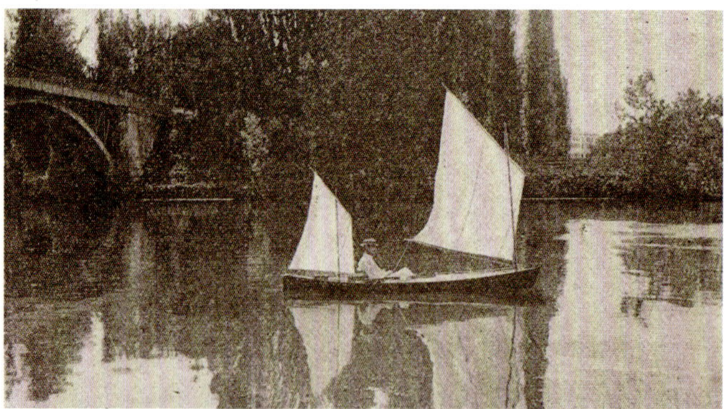

FIG. 22. *The Railway Bridge in Rueil* (*Le pont du chemin de fer à Rueil*), digital print from a late 19th-century postcard. Via Joconde – Portail des collections des musées de France.

FIG. 21. Anonymous, *Gustave Caillebotte and His Fellow Boaters* (*Gustave Caillebotte et ses amis canotiers*), c. 1877–1879. Comité Caillebotte, Paris.

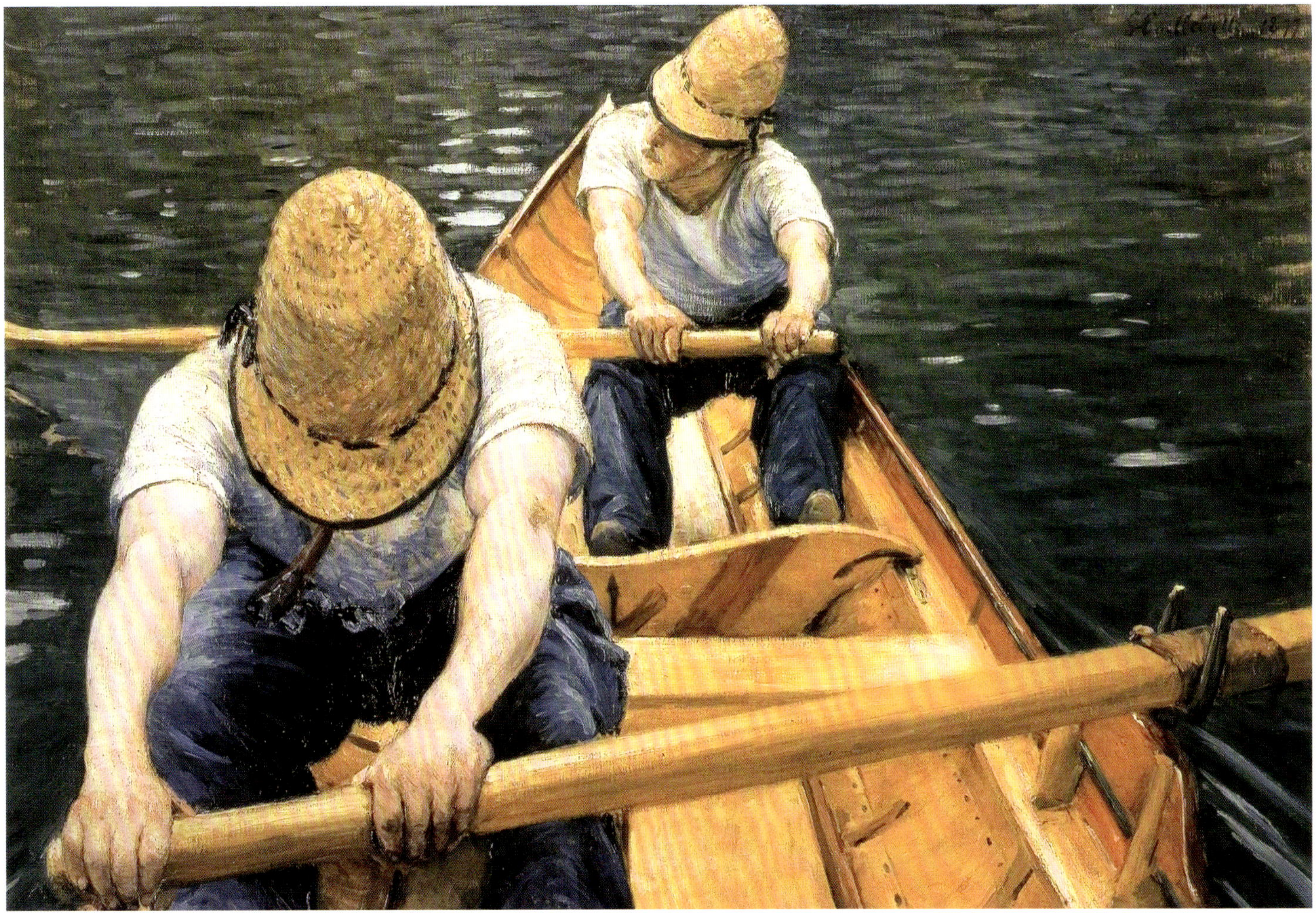

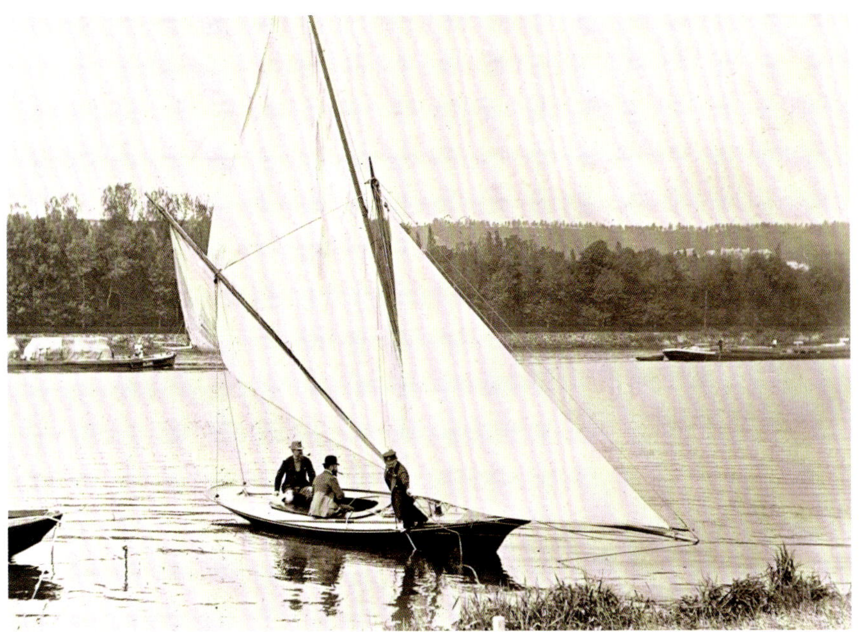

ABOVE
FIG. 23. Gustave Caillebotte,
Oarsmen Rowing on the Yerres
(*Canotiers ramant sur l'Yerres*),
1877, oil on canvas, 24 × 36 in.
(61 × 91.4 cm). Private collection.

LEFT
FIG. 24. Gustave Caillebotte,
*Sailboats Reaching the Shore at
Petit-Gennevilliers* (*Voiliers accostant
sur la rive du Petit-Gennevilliers*).
Comité Caillebotte, Paris.

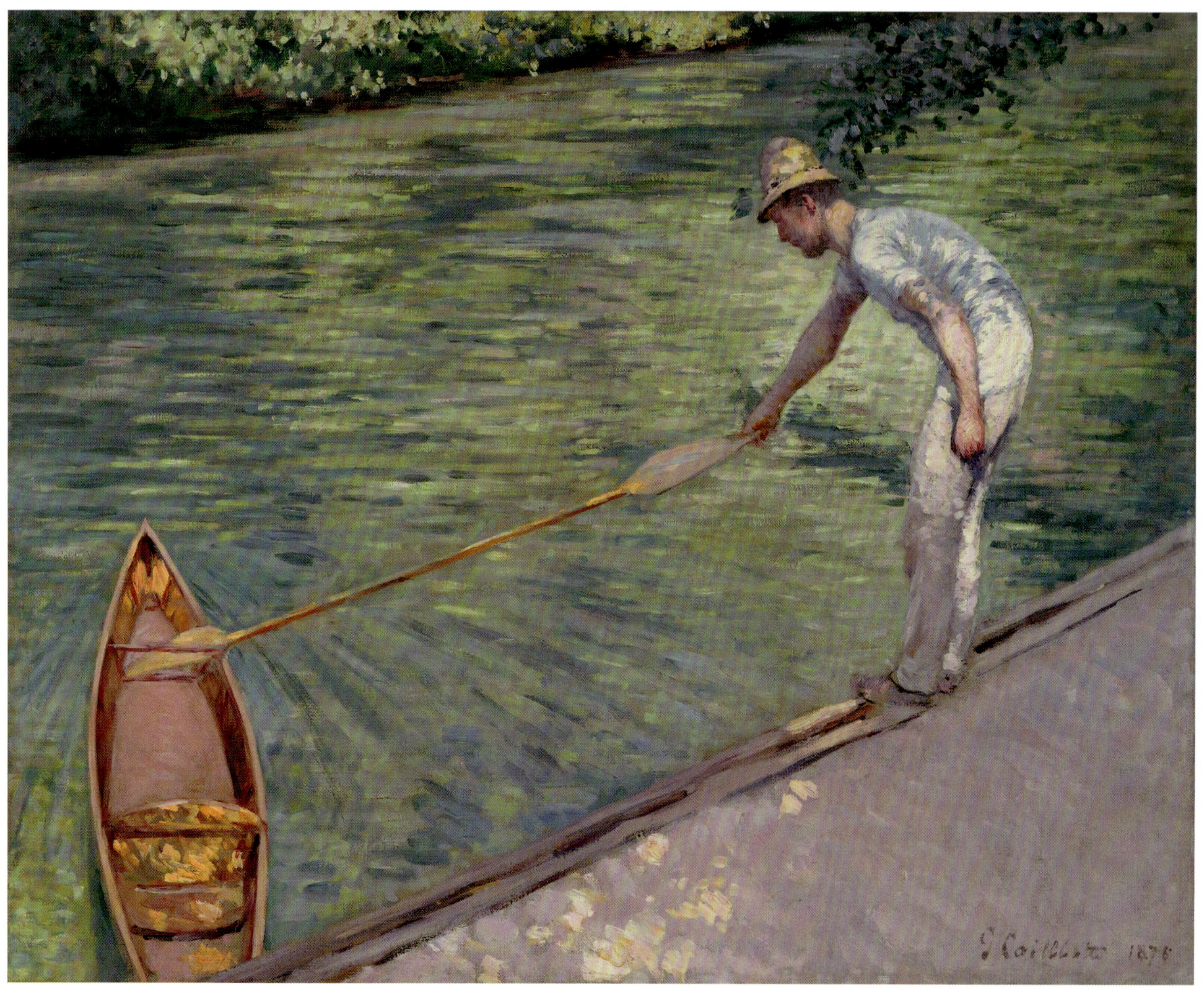

CAT. 33. Gustave Caillebotte, *A Man Docking His Skiff* (*Canotier ramenant sa périssoire bord de l'Yerres*), 1878, oil on canvas, 29 × 36½ in. (73.7 × 92.7 cm). Virginia Museum of Fine Arts, Collection of Mr. & Mrs. Paul Mellon.

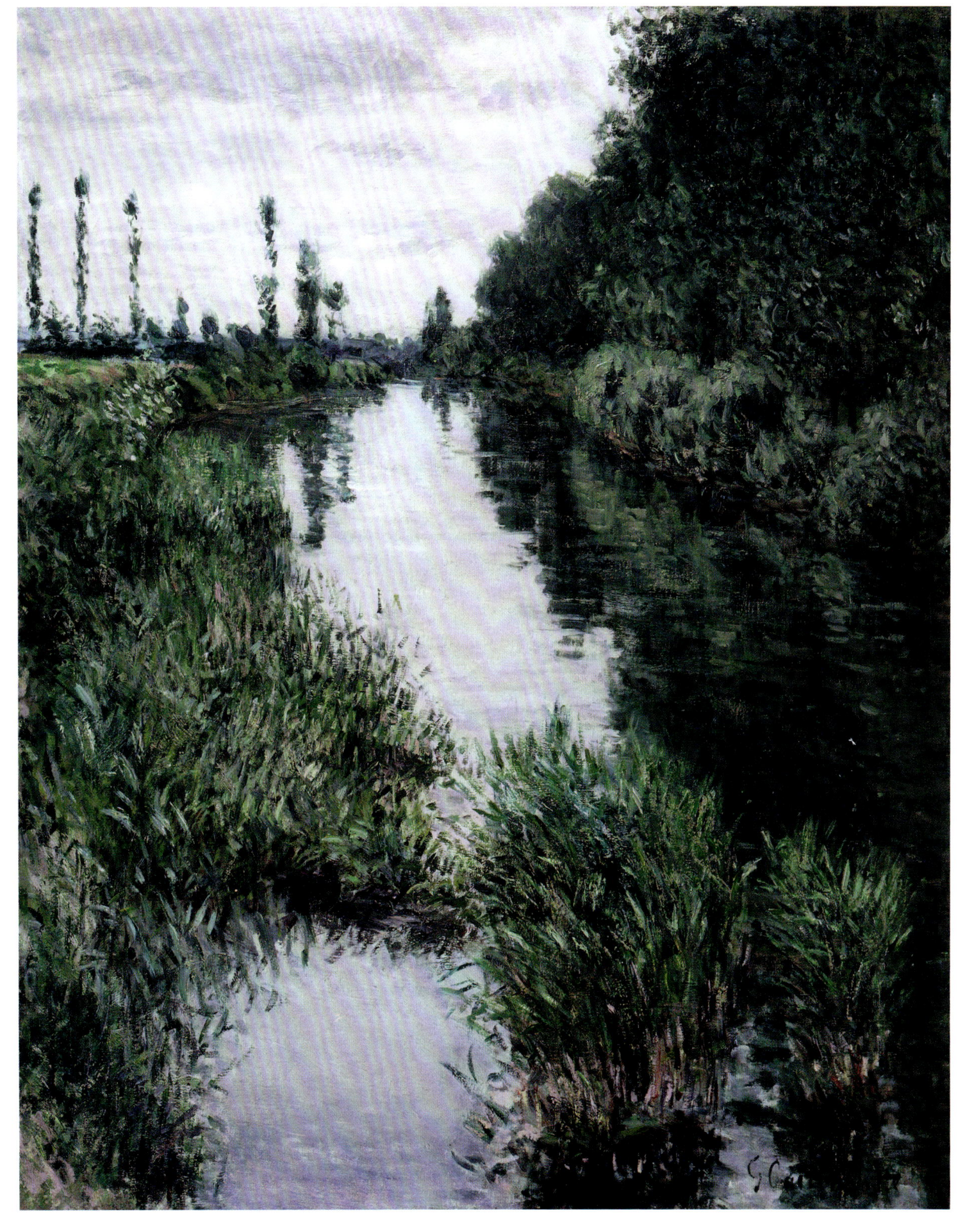

CAT. 34. Gustave Caillebotte, *Small Branch of the Seine at Argenteuil* (*Petit bras de la Seine à Argenteuil*), 1884, oil on canvas, 35 × 28¼ in. (88.9 × 71.8 cm). Private collection.

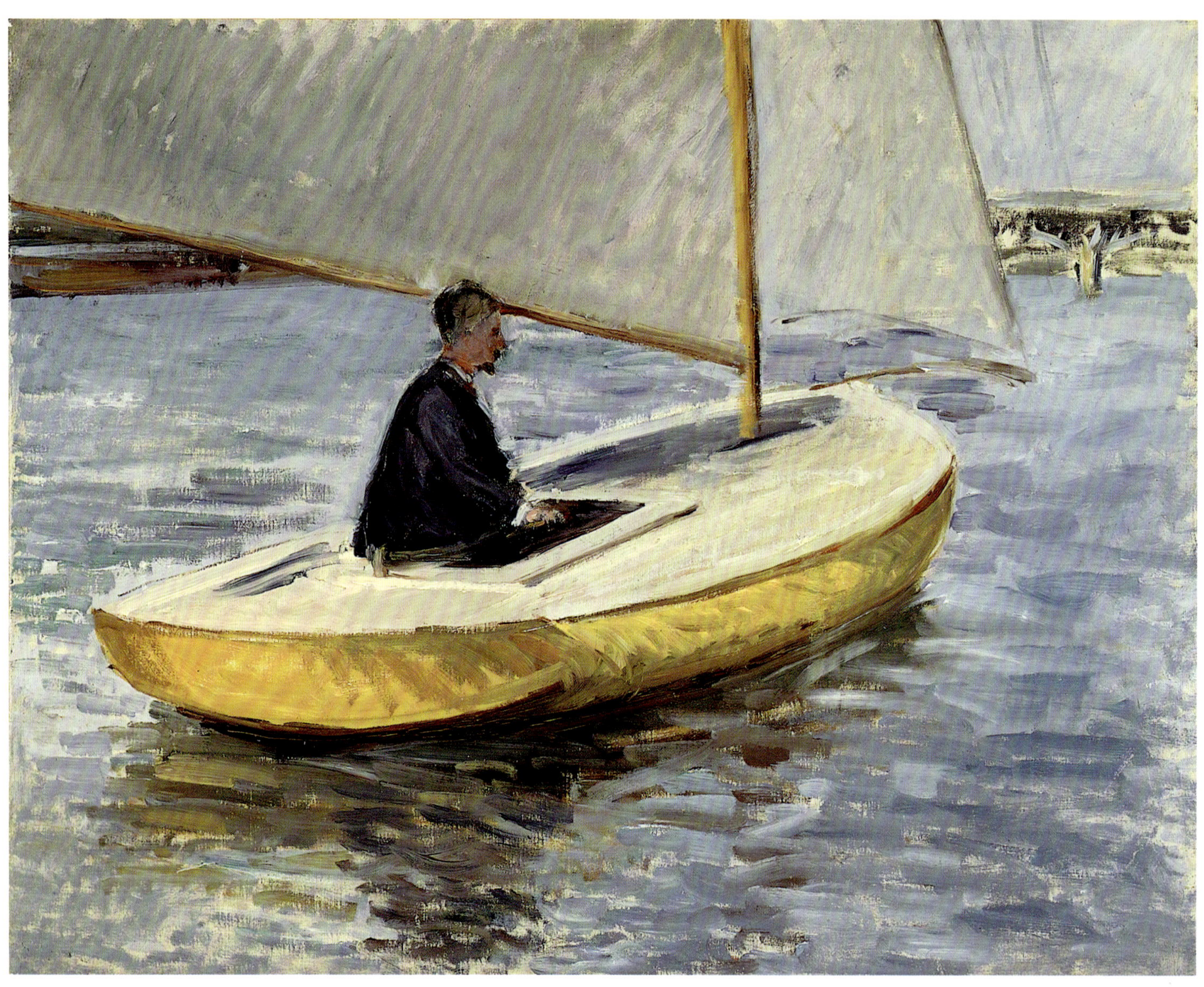

CAT. 35. Gustave Caillebotte, *The Yellow Boat* (*Le Bateau jaune*), 1891, oil on canvas, 28¾ × 36⅜ in. (73 cm × 92.3 cm). The Norton Simon Foundation, Pasadena, CA.

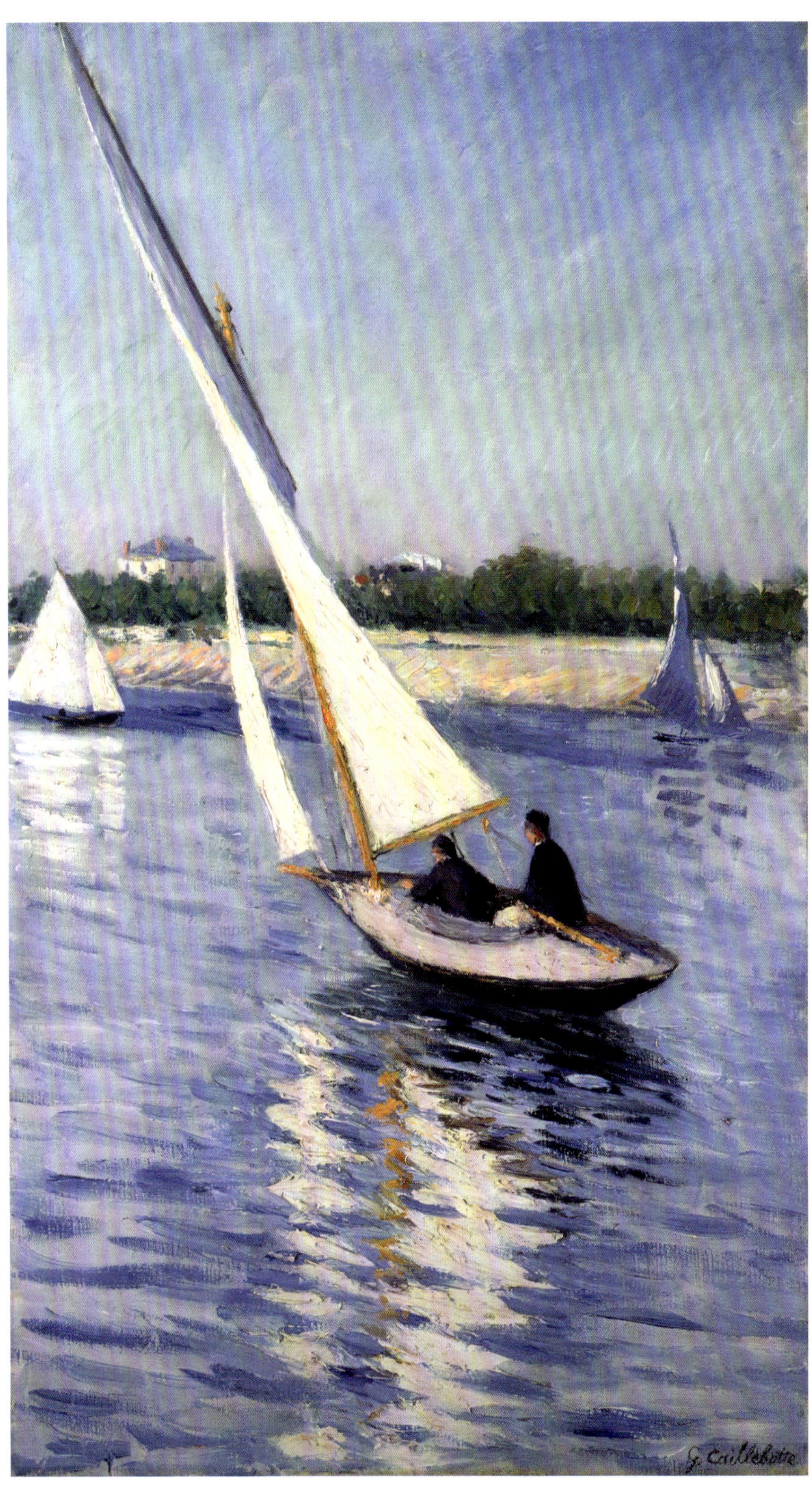

CAT. 36. Gustave Caillebotte,
Sailboats on the Seine at Argenteuil
(*Voiliers sur la Seine à Argenteuil*),
1893, oil on canvas, 28⅞ × 17 in.
(75 × 43.2 cm). Private collection.

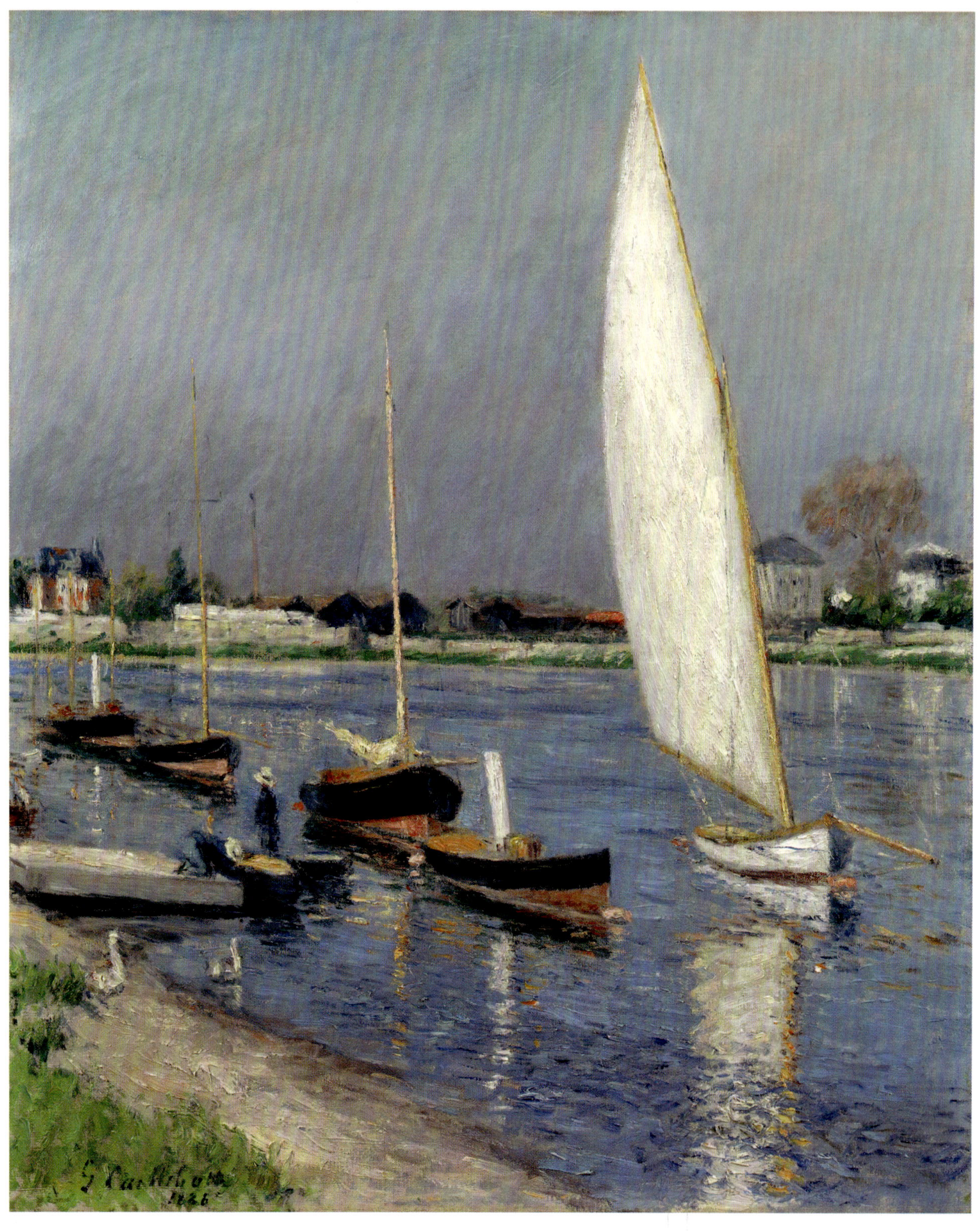

CAT. 37. Gustave Caillebotte, *Sailboats on the Seine at Argenteuil* (*Voiliers sur la Seine à Argenteuil*), 1886, oil on canvas, 25½ × 21¼ in. (65 × 54 cm). Private collection, courtesy of Simon Dickinson Ltd., London.

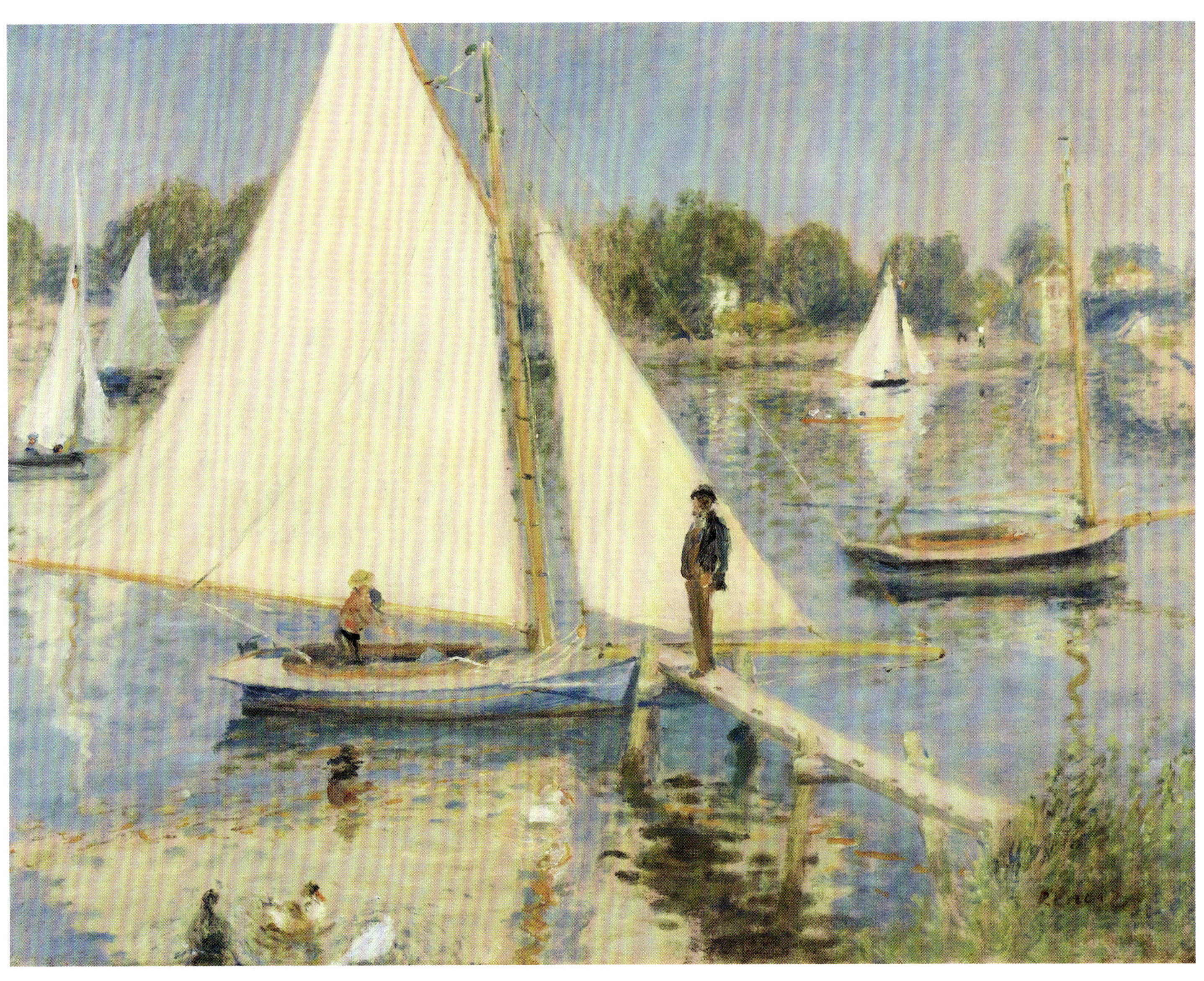

CAT. 38. Pierre-Auguste Renoir, *The Seine at Argenteuil* (*La Seine à Argenteuil*), 1874, oil on canvas, 19¾ × 25¾ in. (50.1 × 65.4 cm). Portland Art Museum, Oregon, Bequest of Winslow B. Ayer, 35.2.

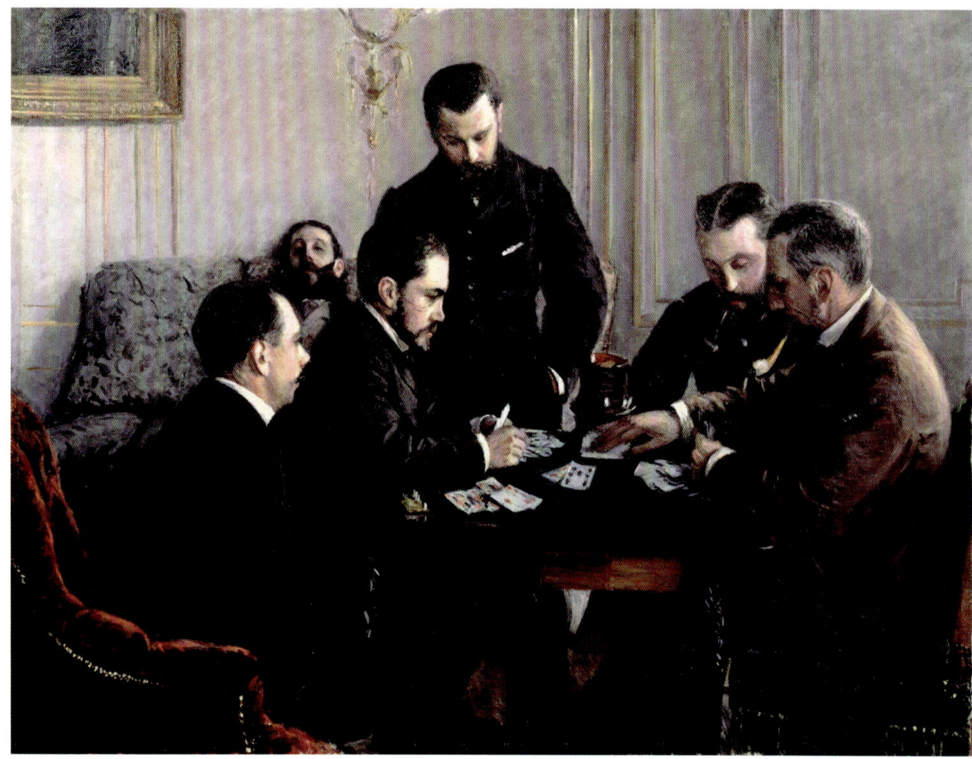

The great masterpiece of the boating genre is, of course, *Luncheon of the Boating Party*, with the two lightly clad, muscled boaters striking masculine poses that anchor and frame the glittering swirl of sociability. Renoir's large-scale, highly ambitious painting "shared the honors of the exhibition" with a multi-figure composition of the same scale and dimensions by Caillebotte at the seventh impressionist show of 1882 (fig. 25).[12] Both paintings featured a group of friends gathered around a table enjoying themselves: Renoir's brilliantly colored rendering of men and women chatting and drinking, abuzz with the warmth of a summer day in a riverside café, found its counterpoint in Caillebotte's *Game of Bezique*, in which the distractions of women, hot sunshine, and alcohol are eschewed as his affluent friends gather in his Parisian flat to focus on an intense game of cards. Dressed in the monochromatic bourgeois male uniform, in the sparsely decorated apartment Caillebotte shared with his brother Martial during the years before the latter married, this group of bachelors gathers in hushed concentration. They are wholly focused on the game, with the exception of Paul Hugot, who slumps on a couch in the background as if exhausted, or

defeated, by play. Against the rhythmic pulse of flirtatious conviviality in Renoir's scene, then, Caillebotte registers that conventional homosocial activity: the men's card game.

The 1882 exhibition was the last artist-organized impressionist show in which either painter participated. Against the vision for the group aggressively advanced by Degas, who sought to open it up to artists whose style did not, in Caillebotte's eyes, align with that of "pure" impressionism, the younger painter agonized over the group's dissolution. The lure of a more stable, assured future embodied by Salon acceptance continued to exert its pull on Monet, Sisley, and particularly Renoir, who had been returning to the Salon since 1879 and coming back to the impressionist group only under extraordinary pressure from Caillebotte. At the same time, the dealer Paul Durand-Ruel began having more success selling their pictures independent of the group shows. Renoir in particular grew closer to Durand-Ruel, who bought *Luncheon of the Boating Party* within weeks of its completion. Writing from a visit to Algiers in 1881, Renoir told Durand-Ruel, "I want to paint stunning pictures that you can sell for very high prices."[13]

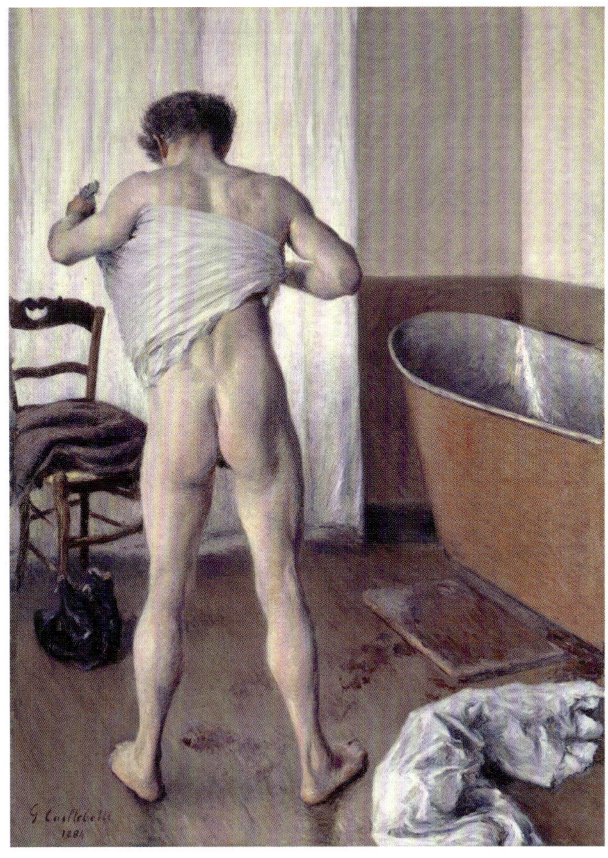

FIG. 26. Gustave Caillebotte, *Man at His Bath* (*Homme au bain*), 1884, oil on canvas, 57 × 45 in. (144.8 × 114.3 cm). Museum of Fine Arts, Boston. Museum purchase with funds by exchange from an Anonymous gift, Bequest of William A. Coolidge, Juliana Cheney Edwards Collection, and from the Charles H. Bayley Picture and Painting Fund, Edward Jackson Holmes Fund, Fanny P. Mason Fund in memory of Alice Thevin, Arthur Gordon Tompkins Fund, Gift of Mrs. Samuel Parkman Oliver—Eliza R. Oliver Fund, Sophie F. Friedman Fund, Robert M. Rosenberg Family Fund, and funds donated in honor of George T. M. Shackelford, Chair, Art of Europe, and Arthur K. Solomon Curator of Modern Art, 1996—2011.

In April 1883, Durand-Ruel gave Renoir a monographic exhibition to which Caillebotte was a major lender.[14] Although, or perhaps because, he was independently wealthy, Caillebotte sympathized with Renoir's mounting financial pressures and continued to support him emotionally, and in all likelihood also financially.[15] But the thrill of changing the course of French painting, the organized, idealistic avant-garde movement of impressionism, had largely dissipated.[16] Manet, the aesthetic father of the group, died during the run of Renoir's exhibition. Later that year, in a conversation with Vollard, Renoir declared impressionism "a blind alley."[17] Caillebotte largely moved away from Paris, spending an increasing amount of time at his estate in Petit-Gennevilliers sailing, boat-designing, gardening, and painting garden- and riverscapes (Cat. 35). The "edgy" pictures of the late 1870s and early 1880s that furthered Manet's realist project of modern urban engagement, that fulfilled Baudelaire's credo to paint the "heroism of modern life" and were promoted by Duranty in his 1876 essay on "The New Painting," shifted to an emphasis on plein-air landscape painting, color experimentation, and the deployment of a free, fragmented touch. It was a shift surely encouraged by Durand-Ruel, who finally started realizing a profit, continuing his monographic exhibitions and, as the decade unfolded, exporting what would become "classic impressionism" to New York.[18]

As the artistic pas de deux between the two artists wound down, Renoir increasingly devoted himself to the female nude and Caillebotte turned to landscapes almost exclusively, both of them leaving behind the urban/suburban genre paintings for which they are most celebrated. In a painting dated 1884, however, Caillebotte produced a work so startling that it seems not to have been exhibited, or barely, for over a hundred years (fig. 26). Where Renoir, alongside Degas, updated the genre of the nude female bather by representing "real" women stepping from contemporary bathtubs or frolicking by the riverside, Caillebotte turned it on its head by supplanting the female body with a "real" male nude. The bather has left wet footprints on the wood floor as he towels himself off, bracing his muscular form against the motion. The physical vitality and glowing flesh of his brilliantly rendered body, almost life-size, mark an aggressive foray into an as-yet-unestablished motif: *l'homme à sa toilette*. The painting was listed first in Caillebotte's suggested group of submissions for Durand-Ruel's 1888 Paris exhibition, although it was not ultimately installed.[19] Later that year, Caillebotte sent it to *Les XX* in Brussels, but even at that most radical of venues, it

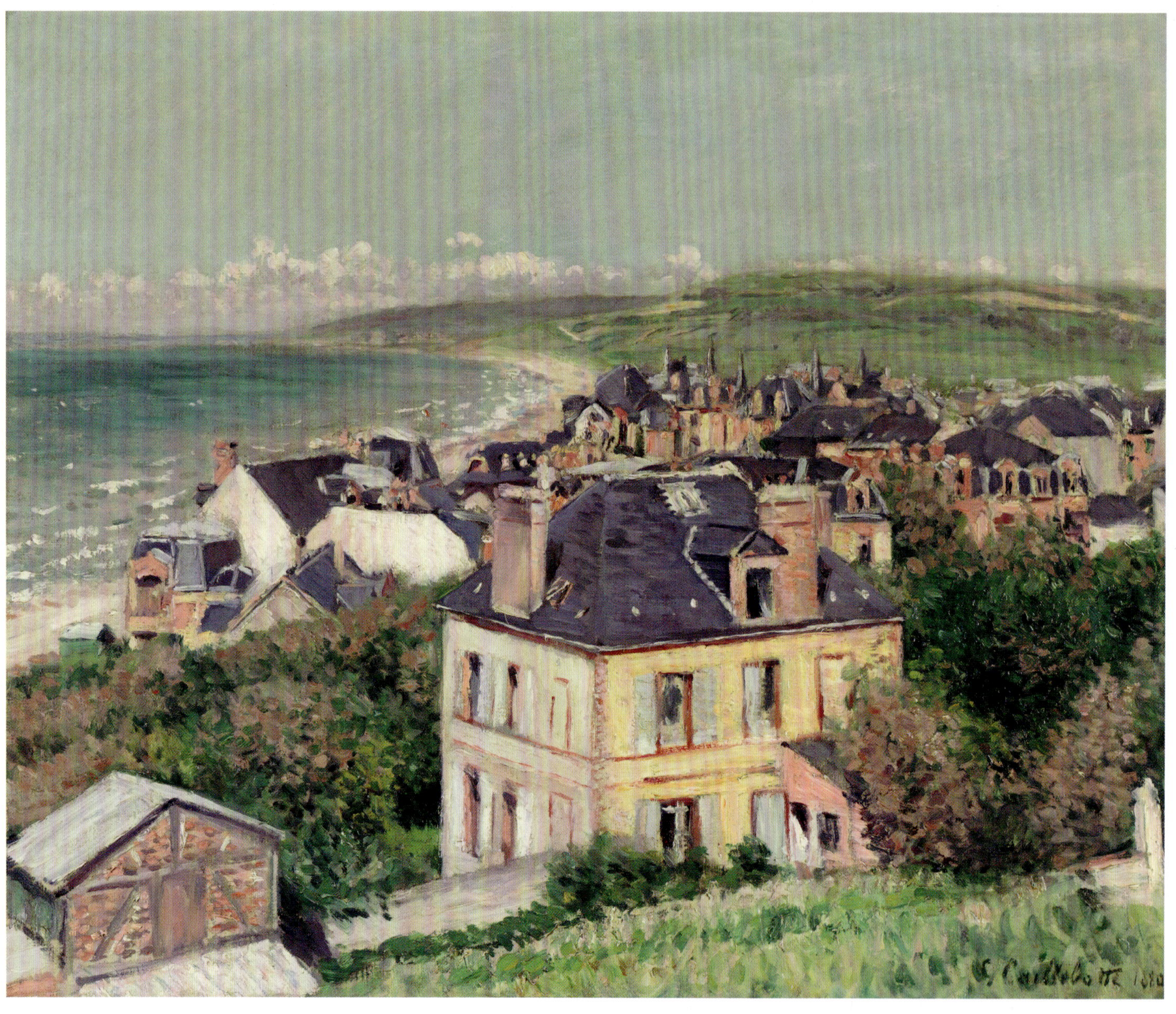

CAT. 39. Gustave Caillebotte, *Villers-sur-Mer*, 1880, oil on canvas, 23⅝ × 28¹¹⁄₁₆ in. (60 × 73 cm).
The Phillips Collection, Washington, D.C., Promised gift of Mr. & Mrs. G. Duane Vieth.

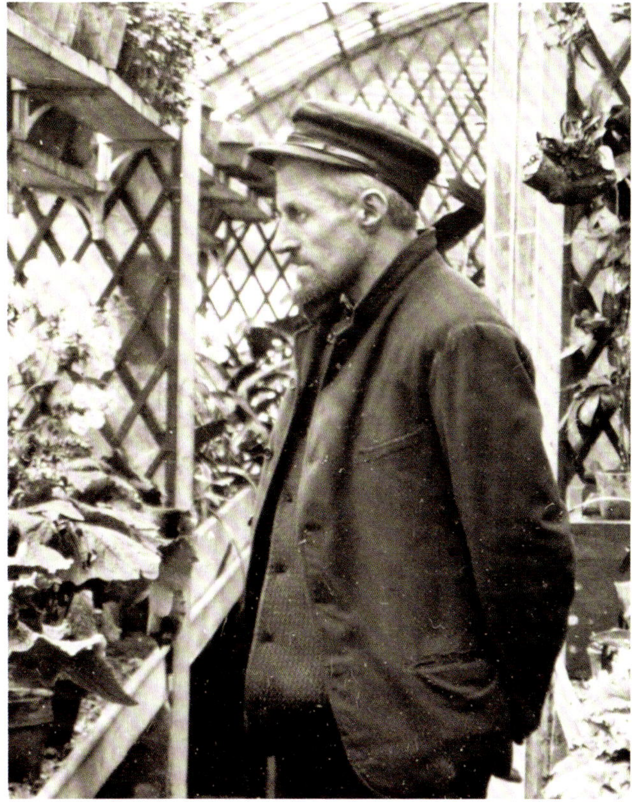

FIG. 27. Martial Caillebotte, *Gustave Caillebotte in his Greenhouse* (*L'Artiste dans la serre*), c. 1892. Comité Caillebotte, Paris.

seems to have been shown in a back room, and may not have hung through the run of the show.[20] One can only wonder what Renoir thought of the painting.

Renoir and Caillebotte maintained their rapport until the latter's untimely death in 1894, when Renoir stepped in to fulfill his role as estate executor assigned to him almost two decades earlier, alongside Gustave's brother Martial. The artists were unlikely friends, from very different social and economic classes, seven years apart in age, with distinct interests and passions. The bond they forged through a shared heroic vision for the future of painting, so dazzlingly commemorated in *Luncheon of the Boating Party*, mellowed but remained intact even as that vision dissipated in the later 1880s and early 1890s.

1. Among the rare firsthand accounts of Caillebotte's social life is Gustave Geffroy's description of Renoir teasing the younger painter at their regular Café Riche gatherings. Secretly enlisting the help of an encyclopedia, Renoir would lure the extraordinarily well-read Caillebotte into discussions on arcane subjects to try to stump him, mocking his responses as Caillebotte's face turned from red to purple. Quoted in Ralph Shikes and Paula Harper, *Pissarro, His Life and Work* (New York: Horizon Press, 1980), p. 273.

2. Musée d'Orsay, Documentation, Fonds Monet, ODO 2007-1-16.

3. Quoted in Pierre Wittmer, "Auguste Renoir and Gustave Caillebotte," in Marchesseau 2014, p. 73.

4. *The Dancer*, 1874, National Gallery of Art, Washington and *La Loge*, 1874, The Courtauld Gallery, London.

5. See the reviews of Jules Claretie and Marc de Montifaud in particular. Reproduced in Berson 1996, pp. 140 and 170. Translations of the critical texts are my own.

6. Georges Rivière, "L'Exposition des impressionnistes," *L'Impressionniste*, April 6, 1877, pp. 2–6, reproduced in Berson 1996, p. 179.

7. See Nienke Bakker et al., *Splendours & Miseries: Images of Prostitution in France, 1850–1910*, exh.

cat., Musée d'Orsay, Paris, and Van Gogh Museum, Amsterdam (Paris: Flammarion, 2015).

8. "Deux silhouettes particulièrement se dessinent : un jeune oisif, précédant une élégante, exquise sous la transparence de son voile moucheté : petite comédie commune, que nous avons tous observée, avec un sourire discret et bienveillant. La figure de l'ouvrier, accoudé sur la balustrade, est audacieuse ; elle coupe l'action. Cependant, elle est une nécessité. Le peintre ne pouvait laisser tout le devant de sa toile complètement vide. C'est du tact que de l'avoir compris." The critic engages in some wordplay and euphemisms which do not translate well into English: "une élégante" signified a female prostitute, and his use of a female pronoun for "*la figure*" instead of using "*il*" for the worker introduces gender ambiguity. Jacques, "Menus propos: exposition impressionniste," *L'Homme libre*, April 12, 1877, pp. 1–2, reproduced in Berson 1996, p. 156.

9. Manet, *Corner of a Café Concert* (National Gallery, London, 1878–1880); *Plum Brandy* (fig. 5), and *A Bar at the Folies-Bergères* (The Courtauld Gallery, London, 1882).

10. See for instance Guy de Maupassant's *Le Père* (1881) and *Yvette* (1884), and Émile Zola's *Thérèse Raquin* (1867).

11. Caillebotte won sailing medals almost every year

from 1879 to 1892, and designed his own race boat.

12. See Paul de Charry's review in *Le Pays*, March 10, 1882, in Berson 1996, pp. 383–384.

13. Knowing he was abandoning his friends, he added, "Please plead my cause with my friends. I send to the Salon for purely commercial reasons." Richard Friedenthal, *Letters of the Great Artists* (New York: Random House, 1963), pp. 133–136.

14. Caillebotte lent *Woman Reading, The Swing, Dance at Le Moulin de la Galette, Landscape,* and *Railway Bridge at Chatou.*

15. In a codicil to his will in November 1883, Caillebotte absolved Renoir of all debts owed him.

16. For more on this shift, see Joel Isaacson, *The Crisis of Impressionism: 1878–1882* (Ann Arbor: University of Michigan Museum of Art, 1980).

17. Vollard 1919, p. 118.

18. See Patry 2015.

19. Handwritten list kept in the Durand-Ruel archives, Paris.

20. For more on Caillebotte's "edgy" oeuvre, see, most recently, Mary Morton and George Shackelford, *Gustave Caillebotte: The Painter's Eye*, exh. cat., National Gallery of Art, Washington, and Kimbell Art Museum, Fort Worth (Chicago, 2015).

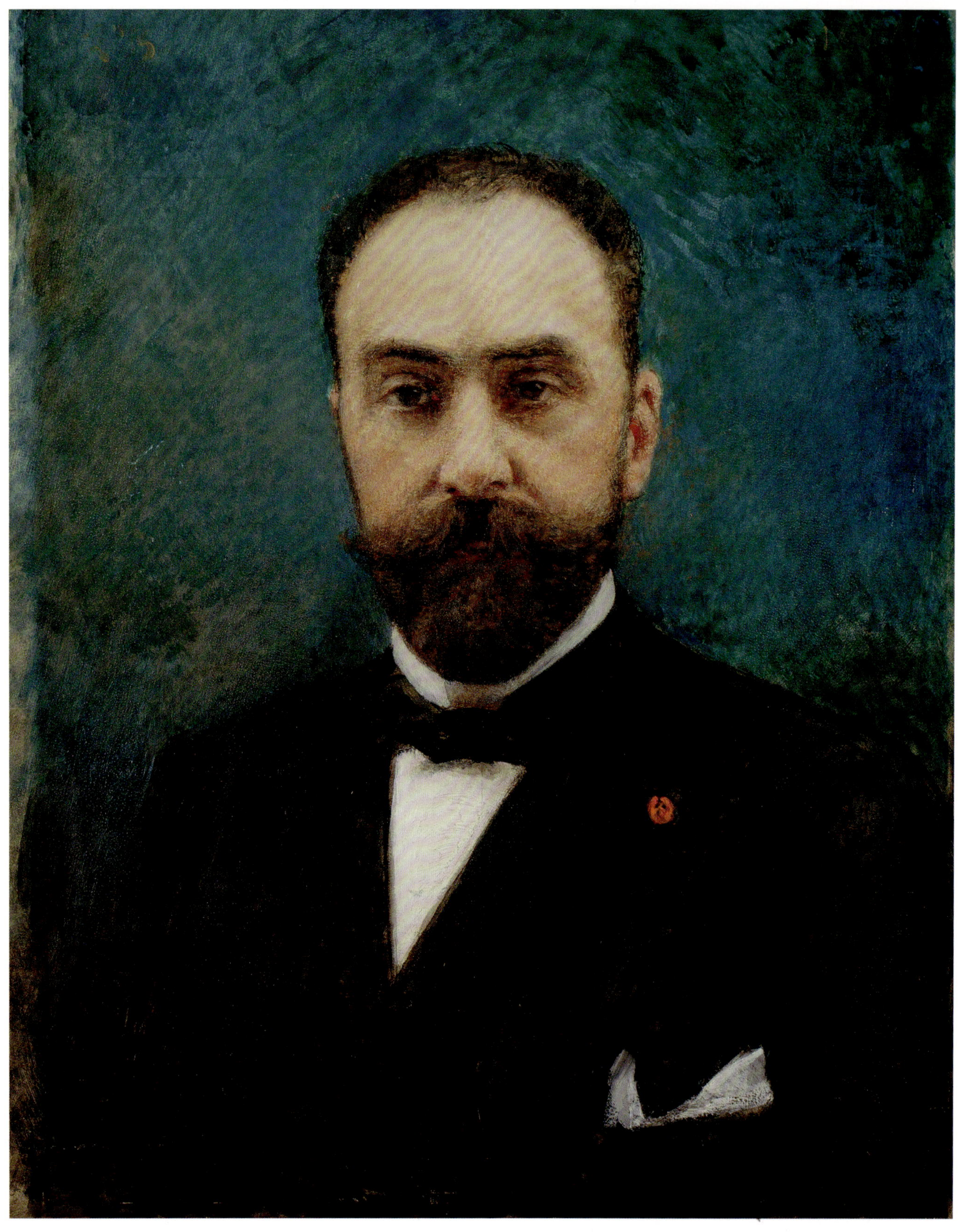

The Elusive Charles Ephrussi: Collector, Critic, and Patron of the Arts

SARA TAS

F EW FIGURES OF THE late nineteenth-century Parisian art world are so omnipresent yet so hard to pin down as Charles Ephrussi. An analysis of this individual, particularly in relation to Renoir, tells us a great deal about the artistic circles and social tensions of the time.

Charles Ephrussi was born in Odessa on December 24, 1849, to a family of grain exporters who became major international bankers.[1] One branch of the family moved to Vienna to run the bank; Charles studied there before leaving for Paris at the age of twenty-one with his family to expand Ephrussi et Cie's European banking empire.[2] This was in 1871, at the start of the Third Republic. As France slowly moved beyond the legacy of the Second Empire and the hangover of defeat in the Franco-Prussian war, conservatism gradually gave way to left-wing Republican ideology. In the art world and

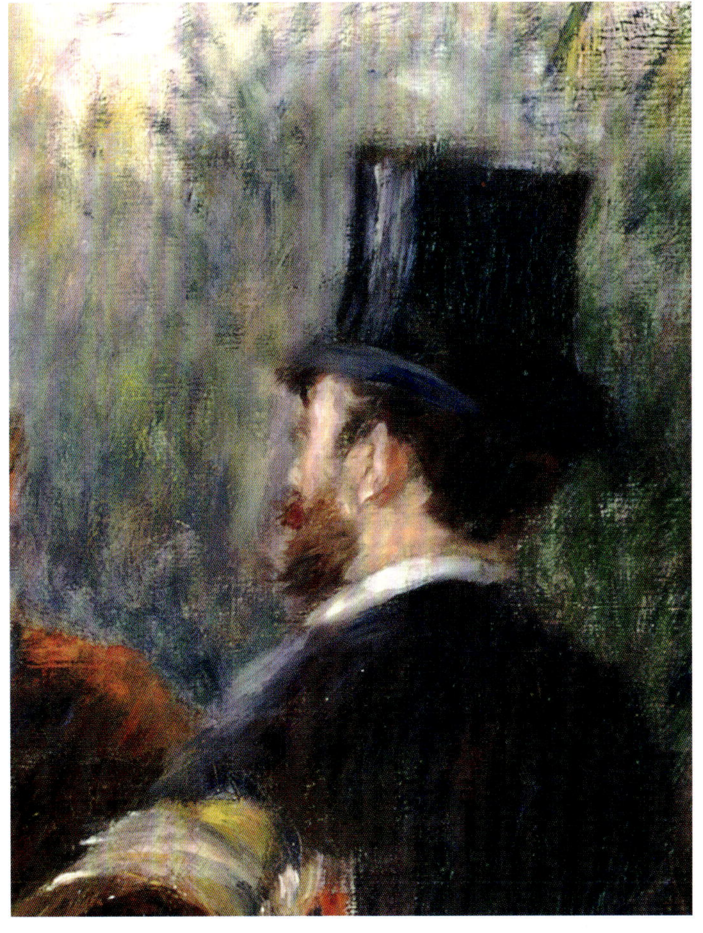

OPPOSITE PAGE
CAT. 40. Léon Bonnat, *Portrait of Charles Ephrussi* (*Portrait de Charles Ephrussi*), 1906, oil on panel, 18 × 15 in. (46 × 38 cm). Private collection.

RIGHT
Detail of Cat. 1, *Luncheon of the Boating Party*: Charles Ephrussi.

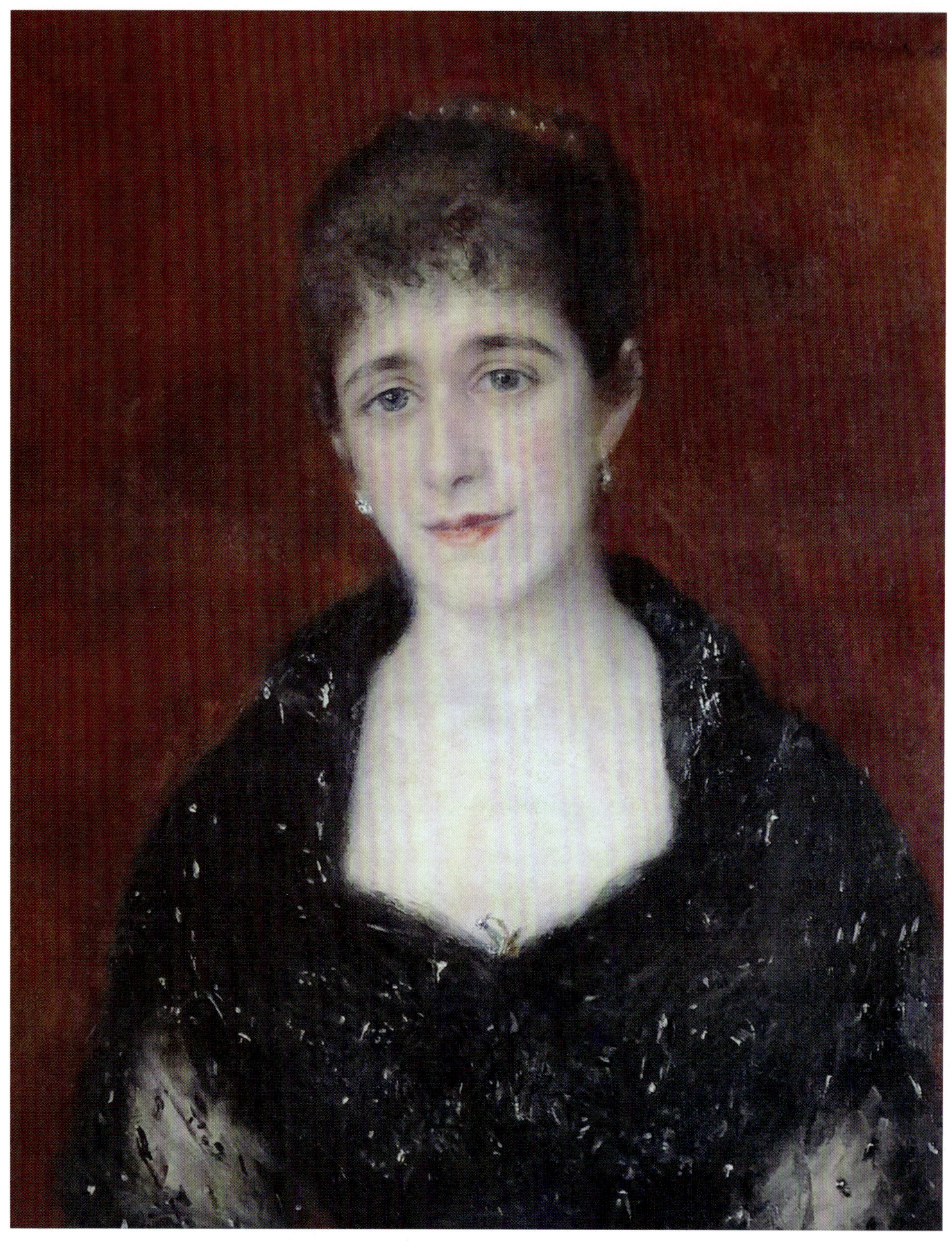

CAT. 41. Pierre-Auguste Renoir, *Portrait of Thérèse Ephrussi – Madame Léon Fould* (*Portrait de Thérèse Ephrussi – madame Léon Fould*), 1880, oil on canvas, 20 × 17½ in. (50.8 × 44.4 cm). Mr. & Mrs. Felipe Propper de Callejon.

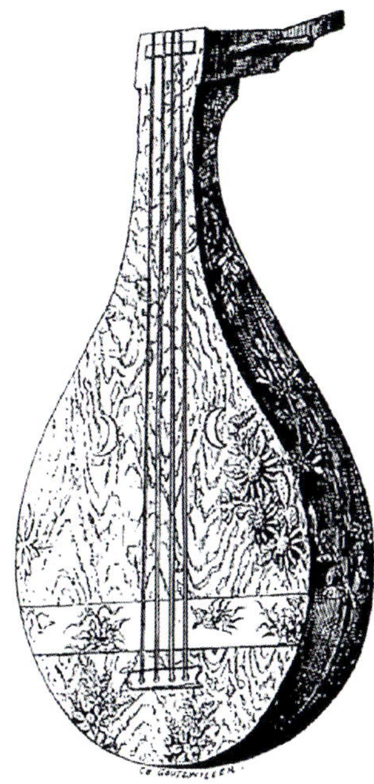

FIG. 28. Japanese lacquer box owned by Charles Ephrussi, 1878, steel engraving, published in Charles Ephrussi, 'Les laques japonaises au Trocadéro,' *Gazette des beaux-arts*, 2ème période, 1878, t. XVIII, pp. 954–968.

beyond, anti-capitalist tendencies—often tied to anti-Semitism—were increasingly influential. Although Charles Ephrussi gained acceptance in this world, the stereotype of the wealthy Jewish banker, exemplified by the Rothschilds, made his position delicate.

Charles lived with his brother Ignace and their mother in a grand house on rue de Monceau.[3] Their newly developed neighborhood was home to the city's nouveaux riches, a group that included many Jews.[4] For nineteenth-century French families of this kind, being Jewish meant being a French citizen with Judaism as a religion. Being accepted in the highest circles of French society was crucial for an immigrant like Charles Ephrussi, so religion played no role in everyday life, at least on the surface; it was limited to the private sphere. Through marriages with other prominent Jewish families, the Ephrussis

went on expanding their empire. Charles's eldest brother Jules married Fanny Pfeiffer in 1876. The other branch of the family, which stemmed from Charles's grandfather's second marriage, was also based in Paris; it included Michel Ephrussi; Maurice Ephrussi, who married Charlotte Béatrice de Rothschild; and Thérèse Ephrussi (Cat. 41), who married Léon Fould. Ignace—who, like Charles, remained a bachelor his entire life—seems to have taken primary responsibility for running the bank. For the next thirty years, Charles was free to immerse himself in the Parisian art world and move in artistic circles.

Collector and critic

Charles Ephrussi became an avid art collector from the moment he arrived in Paris. In his social class, it was normal to own a stately home and to surround yourself with a collection of art and beautiful objects that reflected your identity and interests, but Charles took it further than most and became a significant figure in the Parisian art world. He first became interested in the Italian Renaissance while traveling in Italy in 1872, and brought home tapestries based on cartoons by Raphael and a small sculpture by della Robbia.[5] Japanese art, a new fashion among Western—and more specifically, Parisian—collectors, also drew his attention. At an auction at the Hôtel Drouot on January 25, 1872, he spent 4,587 francs on Japanese art. Two months later, he bought more.[6] In 1878, Ephrussi wrote a long article on the Japanese lacquer boxes on display at the Exposition Universelle, which came from various private collections, including his own (fig. 28).[7] In April 1883, his collection of thirty-three Japanese lacquer boxes and a stoneware vessel formed part of the *Exposition rétrospective de l'art japonais* organized by Louis Gonse and held at the Galerie Georges Petit.[8]

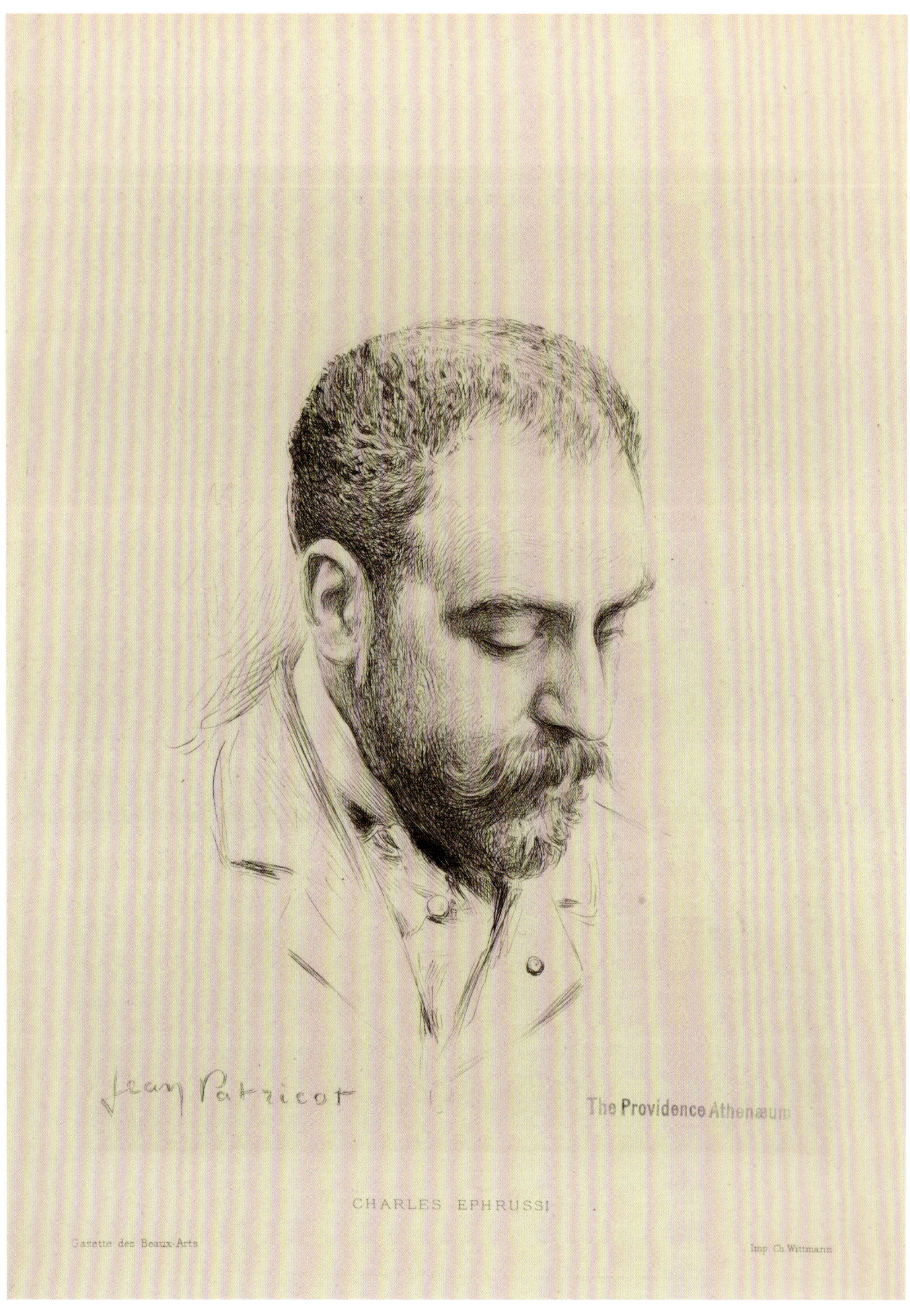

CAT. 42. Jean Patricot, *Charles Ephrussi*, 1905, drypoint, 7³⁄₁₆ × 5¹¹⁄₁₆ in. (18.5 × 14.5 cm).
The Phillips Collection, Washington, D.C., Acquired 2016.

In 1876, at the age of twenty-eight, Ephrussi published an article in the *Gazette des beaux-arts* about the Italian artist Jacopo de' Barbari, making his debut as an art historian in the renowned art journal with which he remained affiliated his entire life. He became its co-owner in 1885 and its director from 1894 until he died in 1905. His publications indicate the tremendous scope of his interests, and he soon became an eminent art historian;[9] his book on the drawings of Albrecht Dürer became a valued reference work.[10] He also co-organized a number of exhibitions;[11] his former secretary Auguste Marguillier wrote in his obituary in the *Gazette* that "there was no artistic or philanthropic initiative that did not call on the aid of his knowledge, his network, and his tireless devotion" (Cat. 42).[12]

Image

Charles Ephrussi's network spanned the entire Parisian intellectual elite. He attended the salons hosted by Princess Mathilde and Marguerite Charpentier and befriended politicians, museum curators, and young artists. His public image and the nature of many of his friendships have been interpreted in diverse ways, however, by both his contemporaries and later art historians. Whether the ultimate opinion of him was good or bad (and this has varied a great deal, with some commentators changing their stance over time), his public persona was often interpreted with a certain duality, which may be connected to the paradoxical life of a French Jew of the period. Jews were, in principle, accepted, especially if they adapted to French Republican values, but they were seldom completely trusted. Charles Ephrussi was known as an "erudite figure, writing in a Chinese dressing gown during the day and dressing up for the Paris salons or the opera in the evening."[13] The notion of Ephrussi's dualistic image is captured in the title coined for him by poet Jules Laforgue, who had served as his secretary and wrote many letters to him from his new position in Berlin. He called Ephrussi—whom he adored, and to whom he owed a great debt of gratitude even though he had worked for him for just a few months—the *bénédictin-dandy* of rue de Monceau.[14] By likening him to a Benedictine monk—an odd association for a Jew—Laforgue wished to emphasize Ephrussi's thorough knowledge and erudition; *dandy* refers to his manner on the boulevards of Paris and in the city's night life.[15] Ephrussi was criticized more harshly than he might otherwise have been for dandyish behavior, for instance by Edmond de Goncourt, who wrote that Ephrussi the Jew went to six or seven parties a night so that he could climb to a position at the Ministry of Fine Arts.[16] Another obviously anti-Semitic description by George D. Painter, Proust's biographer, presented him as intelligent but utterly lacking in charm, and stressed that people made fun of his "Polish Jewish" accent.[17] Some, like Renoir, appreciated Ephrussi's support but expressed ambivalence about his image and taste.

Taste

What do we learn about Charles if we look not at what others have written about him but at the objects he chose to surround himself with? The only conclusion we can be certain of is that his collection was eclectic, and therefore elusive—and in that sense, it may have reflected his personality. The clearest overview of his collection is provided by the catalogue of the auction that took place a few years after his death.[18] It shows that he had accumulated seemingly endless quantities of Dresden, Sèvres, and Meissen porcelain, ceramic figurines, and

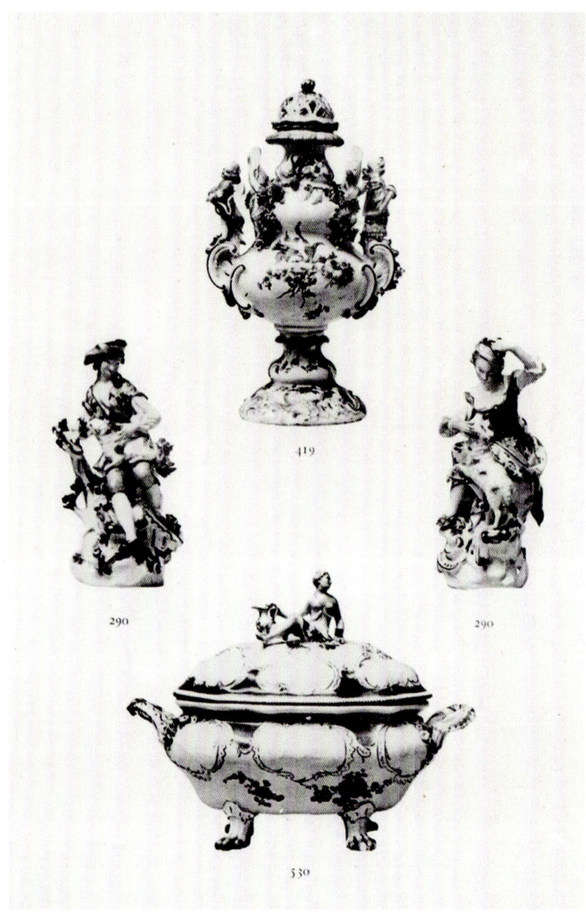

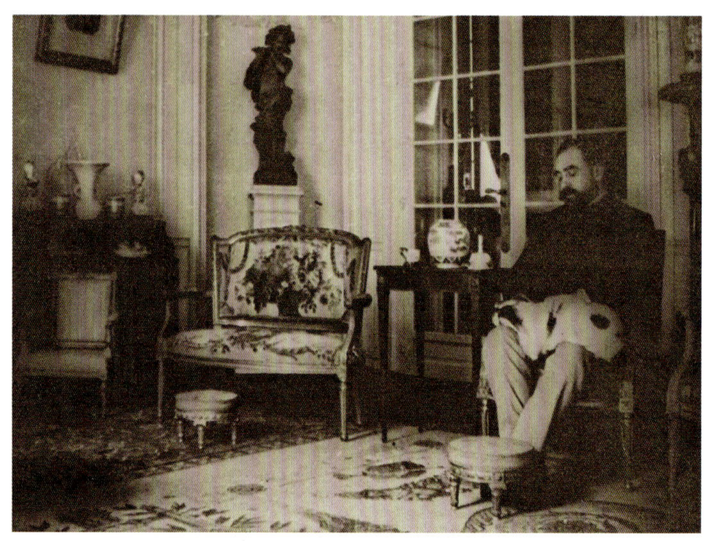

FIG. 29. Porcelain owned by Charles Ephrussi, 1878, steel engraving, as published in *Porcelain owned by Charles Ephrussi*, Paris, Hôtel Drouot, sale no. 10, March 8–13, 1909.

FIG. 30. Charles Ephrussi in his home with a pet on his lap, n.d., Chancellerie des Universités de Paris, Bibliothèque littéraire Jaques Doucet, Paris.

exceptional bronzes and textiles (fig. 29). They must have filled his house. We also know that Ephrussi was a lover of pets, which the only known photograph of the inside of his house shows (fig. 30). He owned a painting of a cat by Renoir[19] and is probably the subject of a pastel by Degas, who portrayed him sitting at his desk, surrounded by three pets.[20]

Ephrussi's painting collection is not included in the auction catalogue of his collection and is more difficult to reconstruct. Goupil & Cie stock books make it clear that he bought work by Narcisse Virgilio Díaz de la Peña, Ernest Meissonier, and Aurelio Tiratelli around 1871. From dealer Paul Durand-Ruel he purchased a work by rococo artist François Boucher in 1873 and about ten works by impressionists in 1881 and 1882.[21]

It was also around this time that he began to write articles about "les indépendants" for the *Gazette des beaux-arts* and the *Chronique des arts et de la curiosité*, a supplement to the *Gazette*. In an 1878 review of a book by Théodore Duret about the impressionists, Ephrussi complained that Duret's praise for them was a little overblown and added that, in his opinion, impressionist paintings were not yet serious enough in their execution. Yet he also emphasized to his readers that this new art movement should not be overlooked, because it represented the spirit of the age.[22] In 1880, when Ephrussi wrote his first longer article on the impressionists, he unmistakably broke a lance for the painters who had chosen that new path.[23] A year later, he again reviewed the *Exposition*

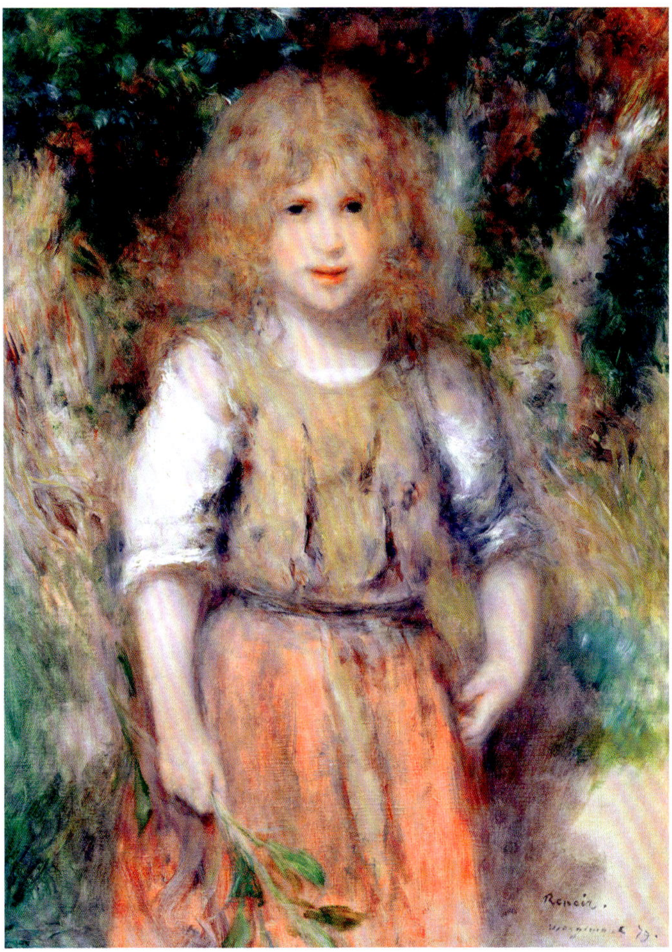

FIG. 31. Pierre-Auguste Renoir, *Gypsy Girl* (*La Sauvageonne*), 1879, oil on canvas, 28⅞ × 21½ in. (73 × 54 cm). Private collection.

des peintres indépendants; this time, he focused on the work of Degas, Cassatt, Morisot, and Pissarro, writing that they wanted to belong to a period of their own and speak a language of their own.[24]

After that, Ephrussi appears to have decided to concentrate on Italian Renaissance and other older art in his publications, though he continued to collect the work of contemporary painters. His painting collection can be largely reconstructed based on his correspondence with Laforgue. Ephrussi's modern art collection made a profound impression on Laforgue, who wrote vivid descriptions of several works—"le Duranty de Degas" (Cat. 43), "la sauvageonne ébouriffée de Renoir" (fig. 31), two fans painted by Pissarro, and work by Cassatt, Monet, Morisot, and Sisley—in a letter in December 1881.[25]

Despite his diverse range of interests, Ephrussi believed that impressionism was the only worthwhile path for the painters of his day. Some of these artists were friends of his, and he sometimes bought paintings from them directly. Opinions varied as to whether he was a good customer. While Monet wrote in June 1881 that Ephrussi wanted to buy his work but was unwilling to pay a reasonable price for it,[26] Manet believed that Ephrussi had paid far too much for his *Asparagus* (Cat. 44), and sent him an additional small painting (Cat. 45) in April 1882 as a token of his gratitude, with the message, "there was one missing from your bunch."[27]

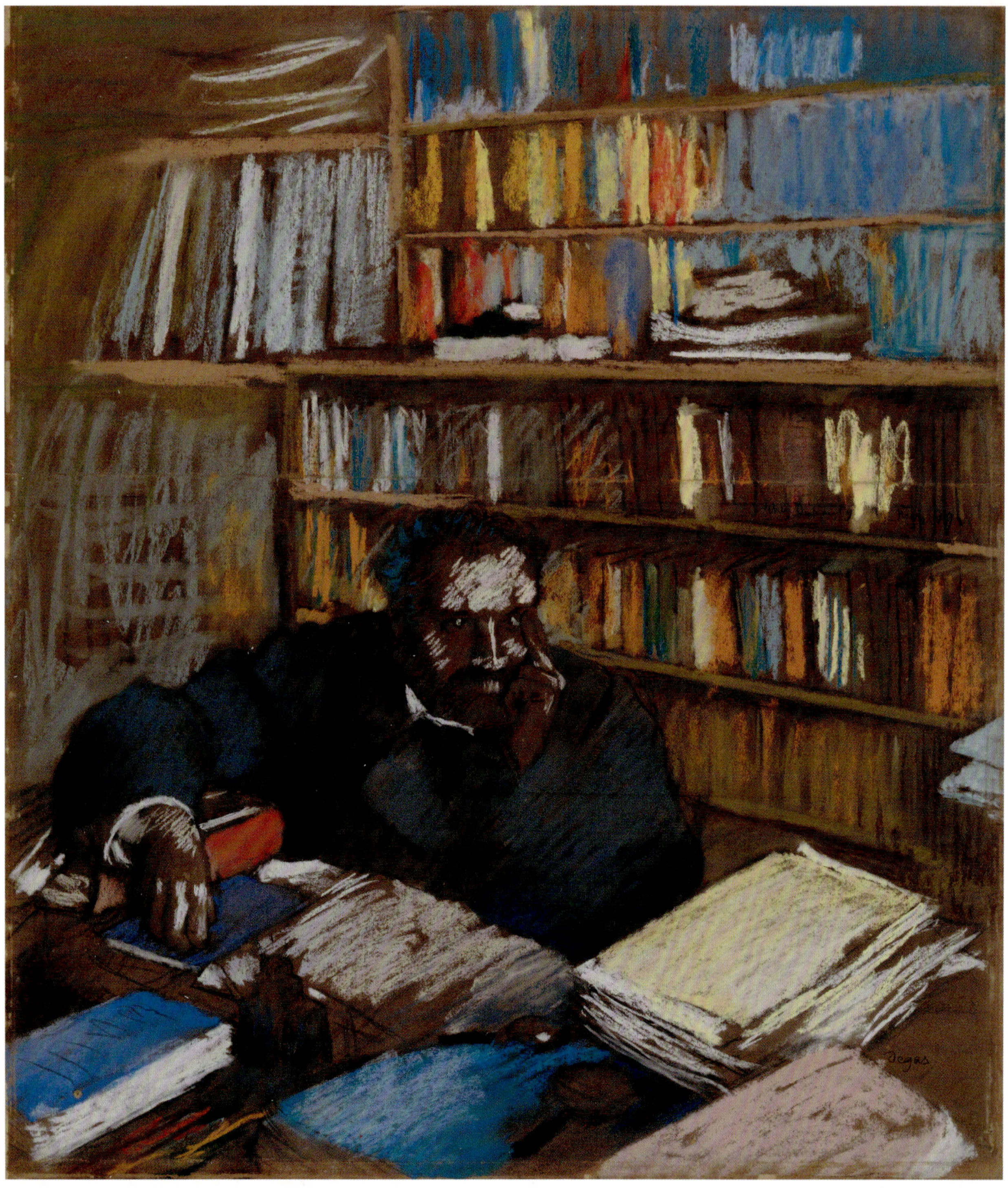

CAT. 43. Edgar Degas, *Portrait of Edmund Duranty* (*Portrait d'Edmund Duranty*), 1879, pastel on paper, 20½ × 17¾ in. (52.1 × 45.1 cm). Private collection.

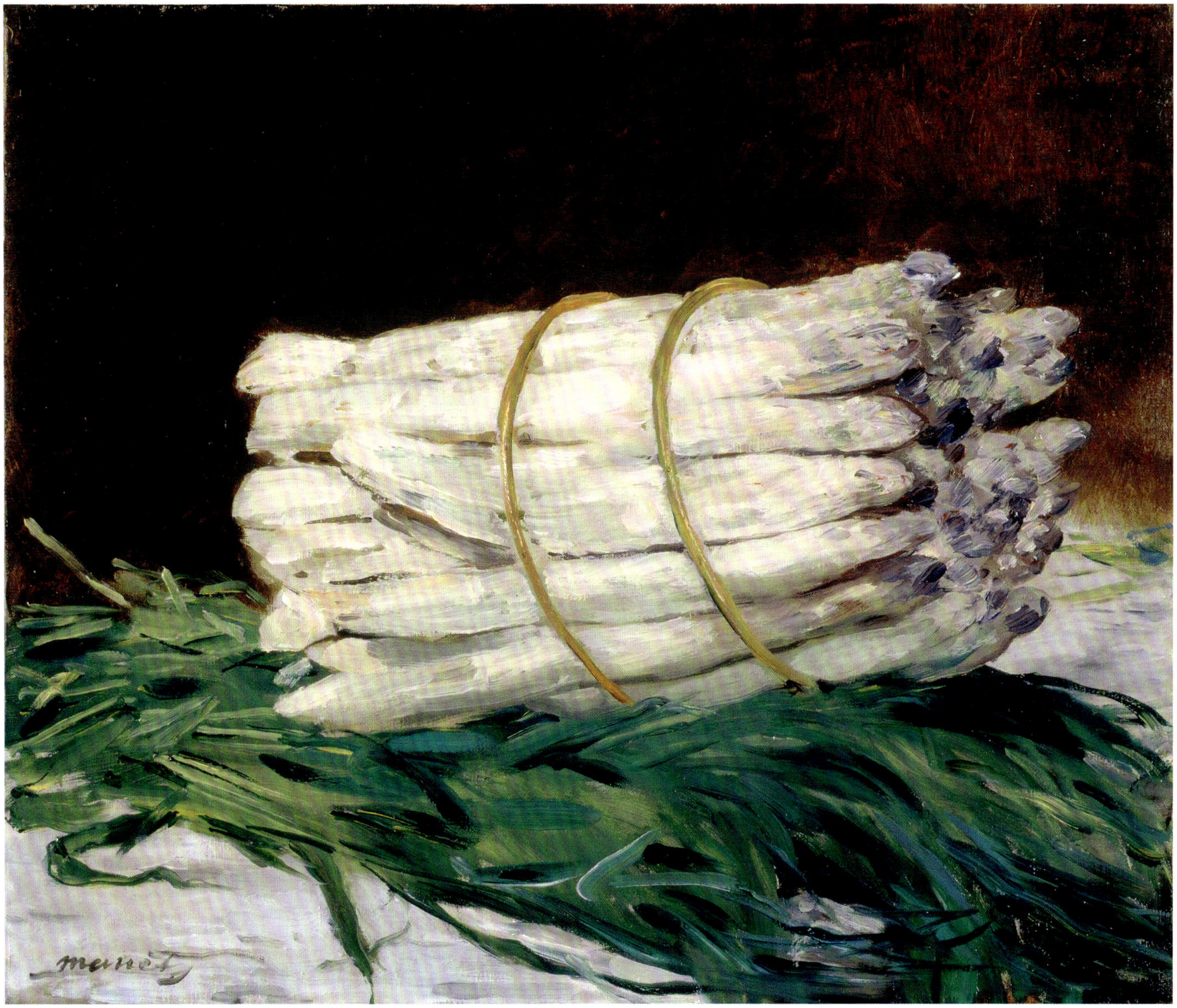

CAT. 44. Édouard Manet, *A Bunch of Asparagus* (*Une botte d'asperges*), 1880, oil on canvas, 18⅑ × 21¹³⁄₂₀ in. (46 × 55 cm). Wallraf-Richartz-Museum & Fondation Corboud, Cologne.

CAT. 45. Édouard Manet, *Asparagus* (*L'Asperge*), 1880, oil on canvas, 6⅜ × 8½ in. (16.5 × 21.5 cm). Musée d'Orsay, Paris, Gift of Sam Salz, 1959.

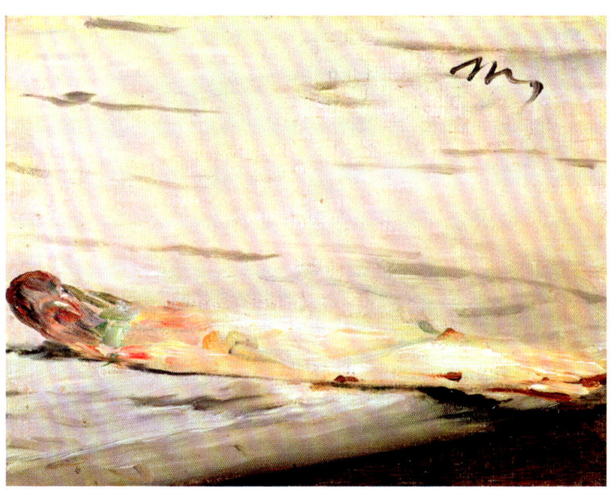

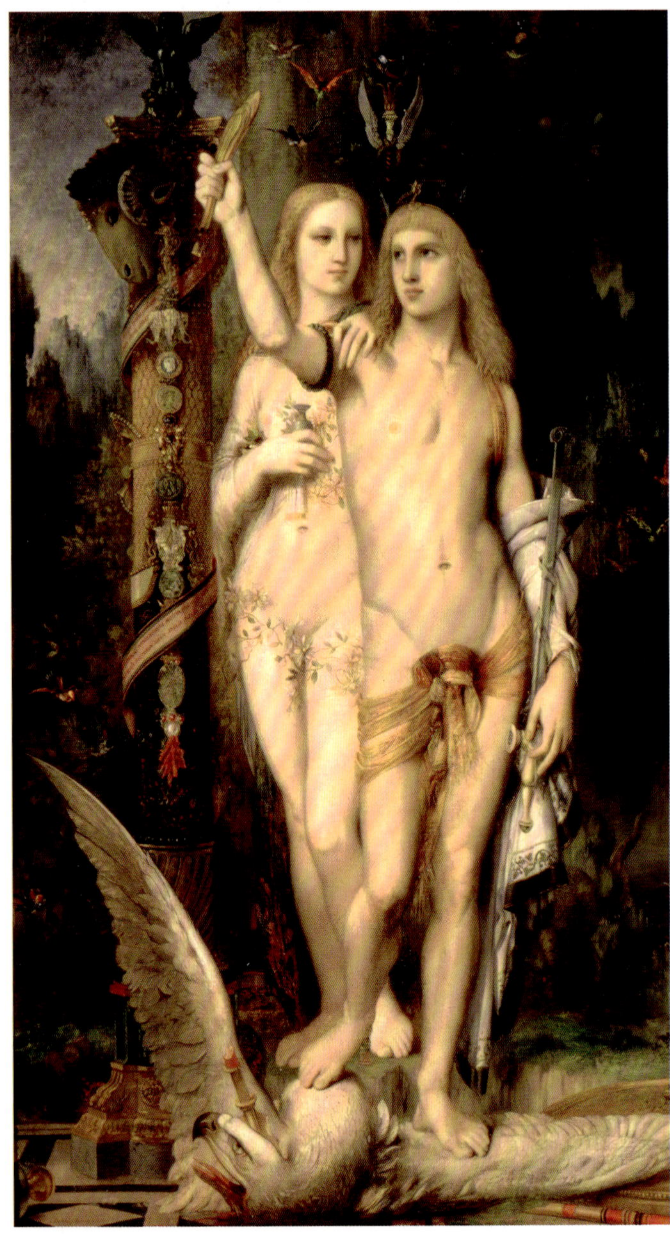

FIG. 32. Gustave Moreau, *Jason*, 1865, oil on canvas, 80⅜ × 45⅝ in. (204 × 116 cm). Musée d'Orsay, Paris.

Ephrussi also purchased works by contemporary artists more accepted by the establishment. His second art historical monograph was the result of his deep admiration for the work of his friend, painter Paul Baudry.[28] In addition, Ephrussi befriended Pierre Puvis de Chavannes and Gustave Moreau, and acquired a number of their works. Puvis de Chavannes often received commissions for paintings in public buildings, and Baudry had been chosen to decorate the Palais Garnier, home to the Paris opera. These established symbolist painters may have constituted a safer choice, more in keeping with "good taste" as it was understood in the Third Republic. Through this deliberate safer choice, Ephrussi could have avoided shocking the sensibilities of the establishment with a collection that was too avant-garde; moreover, it may have been a conscious balance since he had drawn attention for writing about Dürer at a time when appreciation for German art was a delicate matter in France. Ephrussi also bought two paintings from Moreau: *Galatea* (1880–1885) and, in 1880, *Jason* (fig. 32). The latter had been criticized at the Salon of 1865 for being an eclectic set of symbolic objects, "an apotheosis of a collector."[29] It is no wonder Ephrussi fell for the painting, considering its similarity to his eclectic collection. Renoir saw the matter very differently; in his eyes, Moreau was a commercial painter who filled his paintings with golden objects to attract Jewish buyers.[30] He was surprised that this trick had worked on so clever a man as Ephrussi.

It is difficult to determine how Ephrussi's art collection looked as a whole. He probably had some works in his possession for just a short time; he regularly sold works, such as Renoir's *Two Sisters* (see fig. 47).[31] He left a few works to his favorite niece Fanny Kahn and her husband Théodore Reinach, who in turn donated Moreau's *Jason* to the Musée du Luxembourg.[32] Ephrussi's estate documents mention some

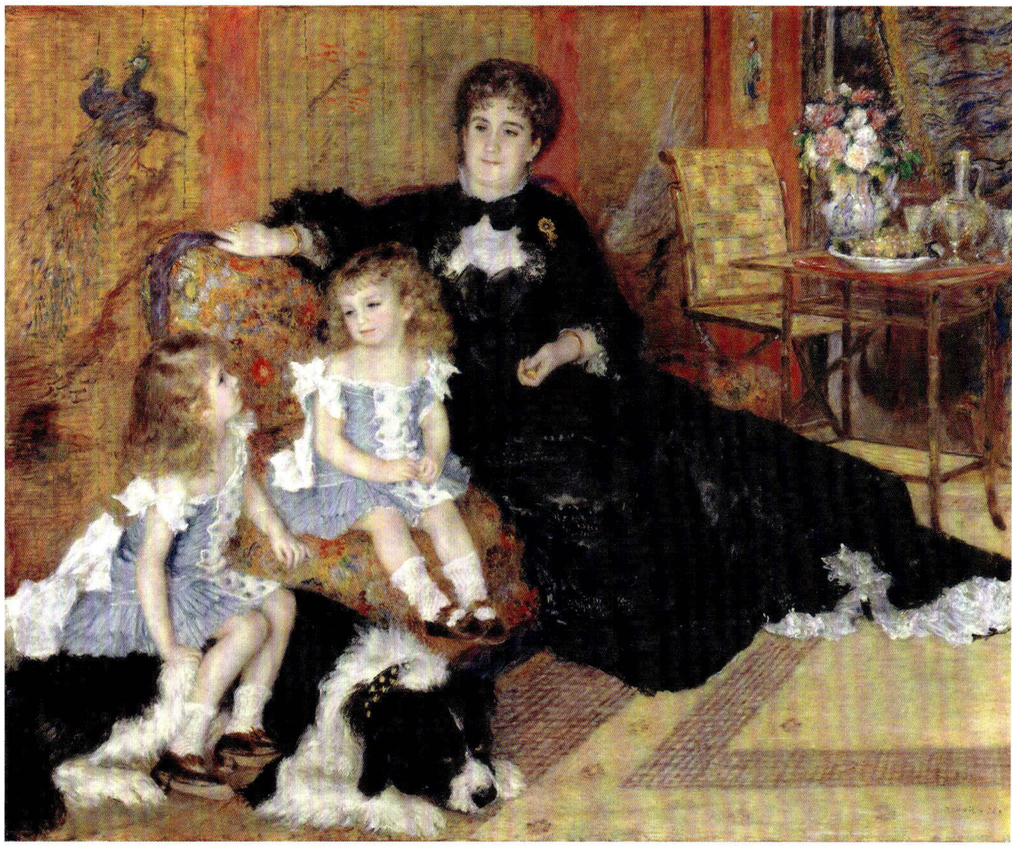

FIG. 33. Pierre-Auguste Renoir, *Madame Georges Charpentier (Marguérite-Louise Lemonnier, 1848–1904) and Her Children, Georgette-Berthe (1872–1945) and Paul-Émile-Charles (1875–1895) (Madame Georges Charpentier et ses enfants)*, 1878, oil on canvas, 60½ × 74⅞ in. (153.7 × 190.2 cm). The Metropolitan Museum of Art, New York, Catharine Lorillard Wolfe Collection, Wolfe Fund, 1907.

works of art in an unsystematic way, including pieces by Paul-Albert Besnard, Pierre Bonnard, Gustave Caillebotte, Eugène Delacroix, and Armand Guillaumin.[33] At the auction of the remainder of his collection in 1909, a few eighteenth-century allegories on panel and six landscapes by the post-impressionist Henri Lebasque were sold. These had probably been permanent elements of his interior decoration. Eclectic collections were not out of the ordinary in those days, but Ephrussi's collection seems extreme. Could he really have been equally drawn to all those styles? Or, as noted above, did he have preferences but also made safe choices as part of his necessary permanent campaign to fit in with society and not be either ostracized as a Jew nor shock people with a collection that was too avant-garde? Did he try in this way to cover all the bases, becoming firmly enmeshed in every aspect of the French cultural world?[34]

Network

Ephrussi was not only a great collector and critic but probably also played an essential role in expanding the clientele of the impressionists. In both Paris and Berlin, Ephrussi won over new buyers to their work. Around 1880–1881, his German cousins Carl and Marcel Bernstein bought a variety of impressionist paintings and watercolors; Ephrussi advised them on the selection.[35]

Renoir and Ephrussi probably became acquainted through common friends, possibly the collector Henri Cernuschi, Ephrussi's neighbor.[36] In March 1879 Renoir invited Ephrussi to visit Madame Charpentier and see his portrait of her and her children (fig. 33).[37] Renoir may have hoped to attract the attention of the establishment or to obtain public commissions through Ephrussi's connections with museum curators.[38]

Although this did not happen, Ephrussi seems to have been impressed with the portrait, and found a new circle of buyers for Renoir among the Jewish elite. In 1880 Renoir painted a portrait of Ephrussi's aunt, Thérèse Fould.[39] Another Jewish couple from the same circle as Ephrussi, the Cahen d'Anvers, had their daughters painted by Renoir not long afterwards, first Irène (fig. 34) and later Élisabeth and Alice (fig. 35).[40]

In 1881, when Renoir was in Algeria, he asked Ephrussi to organize his entry of both paintings of the Cahen d'Anvers girls for the Salon.[41] The following year Renoir asked Paul Berard to organize his entry, saying that he was annoyed with Ephrussi for not spending enough money on a decent frame for his *Bohémienne* (private collection, 1879).[42] The next day, however, he changed his mind and asked Berard to take Ephrussi's advice, because "ce juif plus que bourgeois" had a keen eye for what would be successful at the Salon.[43] His choice of words makes clear that he distrusted the Salon and the Jewish elite in equal measure. After this, his remarks had more frequent anti-Semitic undertones and his relationship with Ephrussi cooled. Nonetheless, Ephrussi's help made a substantial difference at a critical point in Renoir's career. As he gained popularity as a portraitist, among both Jewish and non-Jewish clients,[44] he gradually became able to afford to continue developing his talents and to make ambitious non-commissioned work such as *Luncheon of the Boating Party*.

Luncheon of the Boating Party

Why is it widely believed that the man with the top hat in the background of the painting must be Ephrussi? Only a few contemporary sources point in that direction. The first is Ambroise Vollard, who quotes Renoir—in both his 1919 study of Renoir and in *En écoutant Cézanne, Degas, Renoir* (1938)—

as saying that Ephrussi and Lestringuez[45] had posed together for *Boating Party*.[46]

Another reason to think that Ephrussi was among the models can be found in a letter Renoir wrote to his friend Paul Berard during the project. Renoir told Berard that he had found time to set aside his more decorative work and devote himself to the painting of the boating party, which had been eating at him for some time. He added that he didn't want to spend too much time on it, because the project would cost him too much—but sometimes it takes time to try new things beyond one's capacity. When the painting took up too much of his time after all, Renoir grew impatient and told Berard that he had decided to set aside one more week for the project and then return to his portraits. In the same letter, he wondered whether Ephrussi was back yet.[47] It is not clear where he was returning from or why Renoir wanted to know, but the fact that he was wondering about Ephrussi as he worked on this painting suggests that Ephrussi was involved or needed in some capacity. Ephrussi may not have had much time for modeling, and that may be one of the reasons he is portrayed from behind in a top hat, with his face partly hidden from view. This would have been faster for Renoir and allowed Ephrussi to spend less time posing. Or maybe neither of them wanted Ephrussi to be immediately or widely identifiable. That would be consistent with Renoir's ambivalence toward his "patron." Was Ephrussi doing Renoir a favor by modeling for this expensive project free of charge? Or was Renoir expressing his gratitude to Ephrussi for putting him in contact with new buyers and successfully organizing his entry to the Salon, thus helping to make this ambitious project possible?

Proust's literary work undoubtedly contributed to both the identification and the mystification of Ephrussi's role as a

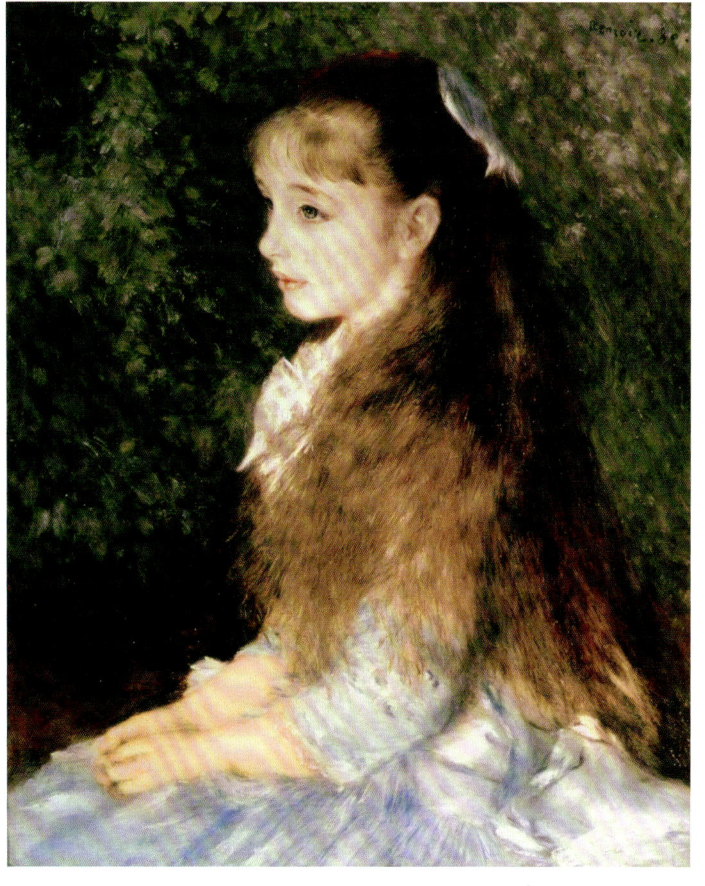

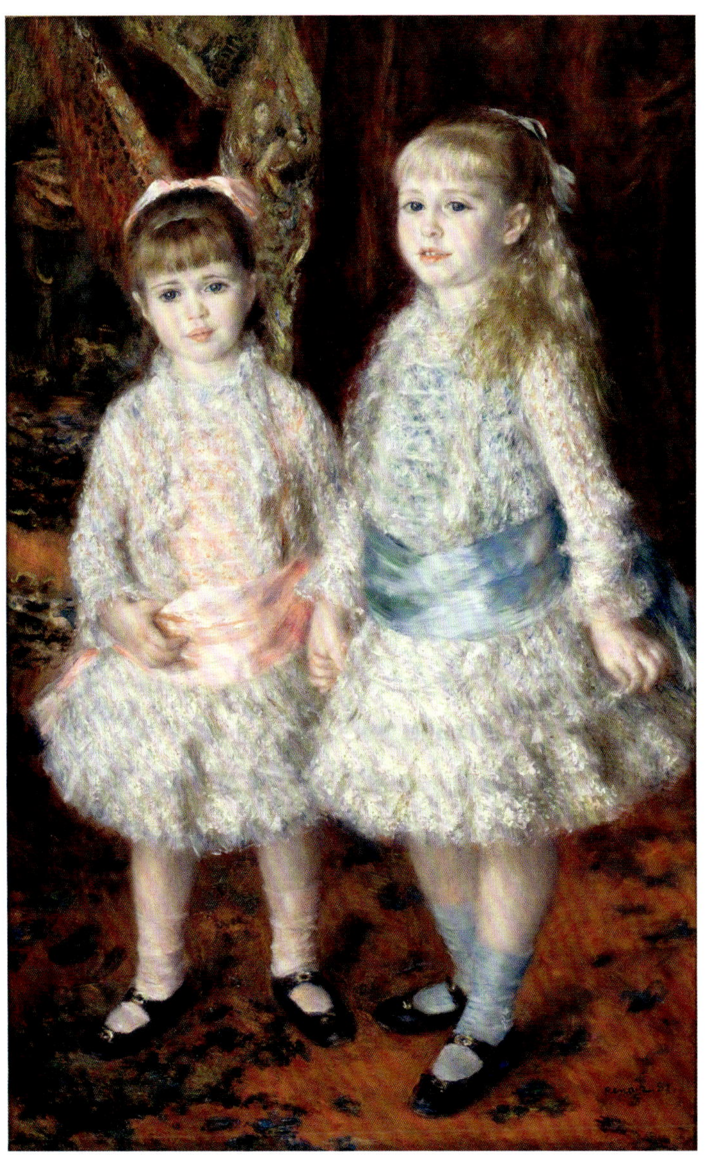

ABOVE
FIG. 34. Pierre-Auguste Renoir, *Portrait of Mademoiselle Irène Cahen d'Anvers* or *Little Irène* (*La Petite Irène*), 1880, oil on canvas, 25½ × 21¼ in. (65 × 54 cm). E.G. Bührle Collection, Zurich.

LEFT
FIG. 35. Pierre-Auguste Renoir, *Pink and Blue – Élisabeth and Alice Cahen d'Anvers* (*Rose et bleu – Élisabeth et Alice Cahen d'Anvers*), 1881, oil on canvas, 46⅞ × 29¾ in. (119 × 75.5 cm). Museu de Arte de São Paulo Assis Chateaubriand, Brazil.

model for both the character of Swann in *À la recherche du temps perdu* and the figure in Renoir's *Luncheon of the Boating Party*. We know from their correspondence that Proust and Ephrussi knew each other well. Proust writes that he spent an entire day with him in April 1899.[48] It is possible that they visited the exhibition at Durand-Ruel together, where *Luncheon of the Boating Party* was on display, and that this experience formed the basis for the following passage from *Le Côté de Guermantes*:

> What I can tell you is that the gentleman you mean has been a sort of Maecenas to Elstir. He launched him and has often helped him out of difficulties by commissioning pictures from him. As a compliment to this man—if you can call it a compliment, it's a matter of taste—he has painted him standing among that crowd, where with his Sunday-go-to-meeting look he creates a distinctly odd effect.[49]

We will never know how much of Ephrussi there is in the character of Swann or in the gentleman Proust describes, nor how much of Renoir there is in Elstir. We can only conclude that Ephrussi was a remarkable and intriguing individual who played a significant role in Renoir's life and career around 1880–1881. The fact that the bond between patron and artist did not last may have to do with Renoir's anti-Semitism, but is probably just as much a result of Ephrussi's eclecticism. Even though Ephrussi was seen as erudite and belonged to the establishment, he was probably always making an effort to adapt to French society, so that he, as a Jewish immigrant, would not find himself out in the cold.

1. For a literary family history, see Edmund de Waal, *The Hare with Amber Eyes: A Hidden Inheritance* (New York: Farrar, Straus and Giroux, 2010).
2. Not long after their arrival, both Charles's sister, Betty, and his father died. Betty had married Max Hirsch Kahn not long before and had a daughter, Fanny Kahn, who later married Théodore Reinach.
3. In 1891, three years after their mother died, Charles and Ignace moved to a new home at 11 avenue d'Iéna.
4. The fact that some leading members of Paris high society were Jewish was the outcome of the French Jewish community's long process of integration, which had begun in 1790–1791 when the Jewish emancipation acts were passed by the Assemblée Constituante "granting Jews full French citizenship". The city's Jewish

population grew from 800 c. 1790 to 2,900 in 1809; 9,000 in 1840 (see Christine Piette, *Les Juifs de Paris (1808–1840): la marche vers l'assimilation* (Québec: Presses de l'Université Laval, 1983), p. 50; 18,000 in 1853; and 30,000 in 1870. From 1880 to 1905 this number continued to grow, but most of the newcomers belonged to less prosperous families who had fled the Russian pogroms. See Cyril Grange, *Une élite parisienne: les familles de la grande bourgeoisie juive (1870–1939)* (Paris: CNRS, 2016), pp. 7–8.
5. Auguste Marguillier, "Charles Ephrussi," *Gazette des beaux-arts, Chronique des arts et de la curiosité*, November 1, 1905, pp. 353–360.
6. For a description of the auctions Ephrussi attended in 1872 and the objects he bought there, see Manuela Moscatiello, *Le Japonisme de Giuseppe De Nittis: un peintre italien en France à la fin du XIXe siècle* (Bern: Peter Lang, 2011), p. 104.

7. Charles Ephrussi, "Les laques japonaises au Trocadéro," *Gazette des beaux-arts* 18 (1878): pp. 954–968.
8. Louis Gonse, *Catalogue de l'exposition rétrospective de l'art japonais* (Paris: A. Quantin, 1883), pp. 193–200.
9. For an overview, see Hélène Lesueur de Givry, "Charles Ephrussi (1849–1905)," Master's thesis, École du Louvre, 2005, and her inventory in the database *Les Critiques d'art francophones des années 1880 à l'Entre-deux-guerres*, forthcoming.
10. Charles Ephrussi, *Albert Dürer et ses dessins* (Paris: A. Quantin, 1882). Partly published earlier in the form of articles in the *Gazette des beaux-arts*.
11. Such as the 1879 exhibition of old master drawings in the École des Beaux-Arts that he co-organized with his friend and fellow collector Gustave Dreyfus (1837–1914), which brought him into contact with Phillipe de Chennevières

and other influential figures in the world of the Musées Nationaux, such as Barbet de Jouy, Clément de Ris, and Louvre curator Léonce Both de Tauzia. Sometimes Ephrussi helped Both de Tauzia with editorial work and acquisitions, such as the major Botticelli frescoes from the Villa Lemmi. In 1878 Ephrussi published a detailed study in the *Gazette* of a large set of old master drawings that had been donated to the Louvre by A.-C.-H. His de la Salle, and he published an inventory of the collection of Queen Marie Antoinette in the Louvre. He co-organized an exhibition on old master drawings of decorative art objects on behalf of the Societé du Musée des Arts Décoratifs, where he had served as a board member since 1877. In 1883 he co-organized an exhibition in the École des Beaux-Arts, *Portraits du siècle (1782–1883)*, which was very successful and raised funds for the Societé Philantropique. Two years later, he organized a reprise of this event. He was also closely involved in the making of the exhibition *Portraits de femmes et d'enfants* in the École des Beaux-Arts in 1897. In 1892 he organized an exhibition of furniture, tapestries, porcelain, and other objets d'art from the First Empire.

12. Marguillier, "Charles Ephrussi."

13. Philippe Kolb and Jean Adhémar, "Charles Ephrussi (1849–1905), ses secrétaires: Laforgue, A. Renan, Proust: 'sa' Gazette des beaux-arts." *Gazette des beaux-arts* 103 (1984): p. 31.

14. Letters published in Jules Laforgue, *Œuvres complètes*, vol. I (Lausanne: L'Âge d'homme, 1986), p. 739.

15. Dottin-Orsini 1991, p. 237.

16. Goncourt, *Journal*, June 15, 1881.

17. George D. Painter, *Marcel Proust: A Biography*, vol. 1 (London: Chatto & Windus, 1959), p. 95.

18. *Catalogue des porcelaines anciennes principalement des manufactures de Saxe et de Sèvres, faïences anciennes diverses, objets d'art et de curiosité, objets divers, tableaux anciens et modernes, sculptures anciennes en bronze et terre cuite, objets de vitrine, bijoux, bronzes d'ameublement du temps de l'empire, étoffes, meubles, etc., provenant de la collection d'un amateur* [Charles Ephrussi], auction at the Hôtel Drouot, Paris, Room 10, Monday, March 8 through Saturday, March 13, 1909.

19. *Chat endormi* (*Sleeping Cat*), c. 1862. Oil on canvas, 24 × 34 cm, location unknown (Guy-Patrice & Douberville Vol. 1, 48), already owned by Ephrussi before 1883 and exhibited at Durand-Ruel's gallery in 1892 as "Le chat qui dort appartient à M. Ch. Ephrussi."

20. *Homme assis lisant* (*Seated Man Reading*), date unknown. Pastel, 38 × 54 cm, location unkown (Lemoisne 655). Ephrussi owned a dog named Carmen. There is a letter addressed by Puvis de Chavannes to Ephrussi's dog dated August 14, 1887 in the archives of the Louvre: Cabinet des arts graphiques, fonds des autographes, C3537. With thanks to Michael Pantazzi.

21. Including Cassatt, Degas, Monet, Manet, and Pissarro, but also Lhermitte and Fantin-Latour. With thanks to Flavie Durand-Ruel.

22. Charles Ephrussi, "*Les Peintres impressionnistes . . . par Théodore Duret*," *Chronique des arts et la curiosité*, May 18, 1878, p. 158.

23. Charles Ephrussi, "L'Exposition des artistes indépendants," *Gazette des beaux-arts* 21 (1880): pp. 485–488.

24. Charles Ephrussi, "Exposition des artistes indépendants," *Chronique des arts et de la curiosité*, April 16, 1881, pp. 126–127, and April 23, 1881, pp. 134–135.

25. Laforgue 1903 [1986], pp. 717–720. A number of works are identified here.

26. Venturi 1939, pp. 222–223.

27. Paris, Musée du Louvre, Cabinet des arts graphiques, fonds des autographes, legs Moreau-Nélaton, A1489, Édouard Manet à Charles Ephrussi, [Versailles, 1881].

28. Charles Ephrussi, *Paul Baudry: sa vie et son œuvre* (Paris: Baschet, 1887).

29. Léo Lagrange, "Salon de 1865," *Le Correspondant* 29 (May 1865): p. 142. "Le *Jason* cacherait-il aussi un symbole? Serait-ce l'apothéose du collectionneur? En effet, voici des médailles, des petits bronzes, des émaux, des armes, des oiseaux, des étoffes: dans ce cas, allez jusqu'au bout, n'oubliez pas les timbres-poste."

30. "Ah! Ce Gustave Moreau, dire qu'on a pris ça au sérieux, un peintre qui n'a jamais su seulement dessiner un pied! Le mépris du monde qu'il avait, et qu'on a tant vanté, moi, j'appelle cela de la paresse. Mais c'était un homme rudement malin, allez, d'avoir imaginé, pour prendre les Juifs, de peindre avec des couleurs d'or . . . jusqu'à Ephrussi, que je croyais, tout de même, un peu sensé! J'arrive, un jour, chez lui: je tombe sur un Gustave Moreau!" In Vollard 1919, pp. 95–96 and Vollard 1938, pp. 196–197.

31. This painting was exhibited in 1883 as the property of Ch. Ephrussi (in the catalogue by Théodore Duret accompanying the Renoir exhibition at Durand-Ruel's gallery), but both before and after that time it was in Durand-Ruel's possession.

32. Letter from Théodore Reinach to Léonce Bénédite, November 19, 1908. Musée du Louvre, Paris, Bibliothèque des Musées Nationaux, Ms 375 (6,1), r. 27-29.

33. Paris, archives départementales. Déclarations de successions de Charles Ephrussi, D.Q7 33398 [Paris, March 29, 1906] and D.Q7 33399 [Paris, April 23, 1906]. I am grateful to Hélène Lesueur de Givry for pointing out this source to me.

34. See also Véronique Long, "Les collectionneurs juifs parisiens sous la Troisième République (1870–1940)," *Archives juives* 42 (1/2009), pp. 84–104.

35. Distel 1989, p. 162.

36. Duret 1924, p. 62.

37. Florisoone 1938, p. 35.

38. As suggested by Elizabeth Melanson, "The Influence of Jewish Patrons on Renoir's Stylistic Transformation in the Mid-1880s," *Nineteenth-Century Art Worldwide* 12, no. 2 (autumn 2013).

39. She and Charles Ephrussi must have been very close, judging by her request to Bonnat, soon after Ephrussi's death, to paint his posthumous portrait. With thanks to Michael Pantazzi.

40. Bailey 1997, p. 181. Goncourt suggested that Charles Ephrussi and Louise Cahen d'Anvers were lovers. Goncourt, *Journal*, October 16, 1878.

41. Letter from Renoir to Théodore Duret, March 4, 1881, published in Butler 2002, p. 114.

42. Letter from Renoir to Berard, from Algiers, early March 1882. Getty Institute. As published in Bailey 1997, p. 344. Renoir regularly stayed in Paul Berard's country house in Wargemont, not far from Dieppe, Normandy. There he painted the *Bohémienne* (*La Petite Bohémienne*)in 1879 and his portrait of Albert Cahen d'Anvers, uncle of the Cahen d'Anvers girls, in 1881.

43. Letter from Renoir to Berard, from Algiers, mid-March 1882. Private collection. As published in Bailey 1997, p. 345.

44. Degas was critical of Renoir's "commercial work" for this circle of Jewish buyers. See Blanche 1927, pp. 62–63.

45. Eugène-Pierre Lestringuez, whose portrait was also painted by Renoir in 1878 (Private collection).

46. Vollard 1919, p. 75, and Vollard 1938, p. 183. It is on this basis that Ephrussi has been identified as one of the models depicted in the painting. That is plausible, but claims by Vollard should be taken with a very large grain of salt.

47. Berard 1968, pp. 54–58.

48. Letter from Proust to Robert de Montesquiou, April 25, 1899. Record: c20680, University of Illinois at Urbana-Champaign, The Kolb-Proust Archive.

49. Marcel Proust, *In Search of Lost Time, Part III: The Guermantes Way* (London: Chatto & Windus, 1992), p. 578.

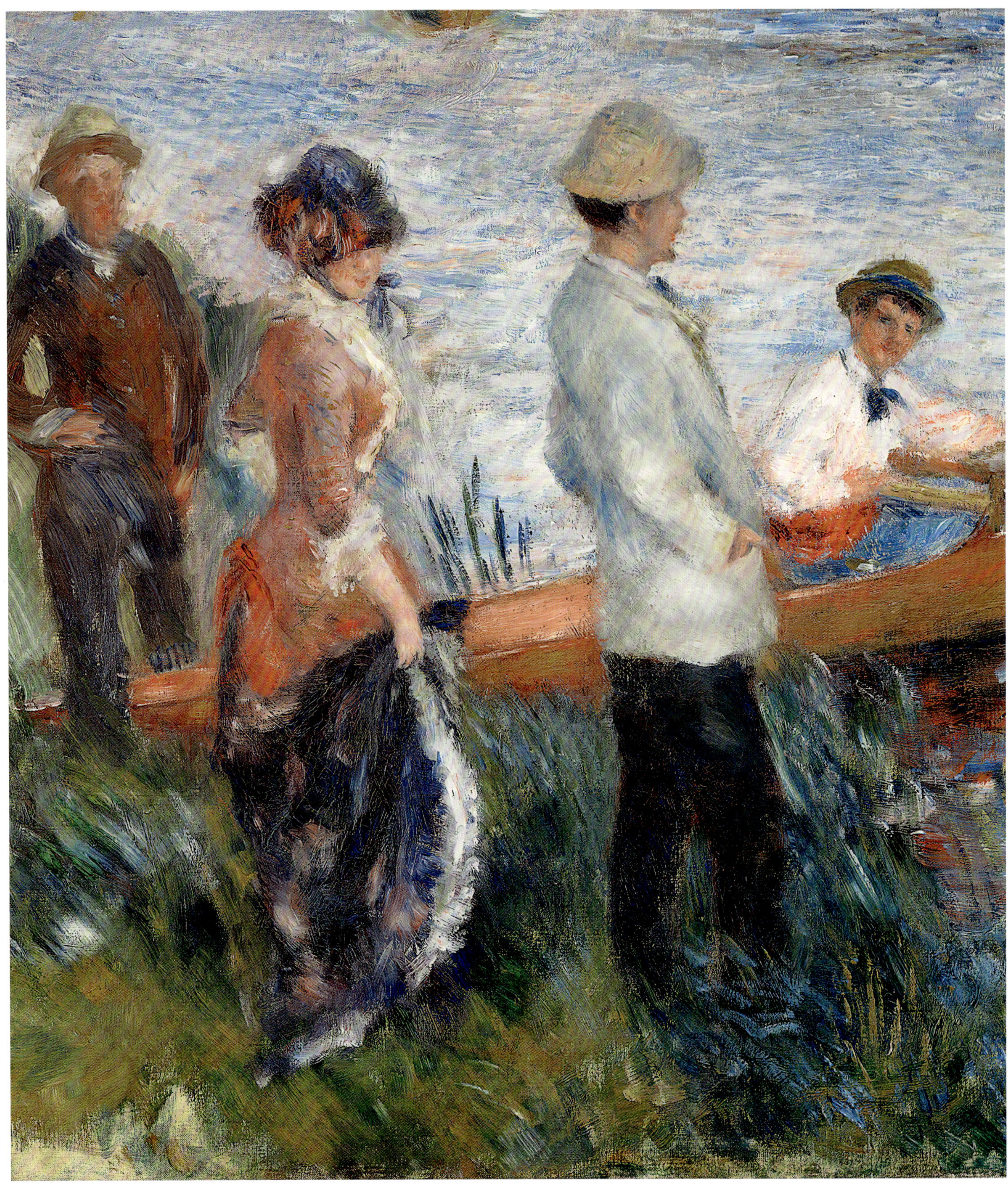

Renoir's Way with Clothes

AILEEN RIBEIRO

SET ON THE UPPER TERRACE of the Restaurant Fournaise on an island in the Seine at Chatou, west of Paris, Renoir's *Luncheon of the Boating Party* is a literal conversation piece, a depiction of that moment when a convivial lunch reaches the stage of fruit and more wine, and people wander around to talk to fellow diners, and to friends and acquaintances who have just joined the party. As Gustave Geoffroy, critic and friend of the impressionists, remarked, we see '"the very essence of the lull in conversation which follows a meal, the uninhibited attitudes, the gay and enthusiastic phrases spoken to women. . . ."[1] At any moment we expect the scene to "unfreeze" and the characters to come alive on the canvas. In a lively and casual public setting, women and men are shown with an equality of attention indicative of a modern, post-monarchical society; to emphasize the point, the artist clothes his main figures (a mixture of friends and professional models) in appropriately informal clothing. "L'Empire de la mode n'existe plus, il est remplacé par la république de la mode," was the comment made in 1873 by the editor of *La Mode illustrée;*[2] this new democracy of appearance was taken up by impressionist artists who liked the opportunities for expansive gestures and the freedom of movement simpler clothing enabled, which is evident in *Luncheon of the Boating Party*.

What was Renoir's attitude to clothes in his art? His father and brother were tailors and his mother a dressmaker, which gave him a professional interest in textiles, and how clothes work on the human body, both at rest and in movement. Although he claimed, according to his son Jean, to prefer relatively simple styles of dress in comparison to the extremes of female fashion (a conventional platitude voiced by artists through the ages), he was attracted to chic Parisiennes, and, after all, contemporary fashions were essential to the modernity which was the leitmotif of impressionism. To this end he took immense trouble to find the right outfits and accessories for the models in his scenes of Parisian life, and—although for portraits he asked sitters to wear *tenue habituelle* (everyday dress, clothing they were comfortable in, so as to create a "faithful picture of modern life")[3]—he was equally skillful in painting a *grande toilette* by Worth if necessary,[4] for human nature often dictated a very special outfit be displayed in a portrait, both for personal satisfaction and for posterity. And yet, apropos of women's dress, Renoir lacks the chic of Manet and Degas with their dispassionate detachment towards clothes; perhaps this is because he was unable to distance himself, as he *felt* fashion rather than coolly observing it. We can only speculate whether this attitude arose from his nervous, restless character—he was a man of little social skill who perhaps loved women not so much *as* women,[5] but for the way dress enhanced their bodies, which he depicted with pleasure and delight.

What about Renoir's own clothes? In his studio he dressed for comfort above all; in his old age, a number of visitors, like his close friend and fellow artist Albert André, recorded his appearance in a loose greatcoat, or bundled up in shawls, feet in woolen slippers, and his head covered up in a flapped cap or a shapeless linen hat.[6] Outside the studio he was never a stylish man but he liked to be modestly fashionable, befitting the son of a tailor; Jean Renoir informs us that his father had three made-to-measure suits "from good English material," two of which were of grey pinstripe cloth.[7] Although he affected (like many artists) to deplore the formal frock coat, claiming that it should only be worn for funerals, a photograph from the 1870s in the Musée Marmottan shows him wearing one.[8] Compared to images of Manet as a fashionable man-about-town, portraits of Renoir suggest an understated and casual taste in dress, which is not to be confused with indifference to appearance. Frédéric Bazille's portrait (fig. 36) of the artist as a young man (though looking somewhat older than his age[9]) shows Renoir unconventionally posed, his feet on the chair on which he sits, hands clasped together over his knees, and dressed in grey

woolen trousers, elastic-sided boots, and an informal, unstructured, comfortable jacket (known as a *veston*) of black cotton velvet.[10] A later unfinished self-portrait (Fogg Art Museum, 1876)—actually more youthful and flattering than the one by Bazille—shows him in another relaxed style, a loose brown *paletot* (sack coat)[11] and a black hat not unlike that worn by Eugène-Pierre Lestringuez in *Luncheon of the Boating Party*.

The clothing depicted—and, indeed, the title of the painting—reflects, as Renoir's friend and chronicler Georges Rivière said, how "à cette époque, le canotage était à la mode."[12] The most prominent figures in *Luncheon* wear clothes linked to rowing, in patriotic shades of blue, white, and red, a celebration, perhaps, of those democratic values espoused by the Third Republic and taken up by the impressionists. Rowing, in particular, could be enjoyed by men and women alike and at nearly every level of society, and women took an active part as well as being decorative passengers in boats and sculls. Articles on river sports such as rowing, sculling, and yachting featured in newspapers and magazines, a frequent subject in *La Vie moderne*; the issue for August 23, 1879, for example, has an essay by Gustave Goetschy on rowing to Chatou; a group of "hardis canotiers aux bras nus, aux bérets écarlates," coxed by expert women "pilotes," reach the Restaurant Fournaise where they celebrate by throwing their red berets in the air, feasting, drinking, and singing, and then dancing at Bougival, "dans le jardin resplendissant de lumière."[13]

Renoir and Gustave Caillebotte enjoyed rowing both as a pastime and as a fruitful subject for painting. Renoir started to paint the Seine in the late 1860s, and to frequent Chatou early in the following decade; two works from the 1870s give some flavor of his fascination with the sport, and the clothing worn: *The Skiff* (fig. 37), and *Oarsmen at Chatou* (Cat. 29). In *The Skiff*

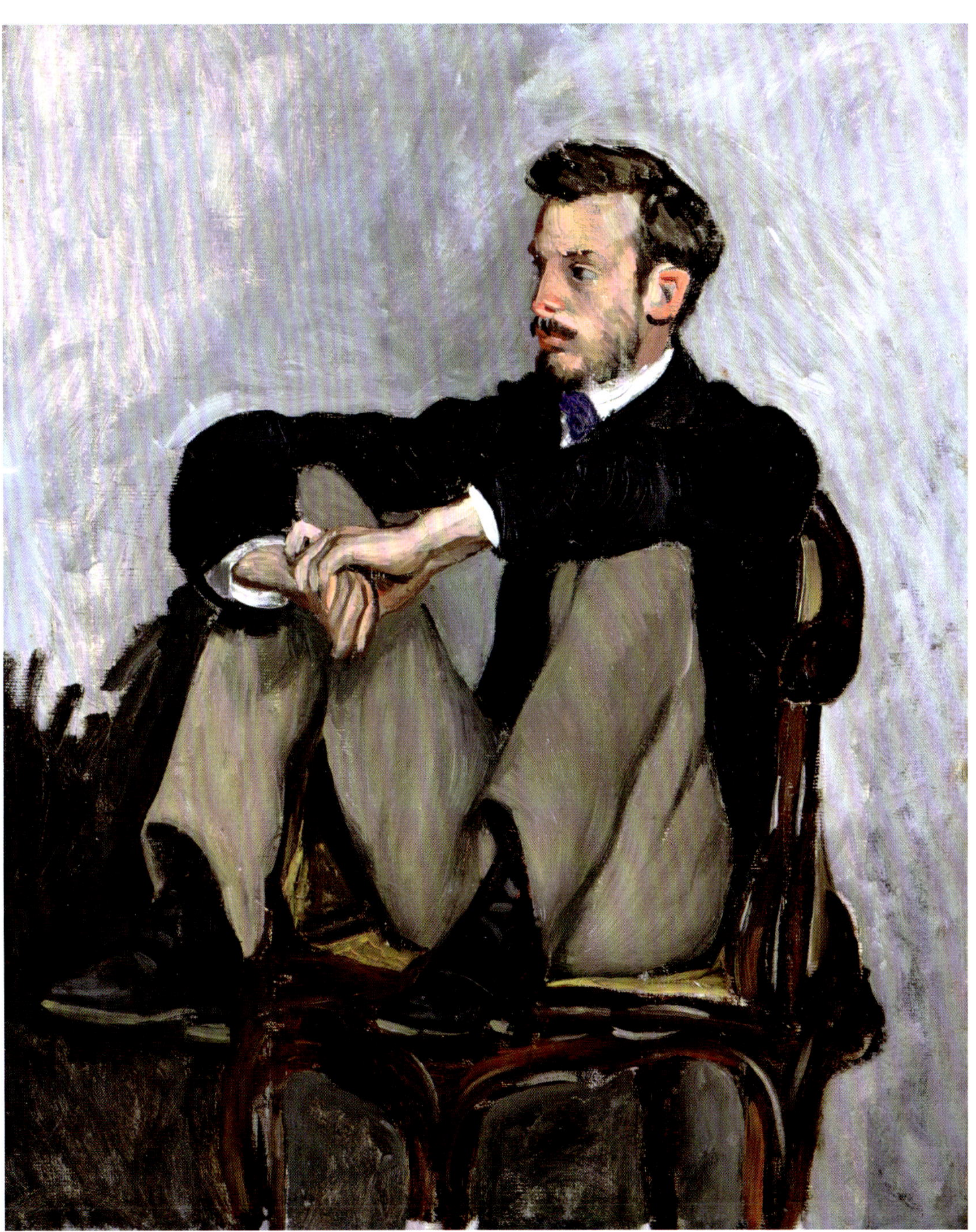

FIG. 36. Frédéric Bazille,
Pierre-Auguste Renoir, 1867,
oil on canvas, 24 × 19¾ in.
(61.2 × 50 cm).
Musée d'Orsay, Paris.

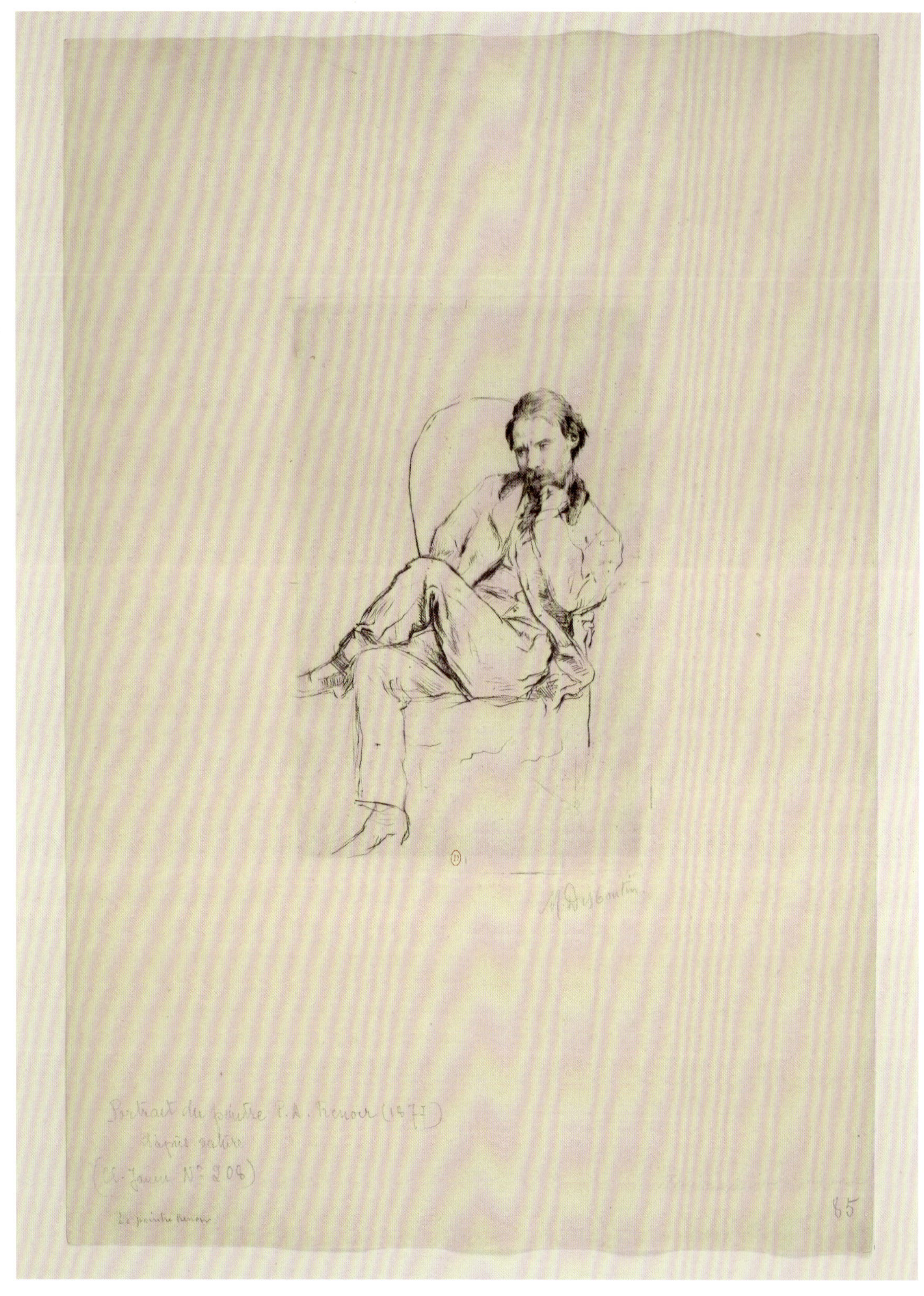

CAT. 46. Marcellin Desboutin, *Renoir, Legs Crossed* (*Portrait du peintre P.A. Renoir, les jambes croisées*), 1877, drypoint, 9 × 5⅞ in. (23.4 × 15.5 cm). Institut national d'histoire de l'art, Paris.

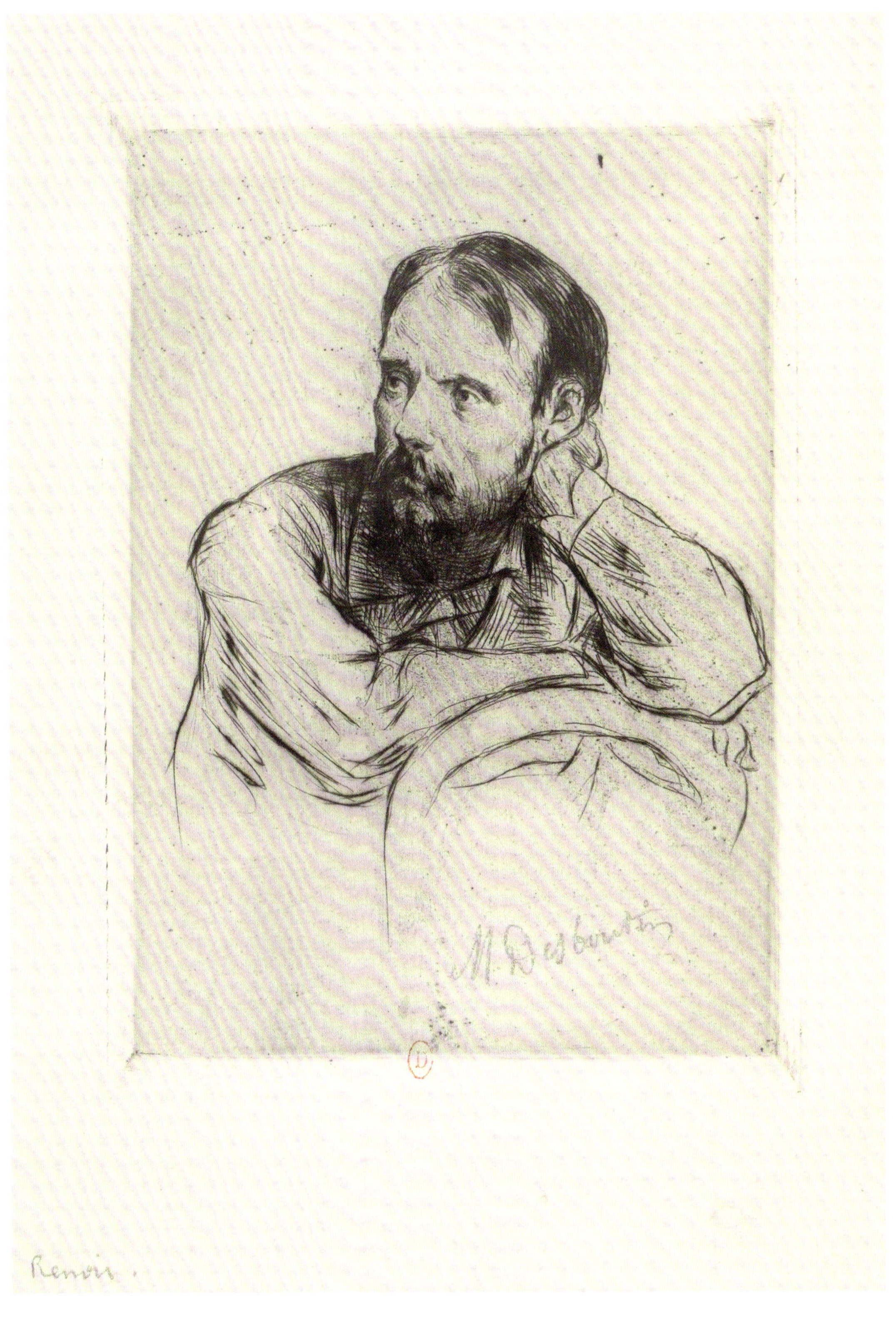

CAT. 47. Marcellin Desboutin, *Renoir* (*Portrait de Renoir*), 1877, drypoint, 5⅞ × 3⅞ in.
(15.2 × 10.8 cm). Institut national d'histoire de l'art, Paris.

(*La Yole*), probably painted at Chatou, fashionable cotton summer dress is depicted; the young woman sculling wears white with a touch of blue at the neck, her passenger in pale pink and white. In *Oarsmen at Chatou* (a somewhat erroneous title), we also see a woman in a red jacket and blue skirt, lifted up to reveal layers of white cotton petticoats, and blue, white, and red feathers in her hat, which is tied under the chin with blue and white ribbons. The man in front of her wears a white cotton or linen jacket, and the seated rower in straw boater, white shirt, and red cummerbund is ready for his passenger— surely the young woman in her modish tricolor ensemble. In

contrast to this lighthearted attire, Renoir sketches in a real working-class boatman in his short dark woolen jacket and trousers, practical clothing for hard physical work.

In *Luncheon of the Boating Party* Renoir focuses our attention on the informal and impromptu aspects of men's rowing clothes,[14] notably the white flannel sleeveless singlets worn by Alphonse Fournaise, standing on the left, and the man seated on the right, who has been not altogether plausibly identified as a youthful Caillebotte.[15] While it's possible that Fournaise, son of the proprietor of the restaurant and accompanying boating enterprise, might have stopped to greet his clients, it

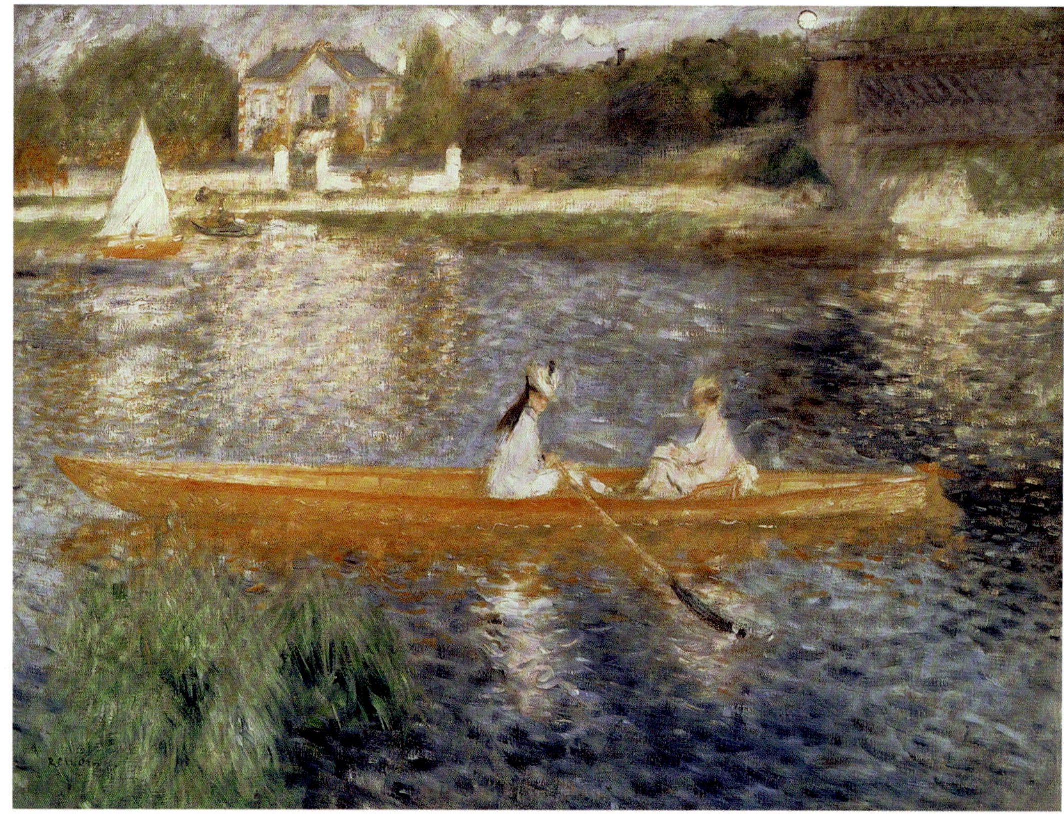

FIG. 37. Pierre-Auguste Renoir, *The Skiff* (*La Yole*), 1875, oil on canvas, 28 × 36¼ in. (71 × 92 cm). National Gallery, London.

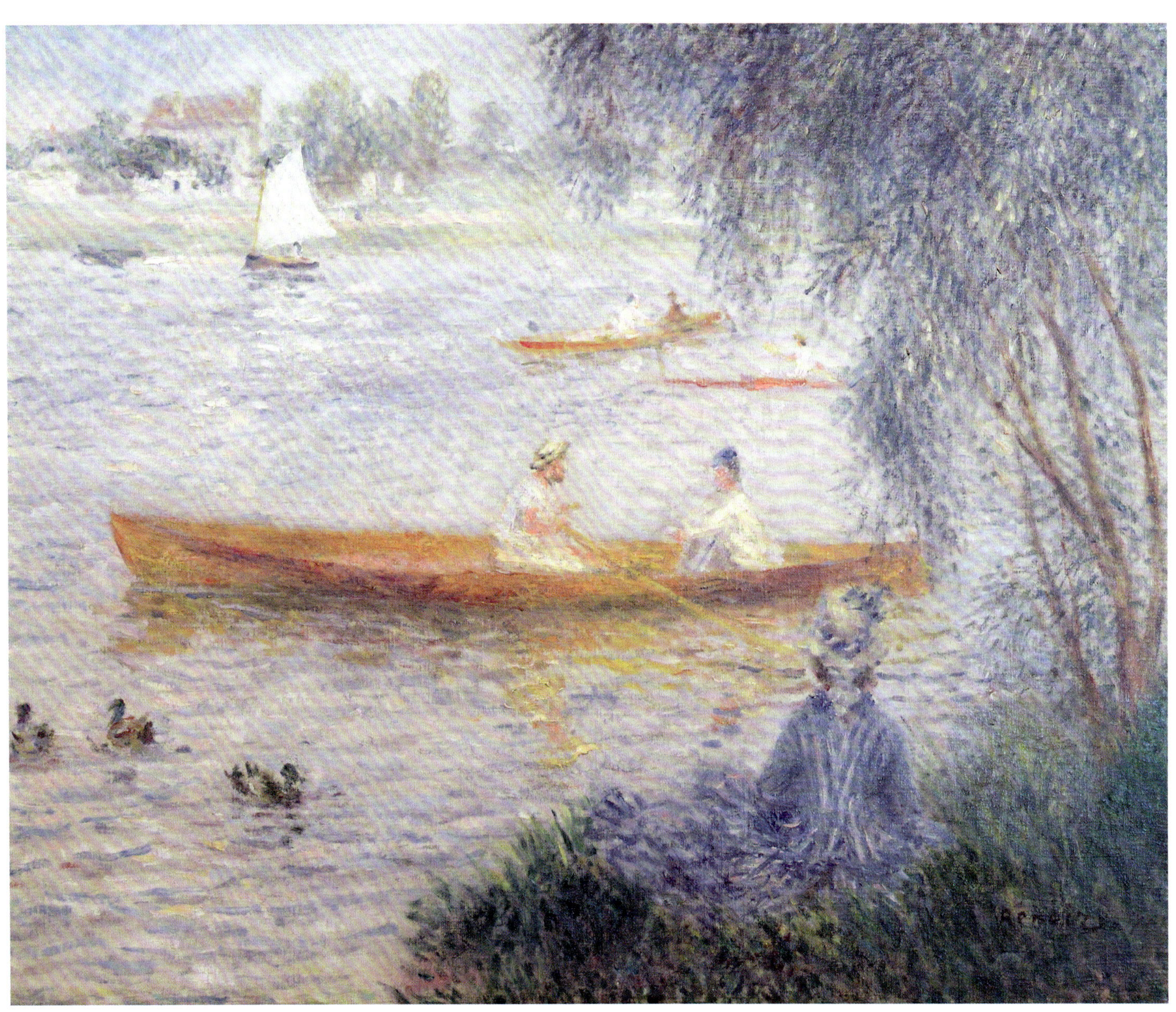

CAT. 48. Pierre-Auguste Renoir, *Boaters of Argenteuil* (*Canotiers d'Argenteuil*), 1873, oil on canvas, 19½ × 24 in. (50 × 61 cm). Larry Ellison Collection.

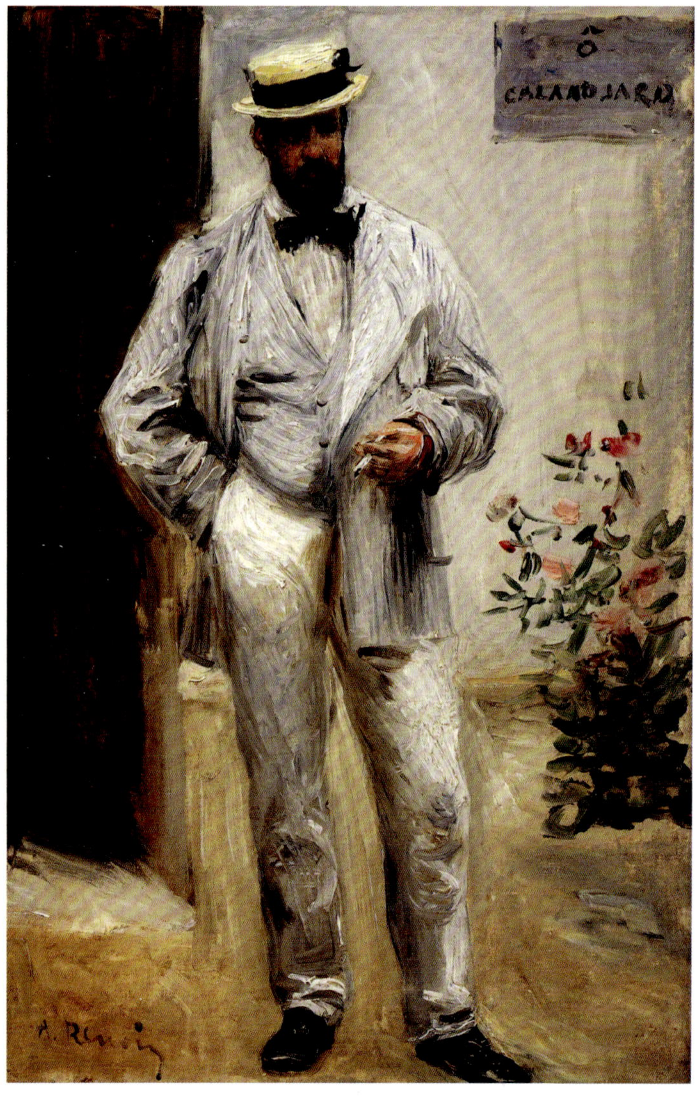

FIG. 38. Pierre-Auguste Renoir, *Charles Le Coeur*, 1874, oil on canvas, 16¾ × 11½ in. (42.8 × 29.2 cm). Musée d'Orsay, Paris.

vests were made either of flannel or of machine-knitted fabrics, both of which, being stretchy, were ideal for exercise. Loose white cotton shirts were also popular, and appear in a number of boating scenes, as do straw hats—both the coarse, rather shapeless kind,[19] and the structured and somewhat more formal straw boater worn by gentleman rowers, such as we see on the figure said to be modelled by Caillebotte, and also in the portrait of the architect Charles Le Coeur (fig. 38).

Shirts and trousers worn for rowing were sometimes striped (or checked) in blue[20] (the color combination was thought suitably nautical), and striped fabrics of linen, cotton, or lightweight wool were associated with river sports as well as seaside wear and informal summer costume.[21] The summer season, claimed the *Journal des tailleurs* in July 1880, brings to menswear "légèreté, élégance, harmonie des couleurs, tout concourt à rendre agréable à l'œil l'ensemble de nos toilettes d'été."[22] It is this kind of harmonious summer ensemble (what the tailoring journals refer to as a "mise négligée") in shades of white, gray, and blue that we see in Renoir's portrait of Le Coeur, including a loose unstructured blue-striped jacket; similar jackets are worn by the unidentified man in *Oarsmen at Chatou* and the journalist Adrien Maggiolo in *Luncheon of the Boating Party* (fig. 39). Maggiolo is almost alone in the painting in not wearing a hat,[23] for even on the most casual occasions some kind of headwear was usually worn; "le couronnement de l'édifice de la toilette est le chapeau," commented the author of *La Comédie de notre temps* (1874), not altogether satirically.[24] The more structured and impractical the hat, the more formal the outfit, such as the top hat and black coat worn by the critic and collector Charles Ephrussi, very much a man of the world, and one possible inspiration for Charles Swann in Proust's *À la recherche du temps perdu*. At the bottom of the social scale was

seems to me unlikely that Caillebotte, very self-aware regarding clothing and personal appearance (described by Rivière as an "homme de goût," a man of taste),[16] would have been at lunch without a jacket over his singlet.[17] Flannel, a soft fabric with an open, loose weave, was a popular choice for sporting (and swimming) clothing. White flannel trousers were often worn for rowing, with short-sleeved round-necked vests very like modern T-shirts (see the figure, possibly of Renoir's brother Edmond, in *Lunch at the Restaurant Fournaise* (Cat. 22)).[18] Such

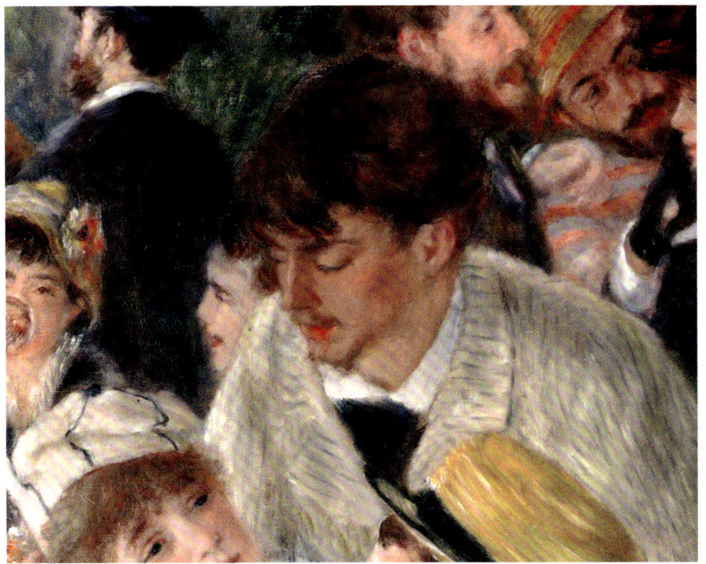

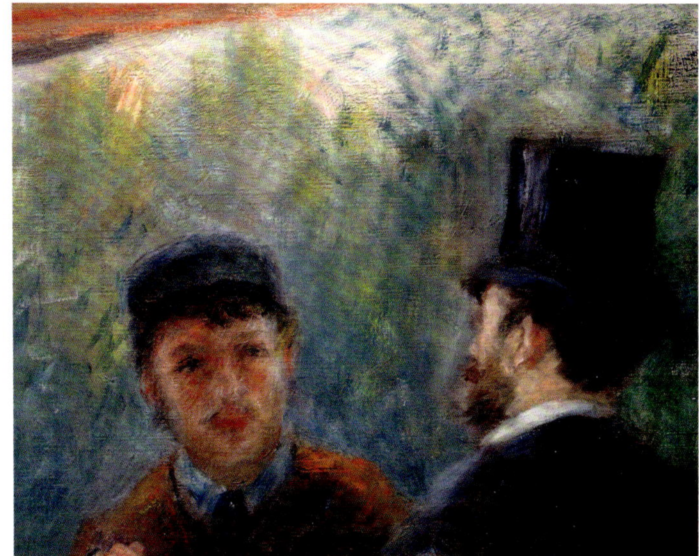

FIG. 39. Detail of *Luncheon of the Boating Party*: Adrien Maggiolo.

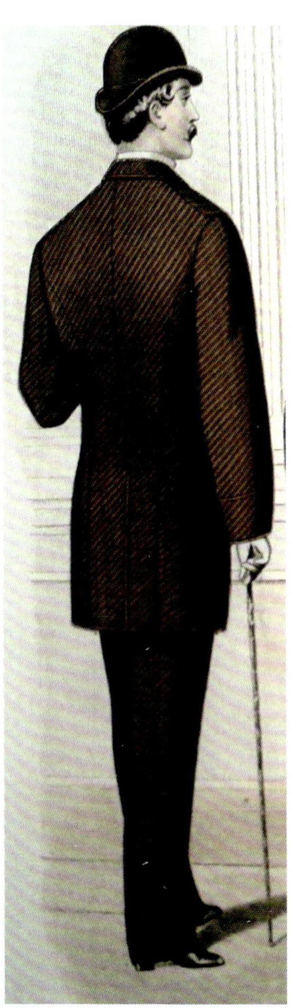

the working man's woolen peaked cap (*casquette*) of the kind worn by the unknown man, literally a blue-collar worker whom Ephrussi talks to, a physical meeting of classes;[25] in between these two extremes are the informal felt hats with narrow brims, worn by Baron Raoul Barbier and Lestringuez. Facing the young woman who leans on the railing (possibly Alphonsine Fournaise, though the identification is disputed) is the seated figure of the former cavalry officer Barbier, whose well-tailored back we see in a brown woolen jacket; shades of brown frequently featured in fashion magazines (*havane*— presumably the color of a Havana cigar—was especially popular), for outdoor wear year-round (fig. 41). The hat worn by Barbier is possibly a low-crowned version of the English bowler hat (a derby in the United States), known as a *melon* in France, with a brim turned up all round.[26]

In the group of figures in the right-side background we see Lestringuez, whose hat, at a rather rakish angle, has a slight dent in the crown and the brim turned down at the front.[27] He

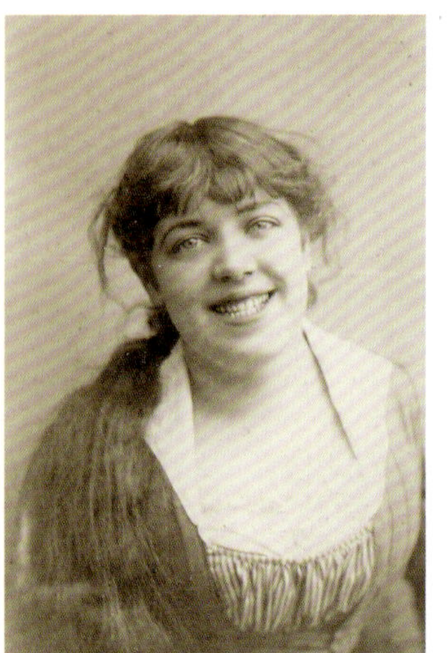

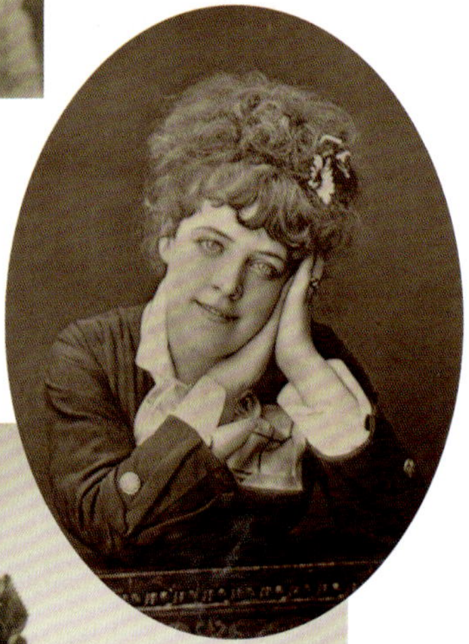

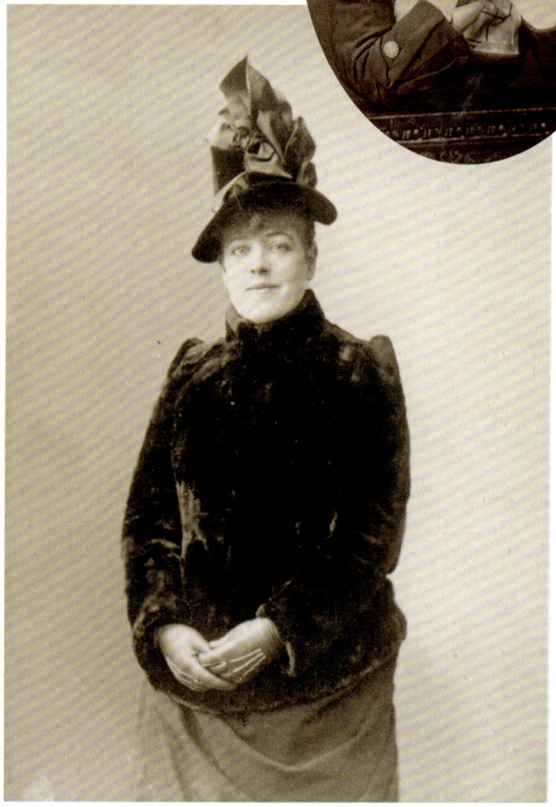

LEFT

FIG. 42. *Jeanne Samary – Smiling*, digital print. Bibliothèque-musée de la Comédie-Française, Paris.

CENTER

FIG. 43. *Jeanne Samary – Face Resting on Hands*, digital print. Bibliothèque-musée de la Comédie-Française, Paris.

BELOW

FIG. 44. *Jeanne Samary – With a Hat*, digital print. Bibliothèque-musée de la Comédie-Française, Paris.

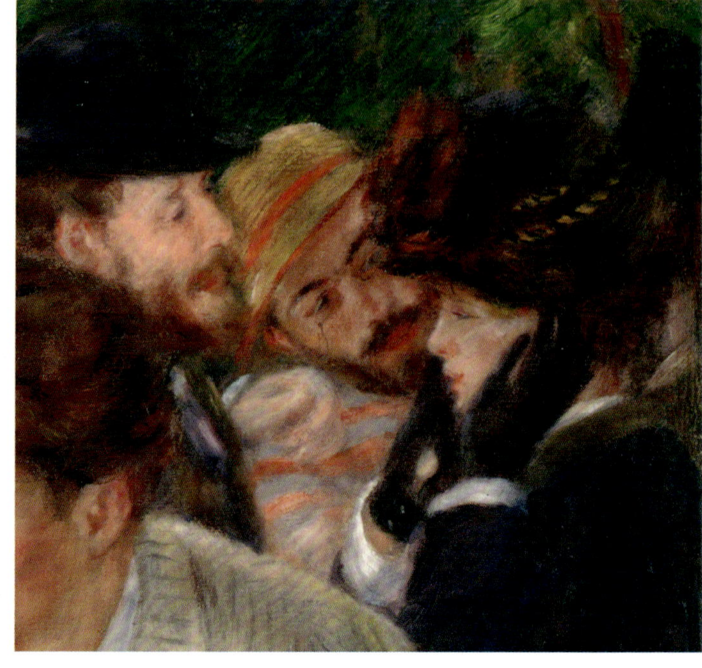

FIG. 45. Detail of *Luncheon of the Boating Party*: Left to right: Eugène-Pierre Lestringuez, Paul Lhote, and Jeanne Samary.

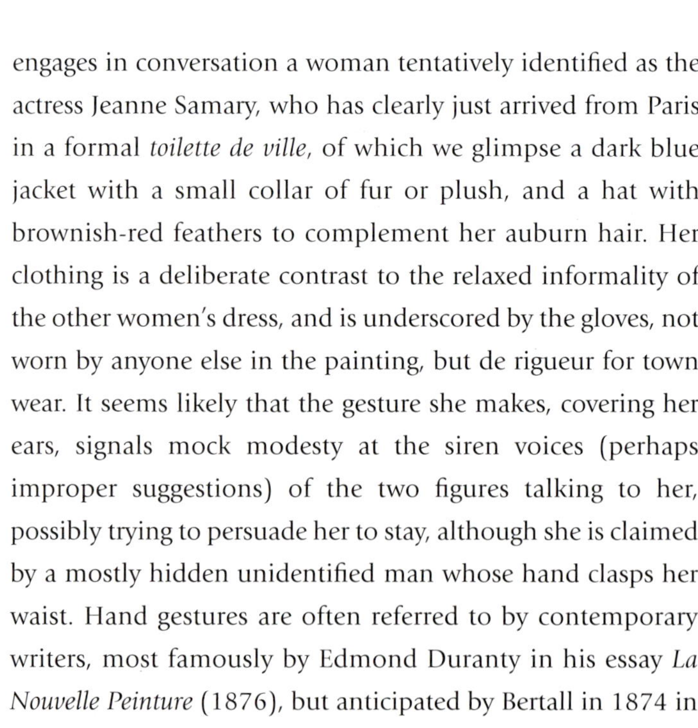

engages in conversation a woman tentatively identified as the actress Jeanne Samary, who has clearly just arrived from Paris in a formal *toilette de ville*, of which we glimpse a dark blue jacket with a small collar of fur or plush, and a hat with brownish-red feathers to complement her auburn hair. Her clothing is a deliberate contrast to the relaxed informality of the other women's dress, and is underscored by the gloves, not worn by anyone else in the painting, but de rigueur for town wear. It seems likely that the gesture she makes, covering her ears, signals mock modesty at the siren voices (perhaps improper suggestions) of the two figures talking to her, possibly trying to persuade her to stay, although she is claimed by a mostly hidden unidentified man whose hand clasps her waist. Hand gestures are often referred to by contemporary writers, most famously by Edmond Duranty in his essay *La Nouvelle Peinture* (1876), but anticipated by Bertall in 1874 in his description of the hand as a kind of prospectus in which a person's origins and character can be read.[28] Renoir applies this theory of the way hands animate character—Samary's gloved hands, the way Aline Charigot holds the small terrier, how "Caillebotte" has his cigarette between thumb and forefinger, and so on. Finally, to the right of Lestringuez we catch a glimpse of Paul Lhote, a friend and frequent model of Renoir's,[29] in the rower's straw hat and striped sweater, bringing us back to our main theme for the *Luncheon of the Boating Party*, rowing-related clothing.

Although there was no specific female costume for the sport, the fashion worn was often blue, white, and red, and included such styles as the sailor collar seen on the white blouse trimmed with red rickrack braid worn by "Alphonsine," similar to that worn by Suzanne Valadon in Renoir's *Dance at Bougival* (see fig. 4).[30] Practical and stylish boating ensembles for the active young woman might also include a jacket and skirt, often of blue, such as we see in Renoir's *Two Sisters* (*On the Terrace*) of 1881 (fig. 47), on a terrace (not the same one) at the Restaurant Fournaise. Here, the elder girl, identified as the eighteen-year-old Marie Darlaud (later a light-comedy actress under the name Jeanne Darlaud) wears a hooded blue flannel jacket and skirt over a white blouse, the tricolor effect completed by a red hat with red roses.[31] Guy de Maupassant's novella *Yvette* (1885) has a description of the costume of female rowers as blue or red flannel,[32] but blue was far more popular, more practical, more nautical, and—above all—more fashionable, and a color Renoir loved.[33] In *Luncheon of the Boating Party*, the two female figures in the foreground—the actress and model Ellen Andrée in her jaunty white cap striped with blue, and Aline Charigot (mistress and future wife of the artist), playing with the small dog—wear blue with touches of

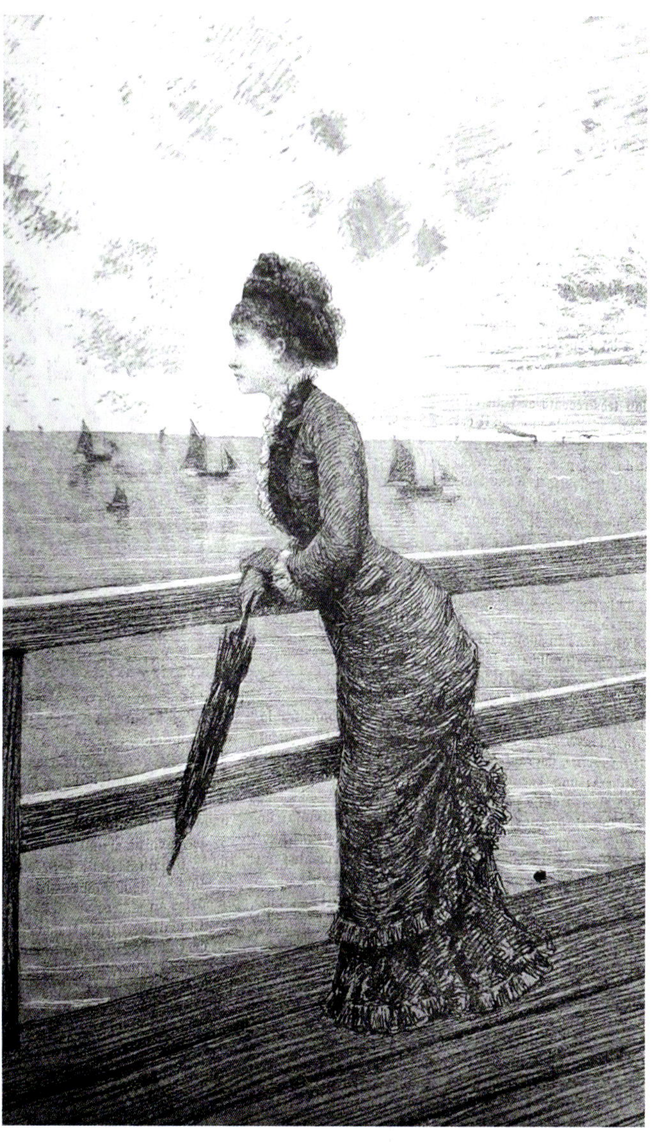

FIG. 46. Maurice Poirson, *On the Jetty* (*Sur la jetée*), 1879, steel engraving, National Art Library, Victoria and Albert Museum, London.

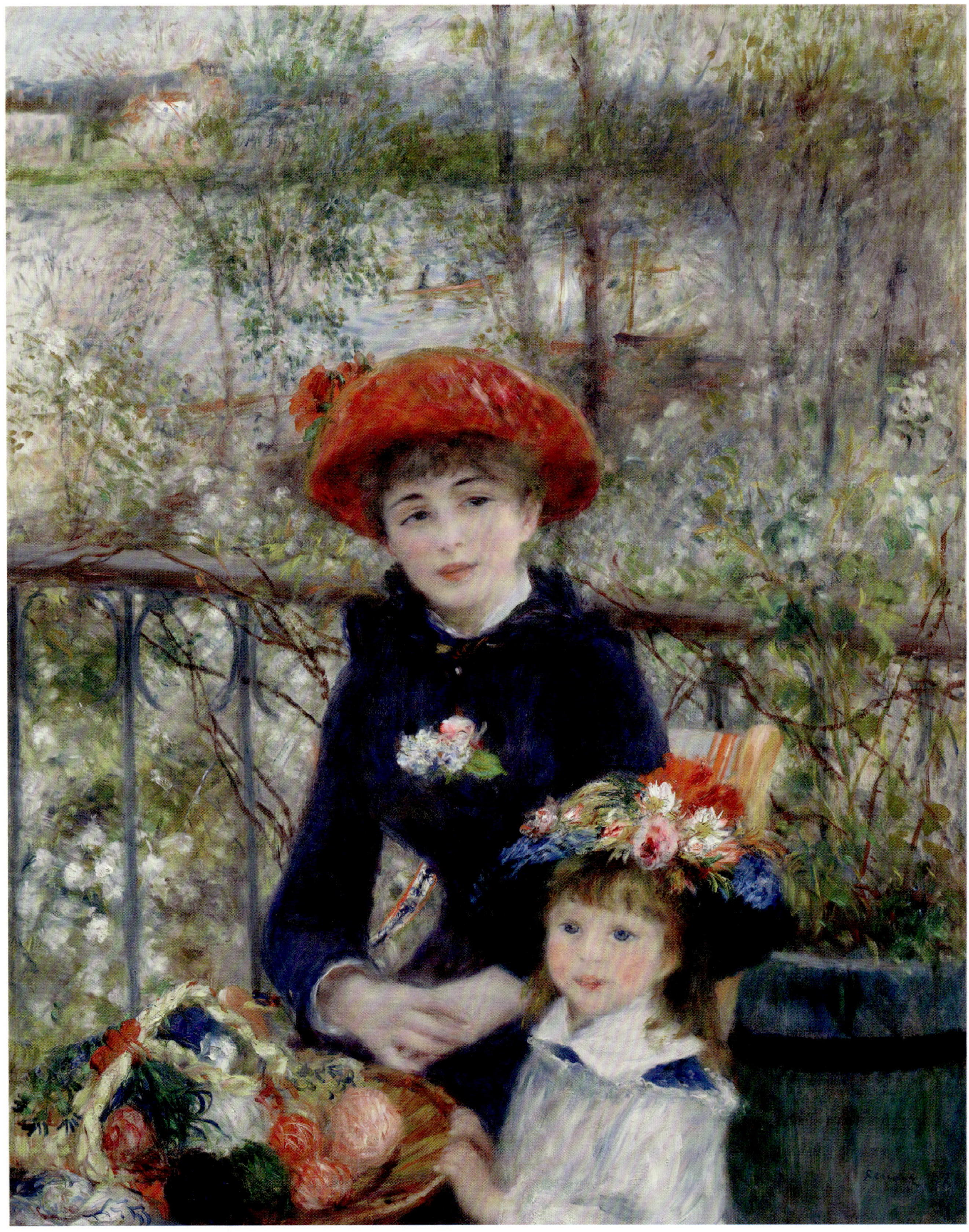

red and white. Charigot's dress isn't easy to read, but seems likely to be a modest version of the fashionable princess line (named by Worth in honor of Alexandra, Princess of Wales), which Renoir could have bought ready-to-wear from an increasing number of department stores by the late 1870s,[34] or which Aline, herself a dressmaker, might have made. Such a dress consisted of a bodice and skirt cut in one, fitted at the waist and with fabric draped over the hips to create slight fullness at the back, an echo of the bustle that had vanished by the late 1870s. When Renoir was pressed to say what his favorite dress was, he replied "la robe princesse qui donne aux femmes cette ligne sinueuse si jolie";[35] and it is this sleek, flattering line that we see in an illustration from *La Vie moderne* (fig. 46), taking the form of a long tunic *en princesse* over a matching skirt. Renoir's paradigm woman, healthy and artless, placid and good-natured, Charigot wears a straw hat decorated with poppies that suggests summer; Renoir loved hats with

flowers, and his studio contained, along with fabrics flung over chairs, a number of "chapeaux fleuris pour ses modèles."[36] This sense of the pastoral, a summer scene where the city met the countryside via the river, seems perfectly suited to *Luncheon of the Boating Party*, and indeed to impressionism in general. Defined by Charles Ephrussi as the "nouvelle école," the impressionists depicted the subtleties of atmosphere, of sensation, of gesture, of light, and of color, achieving "une unité lumineuse" in which apparently irreconcilable elements were brought together to create a general harmony.[37] Thus, in Renoir's *Luncheon of the Boating Party*, the variety of clothing— effectively the range of different social classes—is an essential element. Here is the reverse of paintings Zola referred to as little more than "gravures de mode banales et inintelligentes"; it's a scene alive and imbued with the artist's deep understanding of his own time, "tels que nous sommes, avec nos costumes et nos mœurs."[38]

Acknowledgments: I am grateful to the staffs of the British Library, the National Art Library, and the Courtauld Library (especially Vicky Kontou) for their help. Also to Jenny Lister (Victoria and Albert Museum), Tim Long (Museum of London) and Rosemary Harden and Elaine Uttley (Bath Fashion Museum) for showing me examples of clothing in their collections.

1. Gustave Geoffroy, "Auguste Renoir," *La Vie artistique*, August 1894, quoted in Wadley 1987, p. 191.

2. *La Mode illustrée*, March 16, 1873, p. 87. Two years later the same fashion journal stated that if fashion was to succeed, it had to be "democratic," i.e. worn by the largest number of people (*La Mode illustrée*, February 28, 1875, p. 70). This concept, of course, is the antithesis of fashion, then and now!

3. As recorded by his brother Edmond Renoir in *La Vie moderne*, June 19, 1879, p. 175. For Edmond's comments on his brother's methods of painting portraits, see John Rewald, "Auguste Renoir and his Brother," *Gazette des beaux-arts* 27 (March 1945): pp. 171–188.

4. As in his portrait of *Madame Charpentier and Her Children* (fig. 33), in her black silk dinner dress by Worth. Marguerite Charpentier was instrumental in the founding in April 1879 of *La Vie moderne*, a weekly magazine of art, literature, and fashion, with which Renoir was occasionally associated until early 1886. For Renoir's interest in fashion, see Aileen Ribeiro, *Clothing Art: The Visual Culture of Fashion 1600–1914* (New Haven and London: Yale University Press, 2016) pp. 368, 385.

5. John House comments that Georges Rivière "doubted that Renoir really liked women: 'Though he gave women a beguiling appearance in his paintings, and gave charm to those who had none, he generally took no pleasure in their conversation. With a few exceptions, he only liked women if they were susceptible to becoming his models.'" Arts Council 1985, p. 16.

6. André 1919, p. 18. See also André's portraits of Renoir in old age painting in his studio (1913 and 1919), in the Musée d'Art Moderne de la Ville de Paris.

7. Renoir 1962<1958?>, p. 191.

8. Reproduced in Rathbone 1996, p. 249. The anonymous photographer shows Renoir in a rather strained thoughtful pose, suitable for the formal costume (perhaps his father made the frock coat), but the reverse of the natural gestures which the artist gives to the characters in his paintings.

9. When Georges Rivière met Renoir for the first time (1874) he recorded "son visage sérieux, sillonné de rides, sa barbe courte et rude" (Rivière 1921, p. 3).

10. A *veston* was a simply styled informal jacket, sometimes with no collar or a shawl collar; it had three pockets: two just below the waistline and one on the left breast. A black *veston* is illustrated in the *Journal des tailleurs* for August 1881, p. 8. A similar jacket to the kind Renoir wears (of a kind which in England was sometimes called a smoking jacket) is in the Museum of London, of black velvet with woolen trim (2001.14).

11. Artists liked the comfort of these loose coats and sometimes wore them in the studio. A similar coat to that in Renoir's self-portrait can be seen in John Singer Sargent's portrait of Carolus-Duran (Clark Art Institute, 1879).

12. Rivière 1921, p. 182.

13. Gustave Goetschy, "Les Canotiers," *La Vie moderne*, August 23, 1879, pp. 317–318. Henry Scott's illustrations to this story depict the rowers on the river (women not just as *pilotes*, but also as *canotières*), and the scene at the Restaurant Fournaise.

14. Compared to the more formal and regimented styles of rowing costume in England, notably the blazers designed for collegiate rowing clubs. I'm grateful to Chelsea Eves of the River and Rowing Museum, Henley-on-Thames (Oxfordshire) for her help and for sending me an image of the cream flannel blazer and trousers of c. 1896 worn by rowers from Pembroke College, Oxford.

15. As Anne Distel remarks (Distel 1995, p. 75), only two characters in the painting can be positively identified, Alphonse Fournaise and Aline Charigot. The figure of "Caillebotte" doesn't look like the artist, and thus seems an unlikely tribute by Renoir to a friend and fellow artist.

16. Rivière 1921, p. 34.

17. In the illustration to Goetschy's essay "Les Canotiers" in *La Vie moderne* (see note 13), the scene at the Restaurant Fournaise shows the rowers all wearing jackets (p. 318).

18. The other male figure, M. de Lauradour, a friend of Renoir and regular patron of the Restaurant Fournaise, is shown in a similar vest, under a cream flannel jacket.

19. Probably the kind of straw hat which, according to Ambroise Vollard (who met Renoir in 1895), the artist "was apparently accustomed to crumple in his hands while posing the models" (Vollard 1990, p. 1). Such hats appear in Caillebotte's *Self-Portrait as an Oarsman* (Private collection), and *Oarsmen Rowing on the Yerres* (fig. 23). These cheap and ephemeral straw hats have not survived the passing of time, unlike the sturdier and more costly boaters.

20. The *Journal des tailleurs* (July 1881, p. 2) proposed what appears to be a fanciful (almost fancy dress) "toilette de canotier" of blue striped and checked wool, comprising a tight-fitting jacket (*corsage*) and wide trousers, and completed by a blue beret.

21. Striped suits were so associated with rowing that they are often referred to in the catalogues of costume collections as "boating suits"; an example from c. 1890–1895 in the Victoria and Albert Museum (T 113-1934) comprising jacket, waistcoat, and trousers (known in England as "dittos") of cream flannel pinstriped in blue is thus named. See Jacques-Émile Blanche's portrait of the French novelist and poet Georges de Porto-Riche (Stair Sainty Gallery, London, 1889) in a stylish fine woolen blue-and-white-striped summer suit at the fashionable Anglo-French seaside resort of Dieppe; the emphasis on the detail of the clothes is an interesting contrast to Renoir's painterly image of Charles Le Coeur (fig. 38).

22. *Journal des tailleurs*, July 1880, p. 1.

23. The only other person, just visible to the left of Maggiolo, is a young man who gazes at the model Angèle as she empties her wineglass, seemingly indifferent to his presence.

24. Bertall (Charles Albert d'Arnoux), *La Comédie de notre temps* (Paris: E. Plon et Cie, 1874), p. 71.

25. Sometimes identified as the symbolist poet and critic Jules Laforgue (who was very briefly Ephrussi's secretary until he left for Berlin in November 1881), though this seems unlikely, for images of Laforgue depict a man of fashionable taste in dress, appropriate to his white-collar job as a personal secretary. The man in Renoir's painting (more akin to the humble figure of the boatman in *Oarsmen at Chatou*) wears a blue shirt, brown jacket, and *casquette*. A rare peaked cap from the late nineteenth century (little working-class clothing survives compared to that of the elite classes) is in the collection of the Bath Fashion Museum (BATMC IV.12.3).

26. In Renoir's painting the hat appears to be fairly stiff, but Rivière refers to it as a "chapeau mou," a soft hat (Rivière 1921, p. 186); some confusion is perhaps accounted for by the lapse of forty years between the painting and Rivière's book.

27. This kind of soft felt hat was very popular with artists from the 1870s onwards. From the mid-1890s it was called a trilby in England after the very successful eponymous novel (1894) by George du Maurier, which was set in an artists' studio in the Latin Quarter of Paris.

28. Bertall, *Comédie*, p. 54: "La main est une sorte de prospectus dans lequel sont exposés clairement la nature, les tendances, les aptitudes, l'origine, le passé . . . [et] l'avenir." There is also a discussion of how artists make the hand "speak" in Gabriel Prévost's *Le Nu, le vêtement, la parure chez l'homme et chez la femme* (1884).

29. Renoir used the same models in a number of his paintings; Lhote and Lestringuez, for example, had appeared in *Dance at Le Moulin de la Galette* (fig. 15). Lhote (in an unmatched blue jacket and trousers, *not* a lounge suit) dances with Aline Charigot in *Dance in the Country* (Cat. 27). He is perhaps the man in *Dance at Bougival* (fig. 4) depicted in the demotic clothing of a boatman: a blue knit sweater, mismatched blue jacket and trousers, sturdy shoes reinforced with metal, and a straw hat. Colin Bailey, however, suggests that the dancer in *Bougival* might be Alphonse Fournaise (Bailey 2012, p. 203). And just to add to the identification problems with the figures in *Luncheon of the Boating Party*, Rivière claimed that Lhote was also the man in the top hat, whom most commentators refer to as Ephrussi.

30. The woman may be a composite of Suzanne Valadon and Aline Charigot.

31. The little girl (not identified—they aren't sisters) echoes the tricolor theme in her appearance, wearing a blue dress under a white pinafore, with red and white flowers and blue feathers in her hat.

32. Guy de Maupassant, *Yvette* (Paris: Victor-Havard, 1885), p. 68: "Les canotières en robe de flanelle bleue ou de flanelle rouge . . ."

33. Shades of blue in dress and fabrics feature in Zola's novel *Au Bonheur des Dames* (1883), about a fashionable department store (*grand magasin*), as they do in Renoir's paintings, a notable example being *The Umbrellas* (National Gallery, London, c. 1881–1885).

34. The *grands magasins* catered to the upper and middle classes, but lowlier department stores such as La Samaritaine (founded in 1869) sold some relatively inexpensive ready-to-wear versions of fashionable clothing to non-elite customers.

35. When Ambroise Vollard asked Renoir for his preferences with regard to women's clothes, he famously replied that what he liked best was to see them *un*clothed ("ce que j'aime le mieux, c'est la femme nue"), but if he had to paint a woman dressed, he loved the princess line (Vollard 1938, p. 181). Ernest Hervilly claimed that this style of dress appealed particularly to artists because it emphasized the natural curves of the female body without immodesty and with grace (*La Vie moderne*, October 11, 1879, p. 427).

36. From André 1919, quoted in Butler 2002, p. 23.

37. Charles Ephrussi in the *Gazette des beaux-arts*, May 1, 1880, quoted in Denys Riout, *Les Écrivains devant l'impressionnisme* (Paris: Macula, 1989), p. 233. Huysmans talks of this harmony in Renoir, likening his work to Whistler's *Harmonies* and *Nocturnes*. Joris-Karl Huysmans, *L'Art moderne* (Paris: G. Charpentier, 1883), p. 265.

38. Émile Zola (ed. J.P. Leduc-Adine), *Écrits sur l'art* (Paris: Gallimard, 1991), pp. 206–207.

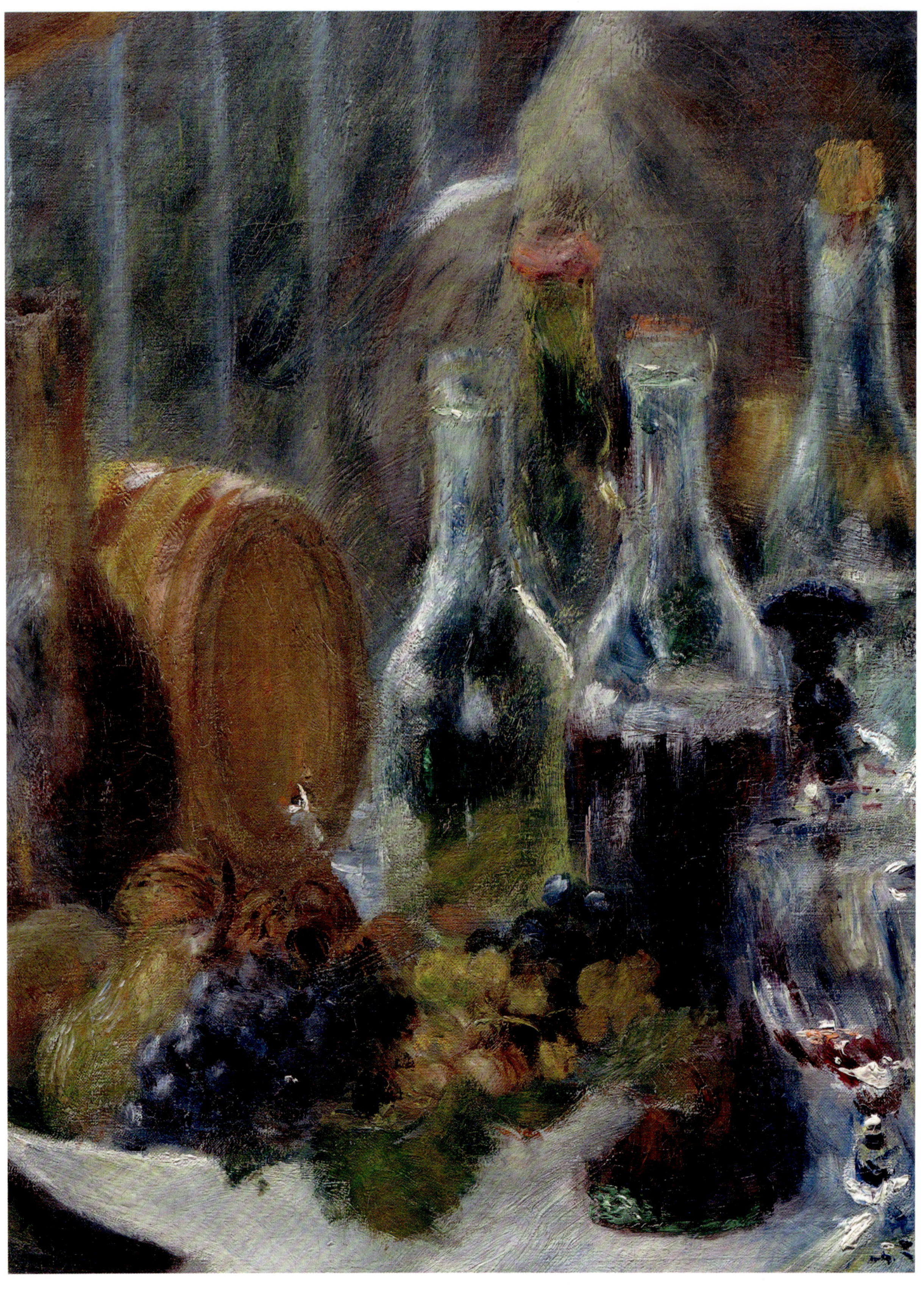

Reevaluation of *Luncheon of the Boating Party*

ELIZABETH STEELE

Paint Analysis by Thomas Lam, Stephanie Barnes,
Jia-Sun Tsang, and Inge Fiedler

THE FIRST TECHNICAL STUDY of Renoir's *Luncheon of the Boating Party* was published in conjunction with The Phillips Collection's 1996 exhibition *Impressionists on the Seine*. Twenty years later, in preparation for *Renoir and Friends*, a fresh assessment of the picture was undertaken using improved X-radiographic and infrared images and new paint cross-sections. While many observations from the previous study remain the same, a second look provided more insight into composition changes than was previously discovered.[1] The allure of the painting lies in Renoir's ability to capture the moment of friends casually enjoying an afternoon at a restaurant on the Seine. What this in-depth examination shows is that he did so only after multiple revisions. We don't know how many people posed at any one sitting, but we assume they came in small groups or perhaps individually.[2] While working on the painting, Renoir wrote to Paul Berard about friends coming and going, complaining about how difficult it was to finish it, since

"Deudon, who was meant to come, has not shown up and I have not seen anyone since your trip. I do not know if Ephrussi is back; I am sacrificing this week too since I have done all I can and I will return to my portraits . . . when I will be able to leave I have no idea and I will not fix a date. I believe I will continue to be delayed and in that case you will be back before me."[3]

Much of the painting's success lies in the convincing interaction that Renoir creates among his models. Their arrangement in twos and threes leads the eye across the table and through the picture to the back of the balcony. It is the complexity of the scene that makes it so intriguing, and demonstrates the painter's mastery of strong compositional skills. No preparatory drawings are known to exist and little underdrawing is apparent in the infrared image; it seems as if the artist developed the work directly on the canvas, making changes as the picture evolved. In the same letter to Berard, he recounts this struggle, saying he had to remove a figure "and I no longer know where I am with it except that it is annoying me more and more."[4] Under raking light, we can identify the passages where changes were made by the textured brushstrokes under the top layer of paint that bear no relationship to the final picture (fig. 48). Earlier states of sitters

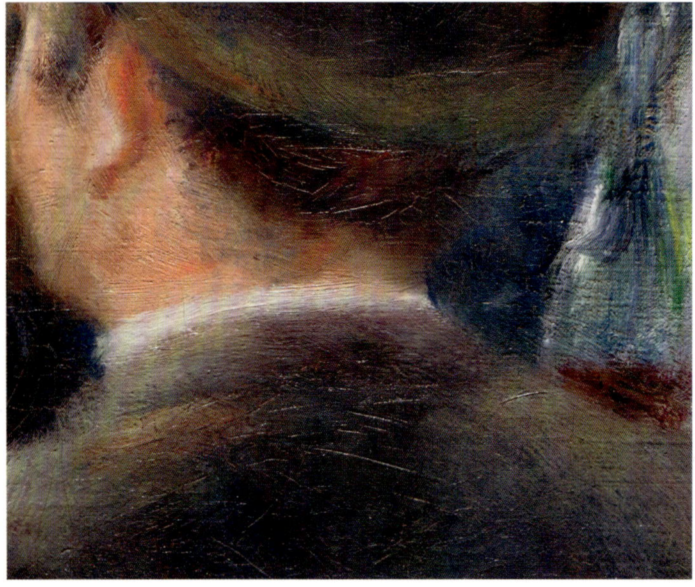

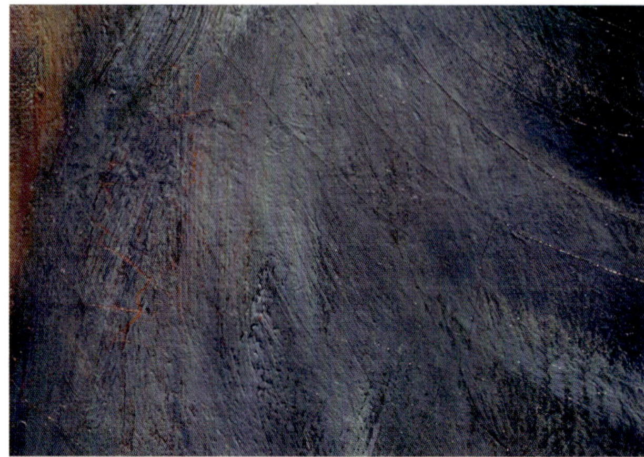

LEFT

FIG. 49. Detail of *Luncheon of the Boating Party*: drying cracks visible in figure's head and back in raking light.

ABOVE

FIG. 50. Detail of *Luncheon of the Boating Party*: red paint showing through cracks of Aline Charigot's dress in raking light.

and alterations throughout the picture are also detectable in the X-radiograph and the infrared image (figs. 62 and 63). When studied under high magnification through a microscope, distinctly different colors in the underlying layers are visible inside drying cracks. The very existence of drying cracks[5] on the surface, formed when Renoir painted over a passage that was not yet dry, attests to his reworking process (fig. 49).

One of the most dramatic changes Renoir made is in the lower left; the woman holding the dog, Aline Charigot, was painted over another figure. In the X-radiograph, a completely different sitter is visible who turns in her chair to face the viewer.[6] She wears a dress with three-quarter-length sleeves and folds her right arm along her torso, holding an object—perhaps a glass or a handkerchief (fig. 51). Elaborating on his annoyance, Renoir tells Berard that "I'm obliged to go on working on this wretched painting because of a high-class cocotte who had the impudence to come to Chatou wanting to pose; that put me a fortnight behind schedule and, in a word, today I've wiped her out."[7] It seems probable that the figure in the X-radiograph is the "high-class cocotte." Red paint is visible in the cracks of Aline Charigot's blue dress, indicating

that the model he painted over wore a red dress (fig. 50). A microscopic sample was taken from an existing loss in the lower left and made into a cross-section, which reveals the paint application in this area (fig. 52). The bottom layer (a) is the lead white ground used to prepare the canvas. Next, a very thin cobalt blue layer (b) is visible, which is most likely Renoir's preliminary sketch applied by brush. On top of this are two to three applications of paint ranging in tone from light pink to a more orange/red color that correspond to the dress worn by the first model. Renoir used lead white and red lake for the lower layers (c) and lead white, vermillion, and red lake with traces of chrome yellow or chrome orange and possibly zinc yellow for the upper layers (d). On top of the red is a layer (e) containing lead white with a small amount of light red (probably vermillion) and yellow pigment particles dispersed throughout. This lighter-colored layer most likely represents a highlight in her dress. The next layer (f) is a thin application of lead white, which the artist presumably used to block out the bright red color. The top two layers (g) are composed mainly of cobalt blue and red lake, and correspond to the dress worn by Aline Charigot.[8] Another clue to the existence of the

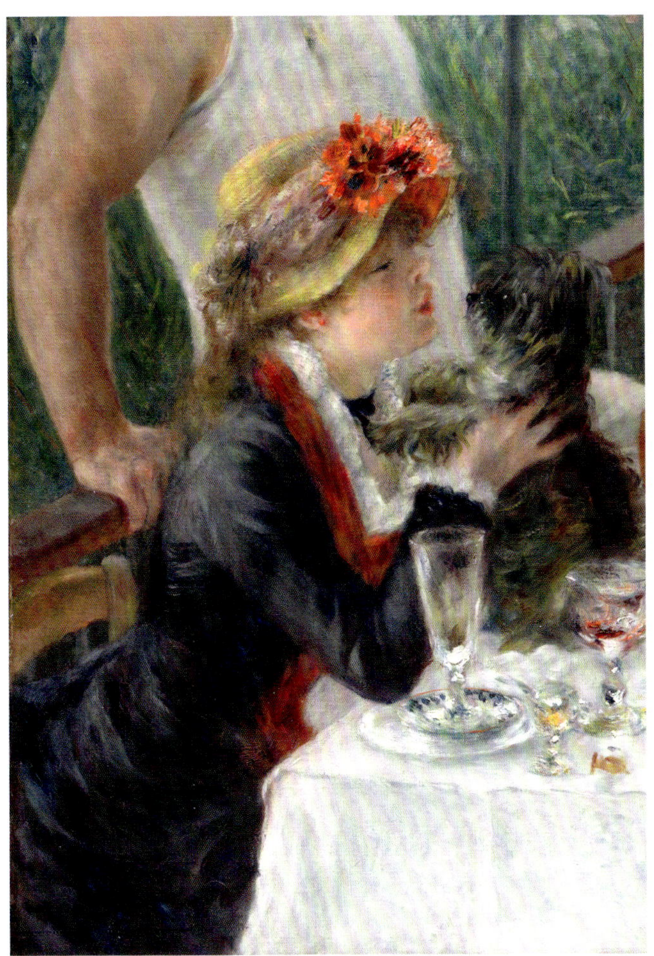

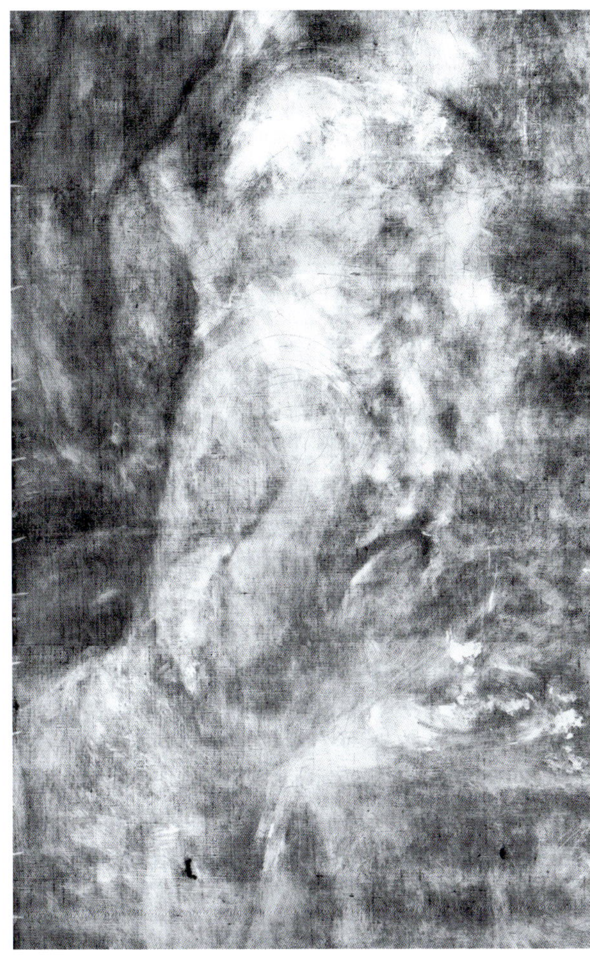

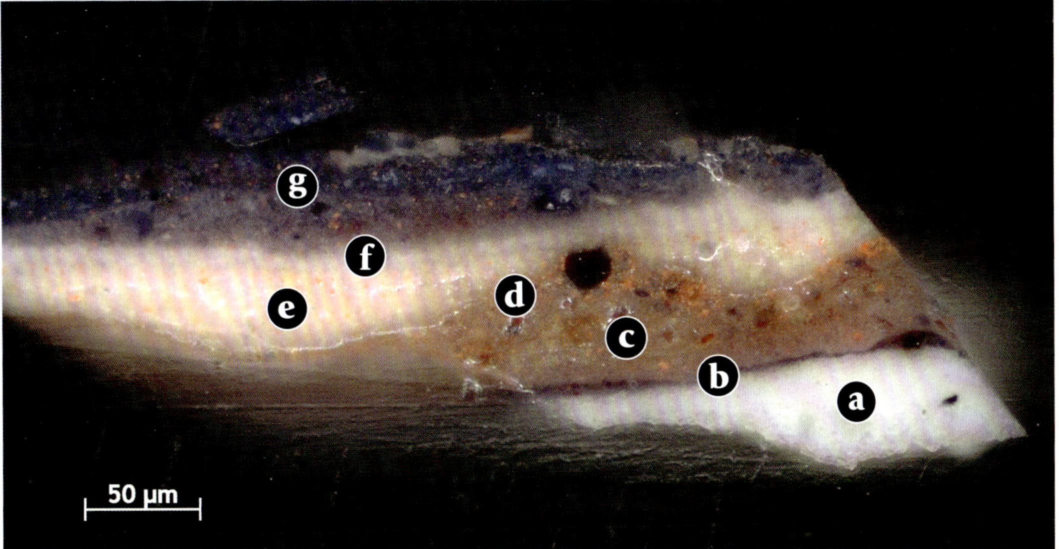

ABOVE

FIG. 51. Detail of *Luncheon of the Boating Party*: Aline Charigot in raking light compared to same area in X-radiograph.

LEFT

FIG. 52. Paint cross-section taken from Aline Charigot's dress in *Luncheon of the Boating Party*. Darkfield Illumination at 200 × original magnification.

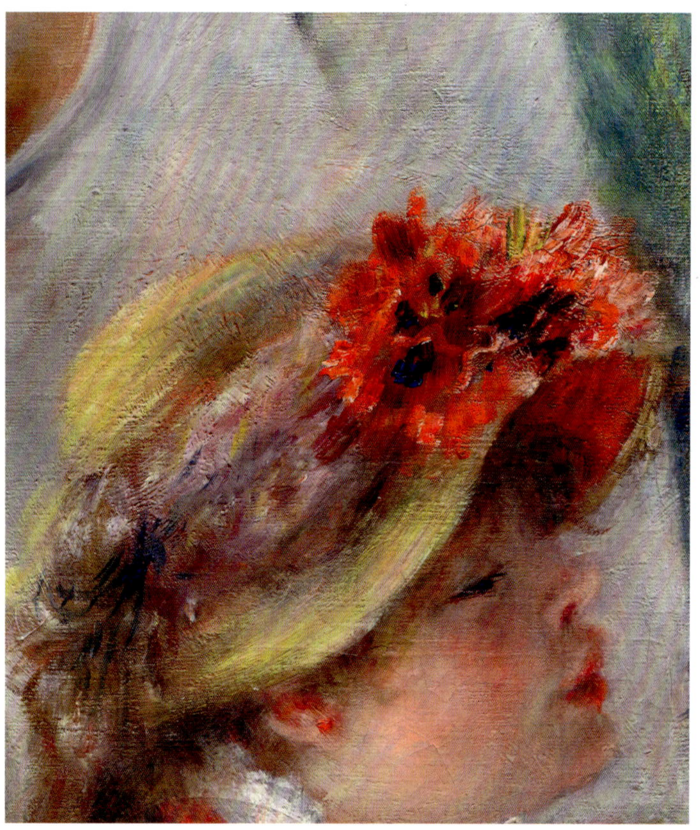

FIG. 53. Detail of *Luncheon of the Boating Party*: area above Charigot's head in raking light.

first sitter can be seen in raking light above Aline Charigot's head (fig. 53). In raking light, we see a more angular hat adorning the head of the first sitter. On close inspection of paint inside the cracks, it too seems to be red. Perhaps the "cocotte" wore a bonnet like the one worn by the woman in *Dance at Bougival* (see fig. 4), which has a similar profile.

Renoir made a surprising rearrangement to the pair of men who stand at the end of the balcony, indicated in raking light by the underlying textured brushstrokes around their heads. The pentimento of an earlier face to the left of the top-hatted figure is also discernible. The revision the artist made becomes clear in the infrared image: Charles Ephrussi, who wears the top hat, initially looked out toward the front of the balcony with his head in three-quarter view (fig. 54). By turning him to face the man to his left, Renoir strengthens their relationship, making

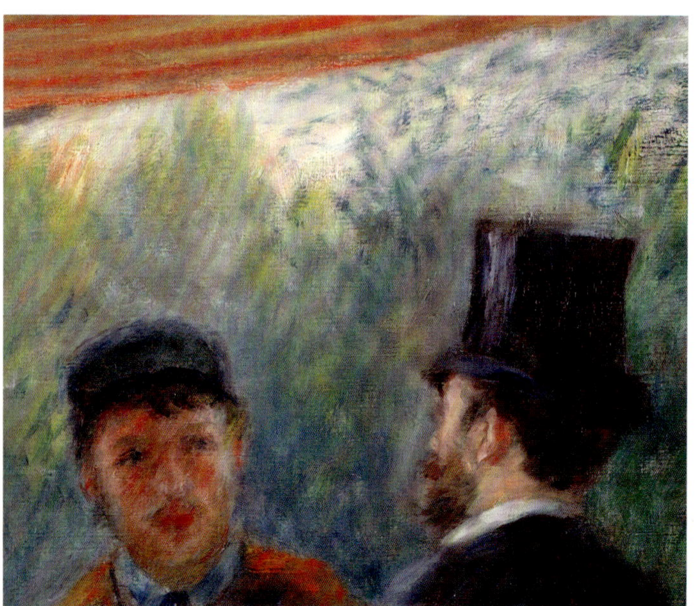

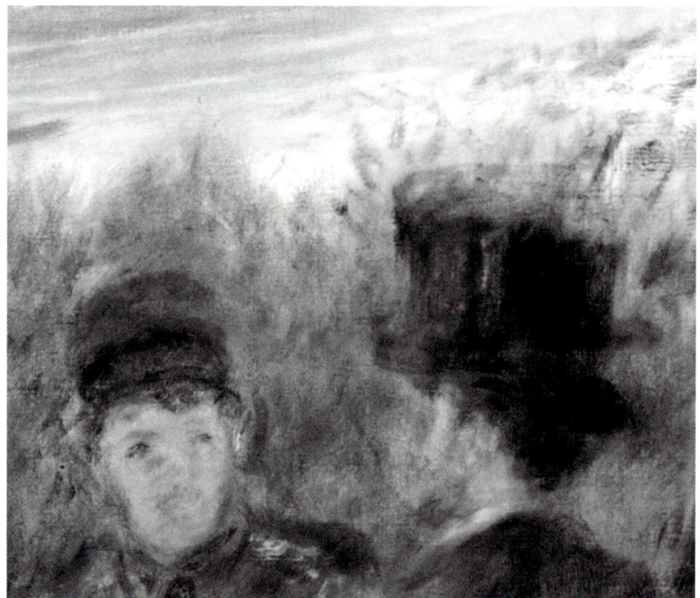

FIG. 54. Detail of *Luncheon of the Boating Party*: Two men in raking light compared to same area in infrared image.

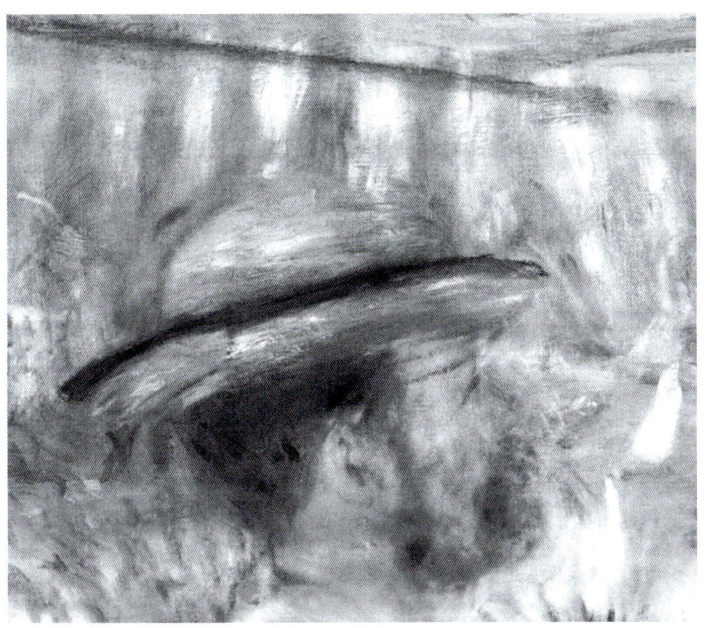

FIG. 55. Detail of *Luncheon of the Boating Party*: head of Alphonse Fournaise in infrared image.

them look more involved in conversation than in the previous configuration. The infrared image also reveals a second set of hats, heads, and shoulders that indicates they were initially positioned higher on the canvas. The same thing happened with Alphonse Fournaise, who leans against the railing on the far left. The downward shift of this figure and the halo-like pentimento around his rower's hat are visible in raking light (fig. 59). The infrared image shows sketched lines across his forehead, revealing that Renoir positioned the hat on his head several times before settling on its final placement (fig. 55).

Renoir probably lowered these figures because of another critical modification to the composition: the addition of the awning. Sweeping textured brushstrokes that do not correspond to the striped fabric are readily visible in the upper left (see fig.

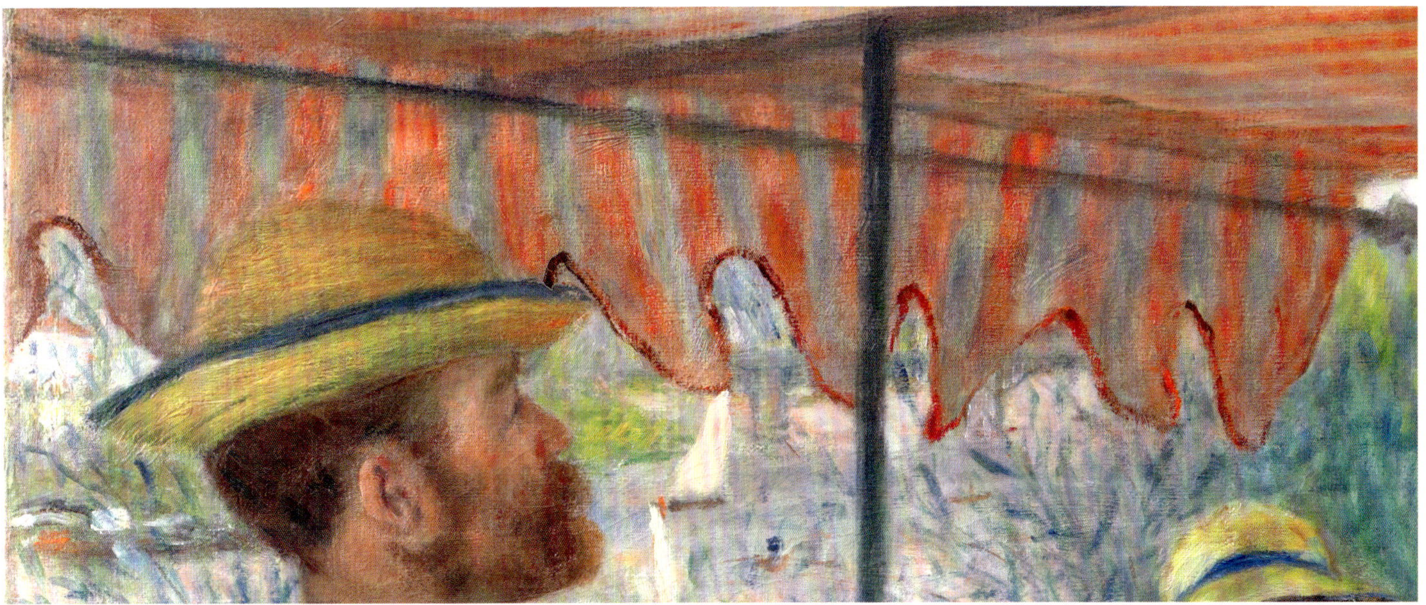

FIG. 56. Detail of *Luncheon of the Boating Party*: awning upper left with head of Alphonse Fournaise in raking light.

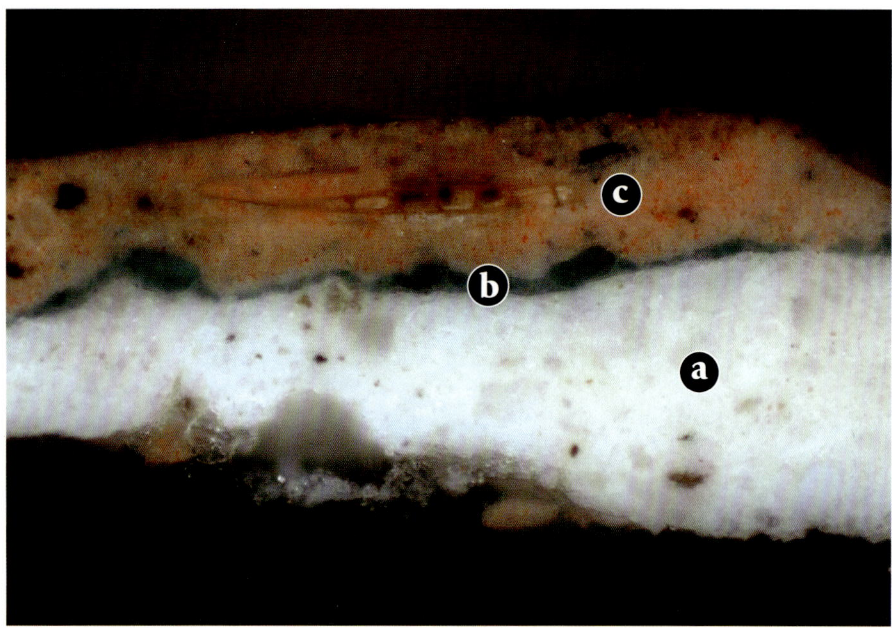

FIG. 57. Paint cross-section taken from along top edge of
Luncheon of the Boating Party. Differential Interference
Contrast Illumination at 200 × original magnification.

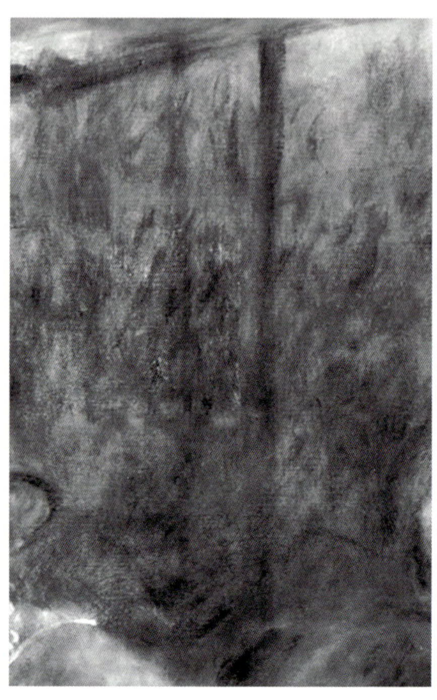

FIG. 58. Detail of *Luncheon of the Boating Party*:
awning poles in infrared image.

56), showing that the landscape and sky initially dominated the top edge of the picture. Upon close inspection, we can see that the railroad bridge was initially visible in its entirety, as well as a dwelling on the far left; yellow, blue, orange, green, and white paint, the same colors used in the foliage below, are discernible beneath the thinly painted striped fabric. A cross-section made from a tiny loss along the upper right edge (fig. 57) reveals viridian green paint (b) under the red (c) used in the awning, which is composed of vermillion, chrome yellow and lead white and provides further proof that he painted the fabric cover on top of a developed landscape as a second thought.[9] The lead white preparation layer (a) lies beneath the green and red layers of paint. There are several small brown specks, including a curious pod-shaped inclusion, seen in fig. 57, which is a highly unusual finding. Their appearance is suggestive of fungal spores, originating from plant material, which may have found their way onto Renoir's palette.[10] The

awning poles were placed before the fabric was painted, and they also lie on top of a somewhat developed landscape; the infrared image shows that Renoir moved the center vertical pole slightly to the right (see fig. 58). Surviving nineteenth-century photographs of the Maison Fournaise show the balcony with and without an awning, although the framework seems to have been fixed so that the covering could be rolled out and in.[11] In the photos the restaurant sports a variety of awnings, some with borders, some without, some striped, others solid; in one image it has a striped awning with a scalloped edge like the one in the painting.[12] Adding an awning after Renoir had painted a considerable amount of the picture must have been a conscious decision to strengthen the composition rather than merely to record the details of the setting. If he had kept an open sky and a distant landscape, the three-dimensional illusion would have been more difficult to create. By enclosing the top edge, the balcony's recession into

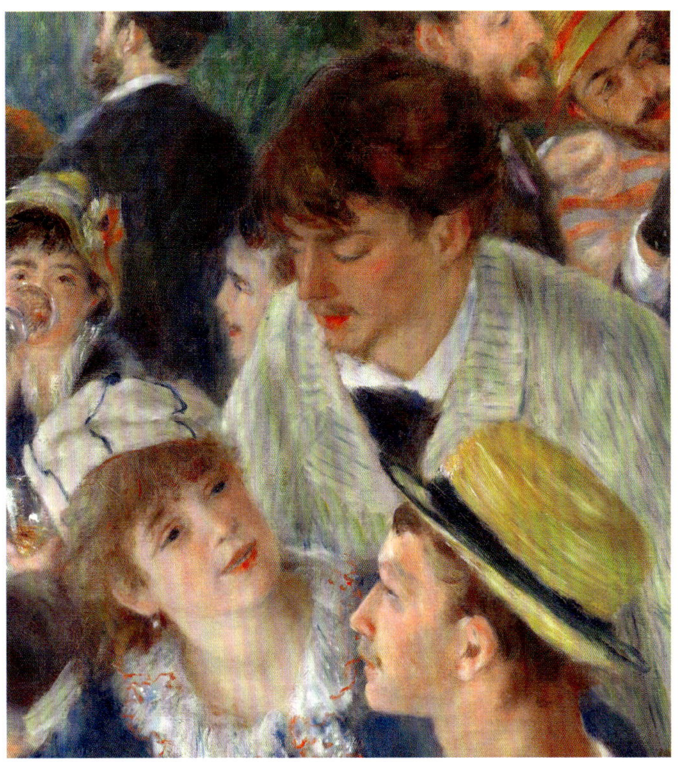

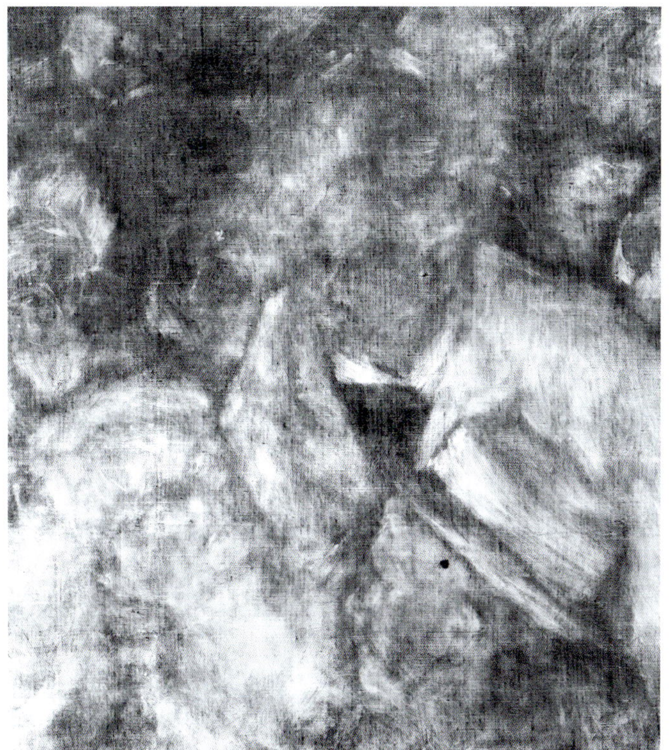

FIG. 59. Detail of *Luncheon of the Boating Party*: right-hand figures in raking light compared to same area in X-radiograph (above right) and infrared image (below right).

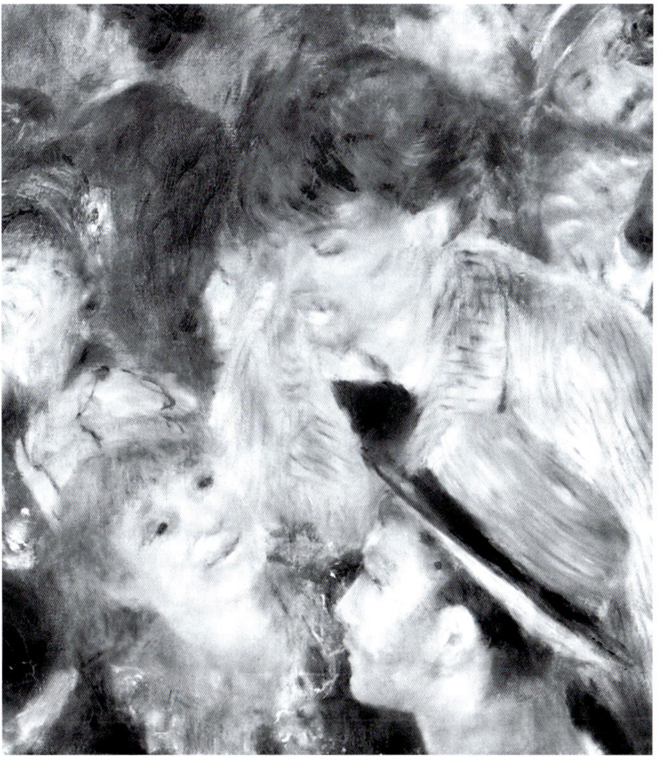

space is more persuasively established, and the sitters are better defined as a group. With the awning in place and the top right corner filled with dense foliage, the luncheon assumes a more intimate feeling that would have been difficult to realize in a more open-air setting.

Inspection in raking light together with the X-radiograph and infrared images shows that Renoir also altered the orientation of the face and neck of the woman seated on the right in a white hat. A second set of eyes is perceptible in both the infrared image and the X-radiograph, and her neck is elongated as she looks up (fig. 59); she originally looked at the man who rests his hand on the back of her chair. It seems probable that Renoir repositioned her gaze in order to connect her with the man straddling the back of the chair next to her, and to create a unified grouping of the three figures. If he had not made this

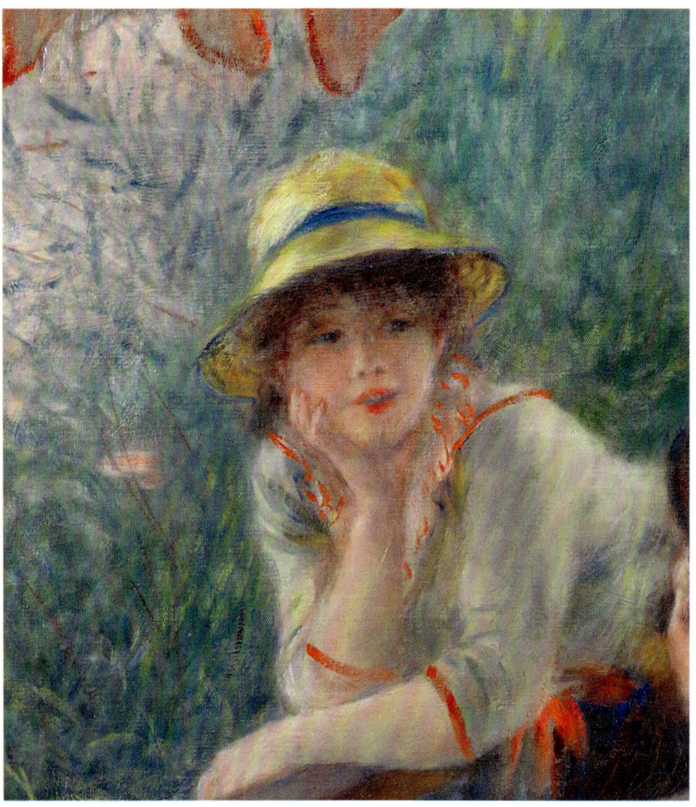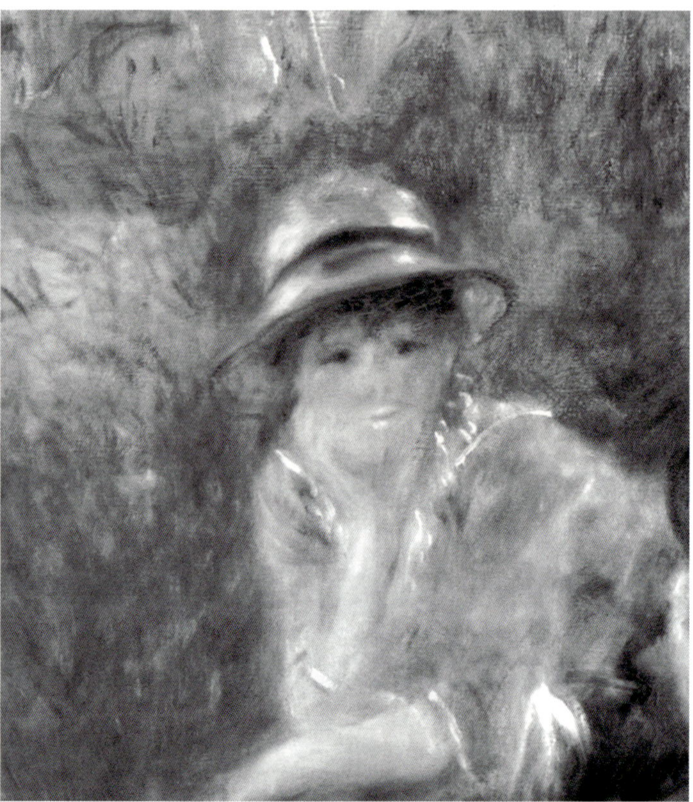

FIG. 60. Detail of *Luncheon of the Boating Party*: woman leaning on railing in raking light compared to same area in infrared image.

change, the man, thought to be modeled by Gustave Caillebotte, would be staring into the distance with little association to anyone else at the table. The X-radiograph also suggests that the man leaning over the other two once wore a hat, since the paint above his head indicates the use of dense pigments that appear too light to correspond with the brown color of his hair, which is X-ray transparent and would appear dark.

Around the head of the woman leaning on the railing, there is again vigorous reworking in the brushwork. Subtle shifts in the placement of her face and the hand under her chin are revealed in the infrared image; her facial features were initially positioned somewhat left of where they are now (see fig. 60). It is plausible that the model originally looked at Renoir while he painted. Her face was later turned slightly to the right,

perhaps to engage Baron Barbier, the man in brown seated in the center with his back turned to the viewer. The drying cracks in his thinly painted jacket are evidence that he was introduced at a later stage over a paint that was still wet (see fig. 49). While the sequence of revisions is difficult to discern, it's possible the young woman's gaze was altered after Barbier was introduced to the scene in order for these two sitters to form a relationship.

The woman who holds her hands to her ears on the far right seems to have once worn a larger, more rounded hat. Red paint inside drying cracks suggests that it was also a different color from the brown and green hat she wears in the final state of the picture. The first hat's light appearance in the X-radiograph points to the use of heavy atomic weight pigments, perhaps similar to the color in the red dress worn by the figure under

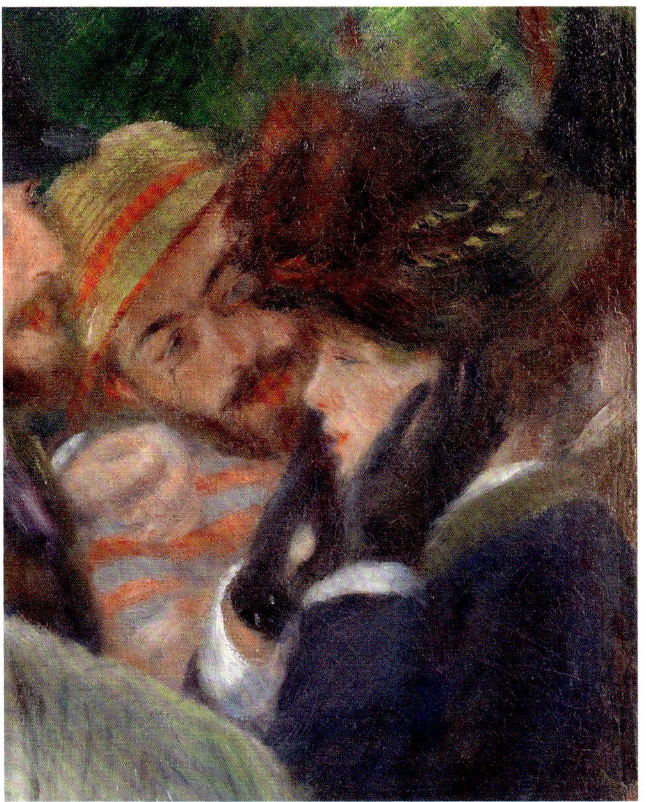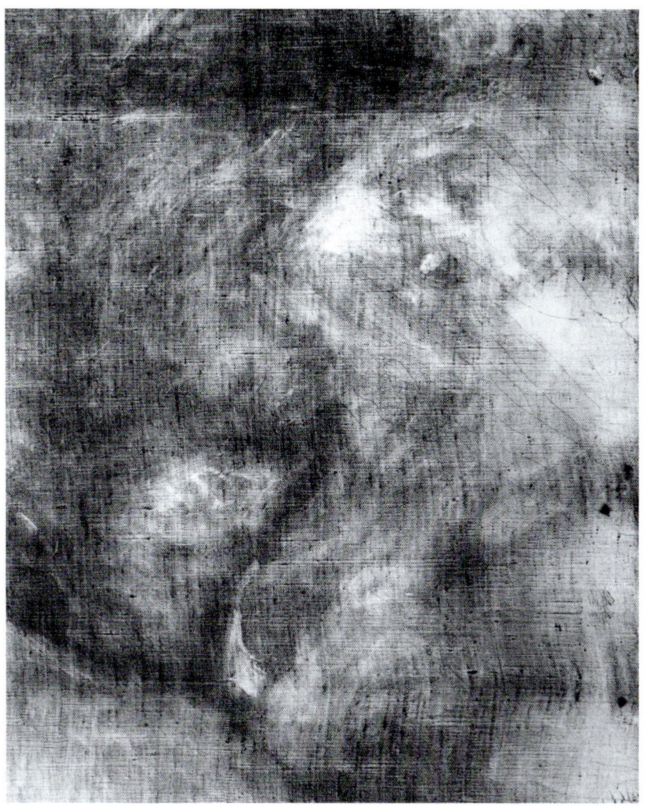

FIG. 61. Detail of *Luncheon of the Boating Party*: woman in brown hat in raking light compared to same area in X-radiograph.

Charigot (fig. 61). Given its shape and color, the hat this model initially wore may be like the one worn by the older woman in *Two Sisters* (*On the Terrace*)[13] (see fig. 47), which Renoir painted using a remarkably similar palette in the same year that he completed *Luncheon of the Boating Party*. The number of hats used and modified in the composition leads us to believe the artist kept a collection of props, including hats, which he reused in this and other pictures. It is curious that Renoir eliminated red apparel on several models. Were these changes another consequence of adding the red-striped awning, to avoid overwhelming the picture with too much of the same color?

Changes to the center of the composition remain a mystery, but improved imaging techniques let us theorize, if not perfectly visualize, a more significant alteration than was perceived in the first technical study.[14] A large shape that appears light in the X-radiograph corresponds to swirling and sweeping brushstrokes in the layers of paint under the bottles and wine cask and around Baron Barbier (see fig. 64). Vastly different colors—red, blue, yellow, and flesh tones—can also be found in thinly painted passages and in the drying cracks in the center of the composition (see figs. 48 and 49). While the salient features of this alteration are not clear in the X-radiograph, contour lines drawn around it might indicate a figure seated with hands resting on the table, looking toward the viewer (see fig. 64). Given the other changes Renoir made and his accounts that friends came and went, it seems plausible that he completely revised the orientation of a sitter (as he did with Ephrussi) or that he replaced one model with another (as he did with Charigot).

127

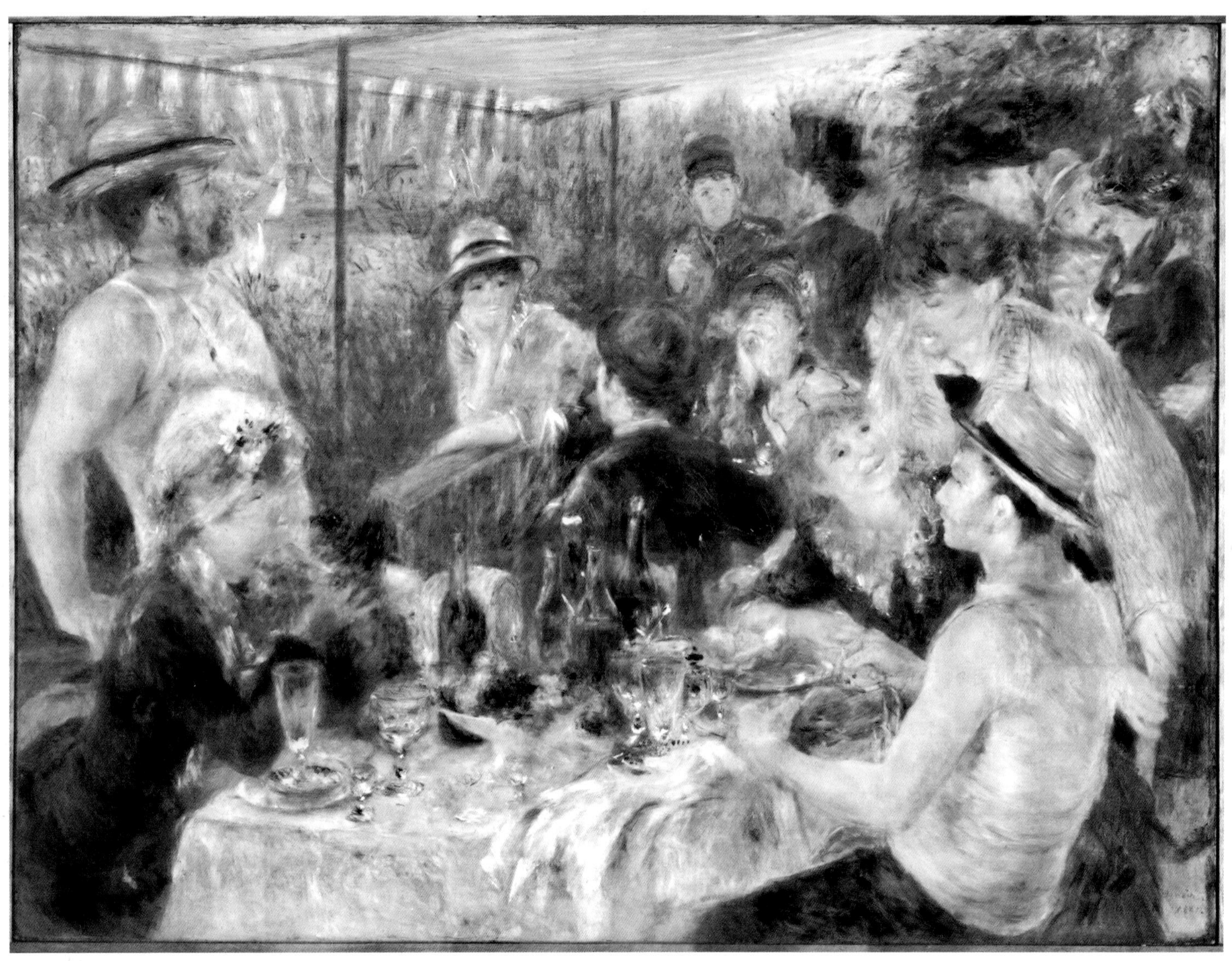

FIG. 62. *Luncheon of the Boating Party*: infrared image.

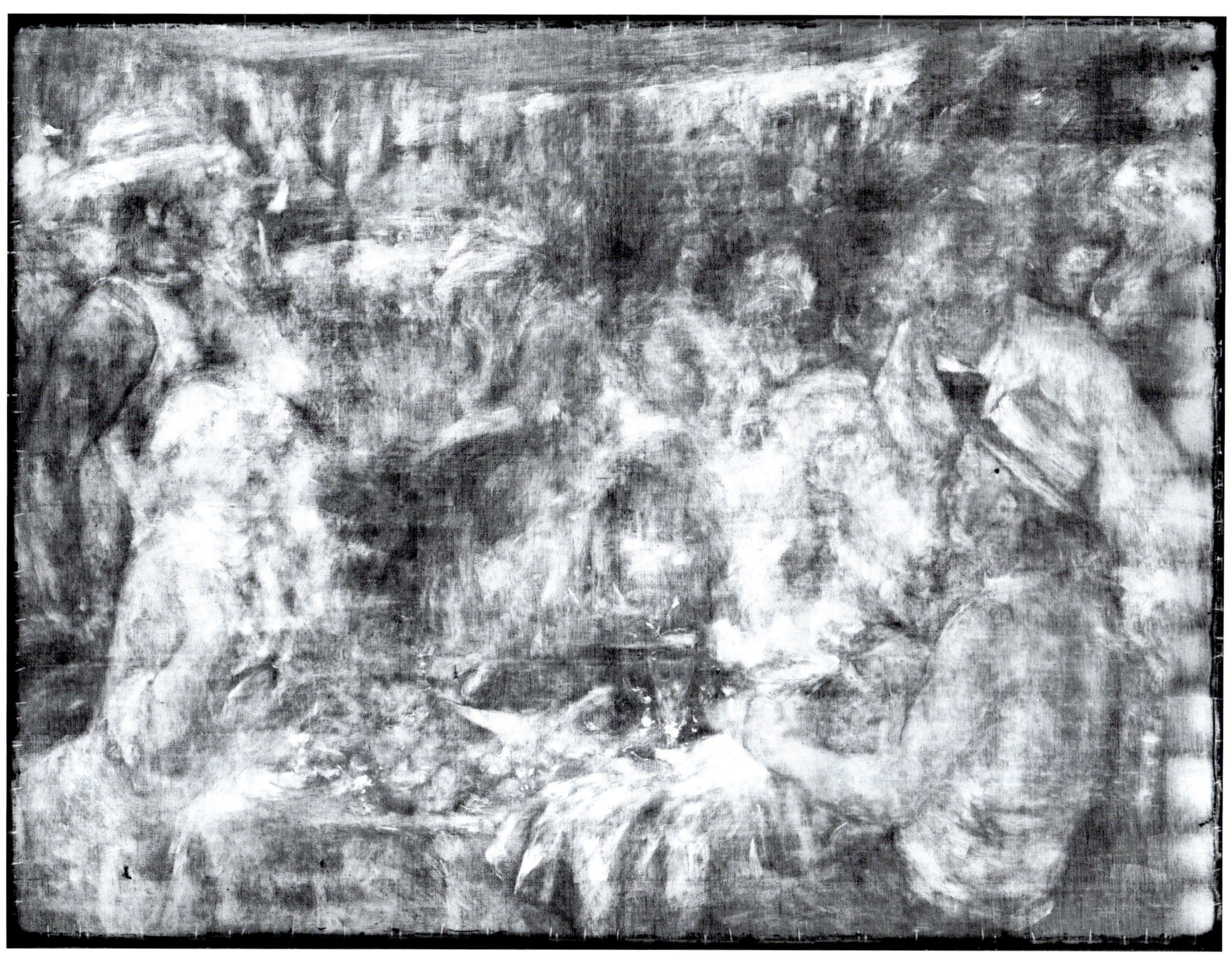

FIG. 63. *Luncheon of the Boating Party*: X-radiograph.

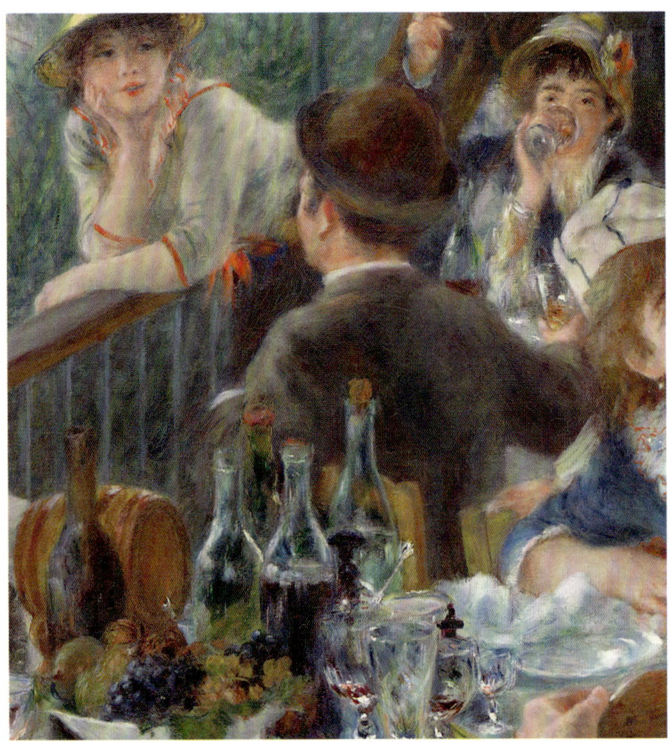

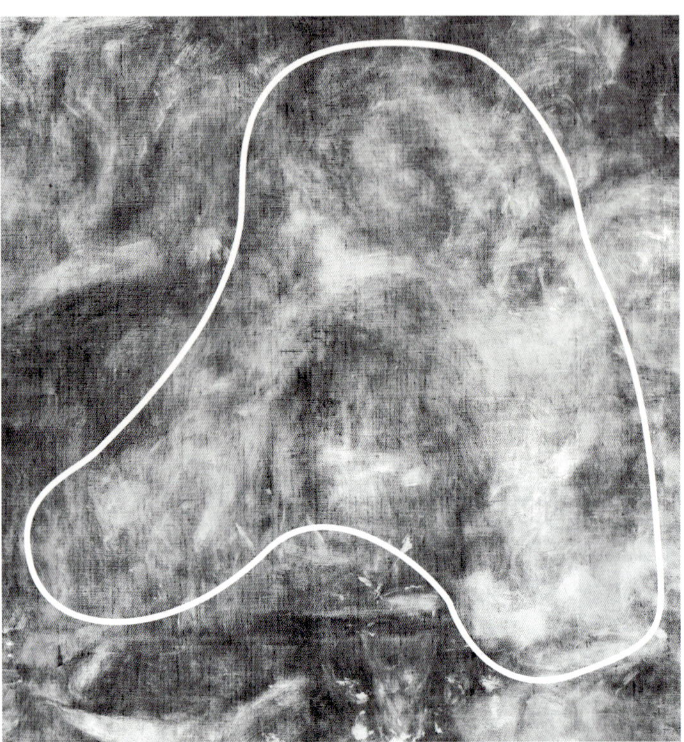

FIG. 64. *Luncheon of the Boating Party*: detail of central section in raking light compared to same area in X-radiograph (above) and infrared image (left).

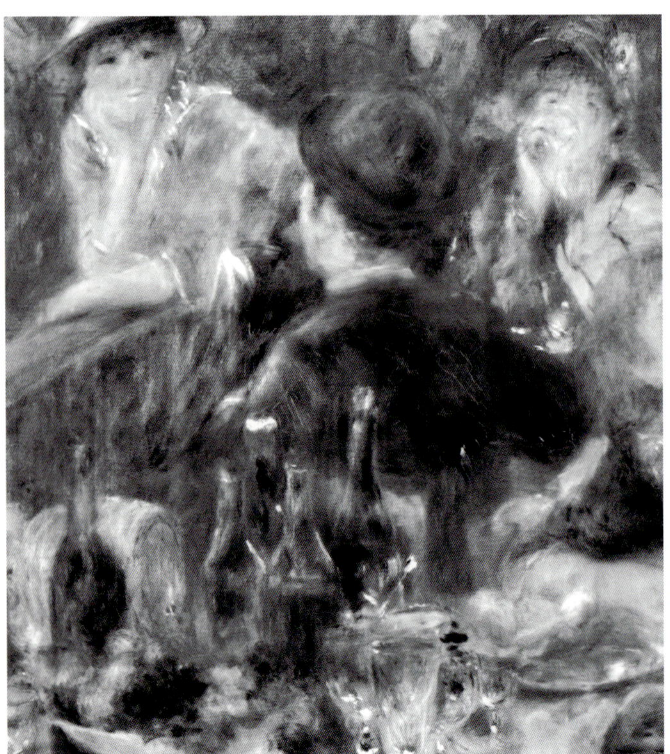

After Renoir put in the man modeled by Barbier, he then painted the wine bottles, cask, glasses, and bowl of fruit. Just as he adjusted the position of his sitters, he tinkered with the placement of objects on the table. A wineglass in front of the cask was painted out (fig. 65a), an aperitif glass was replaced with a small bunch of grapes lying on the table (fig. 65b), another wineglass in front of the fruit bowl was painted out (fig. 65c), and one of the tall glasses on the right was transformed from a stemmed glass (fig. 65d). Although it is conceivable that tableware changed between painting sessions and Renoir faithfully modified his depiction accordingly, these may be deliberate aesthetic choices he made after the fact or in his studio. The revisions in this passage demonstrate how much he labored to perfect the details of his composition.

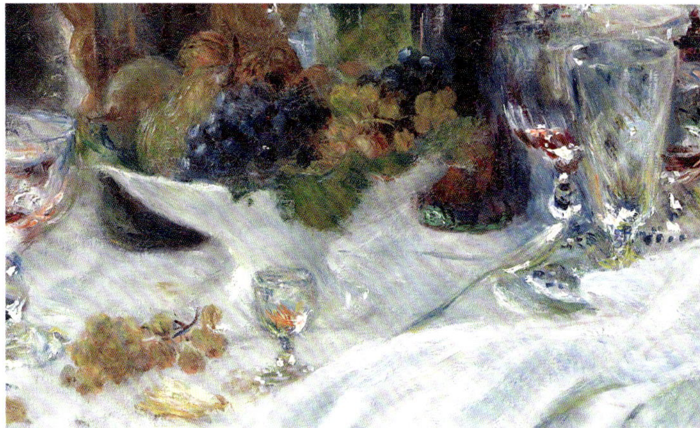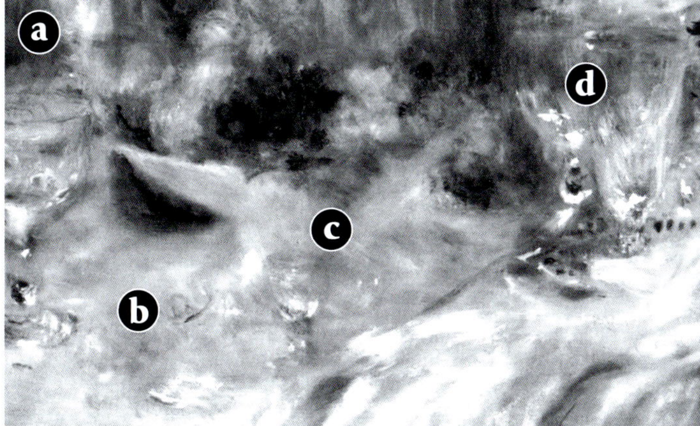

FIG. 65. *Luncheon of the Boating Party*: detail of glasses in raking light compared to same area in infrared image.

Although Renoir beautifully captured the immediacy of the scene, the technical study reveals the great lengths he took to reach this objective. While *Luncheon of the Boating Party* is a masterpiece of impressionism, it was not achieved strictly *en plein air*. While Renoir presumably painted most of the picture on the balcony at the Maison Fournaise, he clearly reevaluated his sitters and their environment several times, and probably did some reworking later in his studio.

1. Portions of the current essay have been drawn from Elizabeth Steele, "Achieving the Composition in *Luncheon of the Boating Party*," in Rathbone 1996, pp. 220–229.
2. House and Dayez-Distel 1985, p. 223.
3. Berard 1968, p. 55.
4. Ibid.
5. These types of cracks are caused by the application of a faster-drying paint on top of a slower-drying or still wet layer of paint. They are generally characterized by a more rounded and less angular appearance.
6. An X-radiograph is a black-and-white image created when low-voltage X-rays are passed through a painting and registered onto a sheet of X-ray-sensitive film. The density or atomic weight of the pigments affects the penetration of X-rays through the painting. Heavier atomic weight pigments absorb X-rays and read as lighter regions on the film, while less dense pigments transmit the X-rays and read as darker regions. The cobalt blue and red lake pigments used in Aline Charigot's dress are less dense than the vermillion and lead white pigments used in the outfit worn by the earlier model, thus the X-radiograph records the image of the latter more readily than the former.
7. Berard 1968, p. 55.
8. Renoir's choice of colors has been well documented in numerous publications, such as Anthea Callen, *The Art of Impressionism: Painting Technique and the Making of Modernity* (New Haven: Yale University Press, 2000), and David Bomford et al., *Art in the Making: Impressionism* (London and New Haven: National Gallery, London and Yale University Press, 1990). The results of paint analysis for this essay conform to previously published studies. The sample taken in the dress came from an existing loss, located 3⅝ in. from the bottom edge and 6¼ in. from the left. I am extremely grateful for the generous support of Thomas Lam, Physical Scientist; Stephanie Barnes, Paintings Conservation Fellow; and Jia-Sun Tsang, Senior Paintings Conservator, from the Smithsonian Museum Conservation Institute, in imaging the cross-sections using a Hirox digital microscope and analyzing the pigments using a Scanning Electron Microscope (SEM-EDS), from which tentative pigment identification can be inferred. I also wish to thank Inge Fiedler, Associate Research Microscopist at the Art Institute of Chicago, for reflected and ultraviolet light imaging of the cross-sections using a Zeiss AxioPlan2 research microscope and for providing her expertise on Renoir's palette to the interpretation of the paint samples.
9. Imaging and analysis provided by colleagues mentioned above at the Smithsonian Museum Conservation Institution and the Art Institute of Chicago.
10. My many thanks to Gary Krupnick, Manuela Dal Forno, and Merinda Nash, botanists from the Smithsonian Institution National Museum of Natural History and to Lisa Canterbury, mycologist from USDA, who offered their expertise to identify the inclusions in the cross-section.
11. Unpublished correspondence between Eliza Rathbone, Henri Claudel, and J. G. Bertauld, Association des Amis de la Maison Fournaise, February 6, 1996, confirms that the awning could be rolled out and in "following the sunlight."
12. Fig. 87, in Rathbone 1996, p. 224.
13. An excellent discussion and technical study of *Two Sisters (On the Terrace)* can be found in Gloria Groom and Jill Shaw, eds. *Renoir: Paintings and Drawings at the Art Institute of Chicago* (Art Institute of Chicago, 2014). https://publications.artic.edu/renoir/reader/paintingsanddrawings/section/135639/135639_anchor (cat. 11).
14. The X-radiograph was digitally reassembled and the stretcher bars were removed, which made the image more legible than when first published in 1996. I am extremely grateful to Annie Schrandt, Conservation Intern, for the diligence she demonstrated in this task. She also composited a new infrared image made using a Sensors Unlimited 320 M-1.7RT Indium Gallium Arsenide camera.

Works in the Exhibition

Léon Bonnat

Portrait of Charles Ephrussi (Portrait de Charles Ephrussi)
1906
Oil on canvas
18 × 15 in. (46 × 38 cm)
Private collection
Cat. 40

Gustave Caillebotte

A Man Docking His Skiff (Canotier ramenant sa périssoire bord de l'Yerres)
1878
Oil on canvas
29 × 36½ in. (73.7 × 92.7 cm)
Virginia Museum of Fine Arts, Collection of Mr. & Mrs. Paul Mellon
Cat. 33

Villers-sur-Mer
1880
Oil on canvas
23⅝ × 28¹¹⁄₁₆ in. (60 × 73 cm)
The Phillips Collection, Washington D.C., Promised gift of Mr. and Mrs G. Duane Vieth
Cat. 39

Sailboats on the Seine at Argenteuil (Voiliers sur la Seine à Argenteuil)
1886
Oil on canvas
25½ × 21¼ in. (65 × 54 cm)
Private collection, courtesy of Simon Dickinson Ltd., London
Cat. 37

Small Branch of the Seine at Argenteuil (Petit bras de la Seine à Argenteuil)
1884
Oil on canvas
35 × 28¼ in. (88.9 × 71.8 cm)
Private collection
Cat. 34

Madame Renoir in the Garden at Petit-Gennevilliers (Madame Renoir dans le jardin du Petit-Gennevilliers)
1891
Oil on canvas
25¼ × 19¾ in. (64.1 × 50.2 cm)
Collection of Bruce Toll
Cat. 32

The Yellow Boat (Le Bateau jaune)
1891
Oil on canvas
28¾ × 36⅜ in. (73 × 92.3 cm)
The Norton Simon Foundation, Pasadena, CA
Cat. 35

Sailboats on the Seine at Argenteuil (Voiliers sur la Seine à Argenteuil)
1893
Oil on canvas
28⅞ × 17 in. (75 × 43.2 cm)
Private collection
Cat. 36

Marcellin Desboutin

Renoir (Portrait de Renoir)
1877
Drypoint
5⅞ × 3⅞ in. (15.2 × 10.8 cm)
Institut national d'histoire de l'art, Paris
Cat. 47

Renoir, Legs Crossed (Portrait du peintre P.A. Renoir, les jambes croisées)
1877
Drypoint
9 × 5⅞ in. (23.4 × 15.5 cm)
Institut national d'histoire de l'art, Paris
Cat. 46

Edgar Degas

Portrait of Ellen Andrée (Portrait d'Ellen Andrée)
c. 1876
Monotype in black and brown ink on ivory paper
8½ × 6¼ in. (21.6 × 16 cm)
The Art Institute of Chicago
Cat. 17

The Actress Ellen Andrée (L'actrice Ellen Andrée)
1879
Drypoint
Platemark: 4⁷⁄₁₆ × 3⅛ in. (11.3 × 7.9 cm)
Sheet: 8⅝ × 6¼ in. (21.9 × 15.8 cm)
Museum of Fine Arts, Boston, Katherine E.
Bullard Fund in memory of Francis Bullard, by
exchange
Cat. 15

Portrait of Edmund Duranty (Portrait d'Edmund Duranty)
1879
Pastel on paper
20½ × 17¾ in. (52.1 × 45.1 cm)
Private collection
Cat. 43

Édouard Manet

A Bunch of Asparagus (Une botte d'asperges)
1880
Oil on canvas
18⅛ × 21¹¹⁄₁₆ in. (46 × 55 cm)
Wallraf-Richartz-Museum & Fondation Corboud
Cologne
Cat. 44

Asparagus (L'Asperge)
1880
Oil on canvas
6⅜ × 8½ in. (16.5 × 21.5 cm)
Musée d'Orsay, Paris, Gift of Sam Salz, 1959
Cat. 45

Portrait of a Young Woman – Mademoiselle Ellen Andrée (Portrait d'une jeune femme – mademoiselle Ellen Andrée)
c. 1880
Oil on canvas
12 × 9¼ in. (33 × 25 cm)
Private collection
Cat. 14

Jean Patricot

Charles Ephrussi
1905
Drypoint
7³⁄₁₆ × 5¹¹⁄₁₆ in. (18.5 × 14.5 cm)
The Phillips Collection, Washington, D.C.,
Acquired 2016
Cat. 42

Pierre-Auguste Renoir

The Seine at Chatou (La Seine à Chatou)
c. 1871
Oil on canvas
18⅛ × 22¹⁄₁₆ in. (46.7 × 56.1 cm)
Art Gallery of Ontario, Toronto, Purchased 1935
Cat. 10

Boaters of Argenteuil (Canotiers d'Argenteuil)
1873
Oil on canvas
19½ × 24 in. (50 × 61 cm)
Larry Ellison Collection
Cat. 48

The Seine at Argenteuil (La Seine à Argenteuil)
1874
Oil on canvas
19¾ × 25¾ in. (50.1 × 65.4 cm)
Portland Art Museum, Oregon, Bequest of
Winslow B. Ayer
Cat. 38

The Seine at Chatou (La Seine à Chatou)
1874
Oil on canvas
20 × 25 in. (50.8 × 63.5 cm)
Dallas Museum of Art, The Wendy and Emery
Reves Collection
Cat. 2

Bridge at Chatou (Pont à Chatou)
c. 1875
Oil on canvas
20¾ × 25⅝ in. (51.1 × 65.4 cm)
Sterling and Francine Clark Art Institute,
Williamstown, MA
Cat. 11

Lunch at the Restaurant Fournaise or The Rowers' Lunch (Déjeuner chez Fournaise or Déjeuner des canotiers)
1875
Oil on canvas
21⅝ × 25¹⁵⁄₁₆ in. (55 × 65.8 cm)
The Art Institute of Chicago, Potter Palmer
Collection
Cat. 22

Self-Portrait (Autoportrait)
c. 1875
Oil on canvas
15⅜ × 12⁷⁄₁₆ in. (39.1 × 31.6 cm)
Sterling and Francine Clark Art Institute,
Williamstown, MA
Cat. 4

Portrait of a Young Man and a Young Woman (Portrait d'un jeune homme et d'une jeune fille)
1876
Oil on canvas
12½ × 18⅛ in. (32 × 46 cm)
Musée de l'Orangerie, Paris, Jean Walter and
Paul Guillaume Collection
Cat. 23

In the Studio (Dans l'atelier) [Georges Rivière and Marguerite Legrand]
1876–1877
Oil on canvas
24¼ × 10⅝ in. (36.2 × 27 cm)
Dallas Museum of Art, The Wendy and Emery Reves Collection
Cat. 19

Man with a Little Hat (L'Homme au petit chapeau)
1877
Oil on canvas
11½ × 11¼ in. (29.4 × 28.5 cm)
Private collection
Cat. 18

Georges Rivière
1877
Oil on cement
14½ × 11⁹⁄₁₆ in. (36.8 × 29.3 cm)
National Gallery of Art, Washington, D.C., Ailsa Mellon Bruce Collection
Cat. 20

On the Shore of the Seine (Paysage bords de Seine)
c. 1879
Oil on linen
5½ × 9⅛ in. (14 × 23.2 cm)
The Baltimore Museum of Art, Saidie A. May Bequest, Courtesy of the Fireman's Fund Insurance Company
Cat. 24

The Dreamer (La Rêveuse)
1879
Oil on canvas
20⅛ × 24⅜ in. (51.1 × 61.9 cm)
Saint Louis Art Museum, Museum purchase
Cat. 13

Alphonsine Fournaise
1879
Oil on canvas
28¹⁵⁄₁₆ × 36⅝ in. (73.5 × 93 cm)
Musée d'Orsay, Paris, Gift of D. David-Weill, 1937
Cat. 21

Young Woman Sewing (Jeune femme cousant)
c. 1879
Oil on canvas
24³⁄₁₆ × 19⅞ in. (61.4 × 50.5 cm)
The Art Institute of Chicago, Mr. & Mrs. Lewis Larned Coburn Memorial Collection
Cat. 6

Woman with a Fan (Femme à l'éventail)
c. 1879
Oil on canvas
25¾ × 21¼ in. (65.4 × 54 cm)
Sterling and Francine Clark Art Institute, Williamstown, MA
Cat. 16

Oarsmen at Chatou (Les Canotiers à Chatou)
1879
Oil on canvas
31¹⁵⁄₁₆ × 39⁷⁄₁₆ in. (81.2 × 100.2 cm)
National Gallery of Art, Washington, D.C., Gift of Sam A. Lewisohn
Cat. 29

Portrait of Thérèse Ephrussi – Madame Léon Fould (Portrait de Thérèse Ephrussi – madame Léon Fould)
1880
Oil on canvas
20 × 17½ in. (50.8 × 44.4 cm)
Mr. & Mrs. Felipe Propper de Callejon
Cat. 41

Young Woman Reading an Illustrated Journal (Jeune femme lisant un journal illustré)
c. 1880
Oil on canvas
18¼ × 22 in. (46.4 × 57.1 cm)
Museum of Art, Rhode Island School of Design, Providence, RI, Museum Appropriation Fund
Cat. 7

Madame Renoir with a Dog (Madame Renoir au chien)
1880
Oil on canvas
12¼ × 16⅛ in. (31 × 41 cm)
Private collection, in cooperation with Durand-Ruel & Cie., Paris
Cat. 9

Boating Couple (Les Canotiers)
1880–1881
Pastel on paper
17¾ × 23 in. (45 × 58.4 cm)
Museum of Fine Arts, Boston, Given in memory of Governor Alvan T. Fuller by the Fuller Foundation
Cat. 8

Luncheon of the Boating Party (Le Déjeuner des canotiers)
1880–1881
Oil on canvas
51¾ × 69⅛ in. (130.2 × 175.6 cm)
The Phillips Collection, Washington, D.C., Acquired 1923
Cat. 1

Albert Cahen d'Anvers
1881
Oil on canvas
31½ × 25⅛ in. (80 × 63.8 cm)
The J. Paul Getty Museum, Los Angeles
Cat. 3

Dancing Couple (study for Dance at Bougival [Danse à Bougival])
1883
Pen and ink on white wove paper
11¹⁵⁄₁₆ × 7⁹⁄₁₆ in. (30.3 × 19.2 cm)
Philadelphia Museum of Art, The Henry P. McIlhenny Collection in Memory of Frances P. McIlhenny, 1986
Cat. 12

Mademoiselle Charlotte Berthier
1883
Oil on canvas
36¼ × 28¾ in. (92.1 × 73 cm)
National Gallery of Art, Washington, D.C., Gift of Angellika Wertheim Frink
Cat. 5

Dance in the Country (*Danse à la campagne*)
1883 or later
Brush and brown, blue, and black wash over
black chalk or graphite
19½ × 12 in. (49.5 × 30.5 cm)
Yale University Art Gallery, New Haven, CT,
Bequest of Edith Malvina K. Wetmore
Cat. 26

Dance in the Country (*Danse à la campagne*)
1883
Pen, brush, and gray ink on wove paper
18¾ × 11⅞ in. (47.6 × 30.2 cm)
National Gallery of Art, Washington, D.C.,
Collection of Mr. & Mrs. Paul Mellon, 1995
Cat. 25

Dance in the Country (*Danse à la campagne*)
1883
Oil on canvas
70⅞ × 35⁷⁄₁₆ in. (180 × 90 cm)
Musée d'Orsay, Paris
Cat. 27

Portrait of Madame Renoir (*Portrait de madame
Renoir*)
c. 1885
Oil on canvas
25¾ × 21¼ in. (65.4 × 54 cm)
Philadelphia Museum of Art, Purchased with the
W.P. Wilstach Fund
Cat. 30

Dance in the Country (*Danse à la campagne*)
c. 1890
Soft-ground etching on paper
12¾ × 9¾ in. (32.4 × 24.8 cm)
The Phillips Collection, Washington, D.C.,
Acquired 1949
Cat. 28

Pierre-Auguste Renoir and Richard Guino
Mother and Child (*Mère et enfant*)
1916
Bronze
21½ × 8 × 8½ in. (54.6 × 20.3 × 21.5 cm)
The Phillips Collection, Washington, D.C.,
Acquired 1940
Cat. 31

PHOTOGRAPHS

Jeanne Samary – Face Resting on Hands
Digital print from a 19th-century original
Comédie-Française Bibliothèque-musée, Paris
Fig. 43

Jeanne Samary – Smiling
Digital print from a 19th-century original
Comédie-Française Bibliothèque-musée, Paris
Fig. 42

Jeanne Samary – With a Hat
Digital print from a 19th-century original
Comédie-Française Bibliothèque-musée, Paris
Fig. 44

The Railway Bridge in Rueil (*Le pont du chemin
de fer à Rueil*)
Digital print from a late 19th-century postcard
Via Joconde – Portail des collections des musées
de France
Fig. 22

Chatou – Restaurant Fournaise
Digital print from an early 20th-century postcard
Via Joconde – Portail des collections des musées
de France
Fig. 3

Chatou – Garage Fournaise
Digital print from an early 20th-century postcard
Via Joconde – Portail des collections des musées
de France
Fig. 1

Nadar (Gaspar-Félix Tournachon)
Ellen Andrée, Actress (*Ellen Andrée, comédienne*)
1879
Modern silver gelatin print from a 19th-century
original
Bibliothèque Nationale de France, Paris
Fig. 6

Nadar (Gaspar-Félix Tournachon)
Angèle
Modern silver gelatin print from an original of
c. 1878
Caisse Nationale des Monuments Historiques et
des Sites, Paris
Fig. 5

Martial Caillebotte
Gustave Caillebotte in his Greenhouse (*L'Artiste
dans la serre*)
c. 1892
Comité Caillebotte, Paris
Fig. 27

Gustave Caillebotte
Sailboats Reaching the Shore at Petit-Gennevilliers
(*Voiliers accostant sur la rive du Petit-
Gennevilliers*)
Comité Caillebotte, Paris
Fig. 24

Anonymous
Gustave Caillebotte and His Fellow Boaters
(*Gustave Caillebotte et ses amis canotiers*)
c. 1877–1879
Comité Caillebotte, Paris
Fig. 21

PUBLICATIONS

Charles Ephrussi
Étude sur le triptych d'Albert Dürer
1876
Collection of Edmund de Waal

Gazette des beaux-arts
May 1, 1880
(Ephrussi review)
National Gallery of Art, Washington, D.C.

Gazette des beaux-arts
July 1, 1880
(Ephrussi review)
National Gallery of Art, Washington, D.C.

Charles Ephrussi
Albert Dürer et ses dessins
1882
Collection of Edmund de Waal

Gazette des beaux-arts
1885
Collection of Edmund de Waal

Charles Ephrussi
Paul Baudry: sa vie et son œuvre
1887
Collection of Edmund de Waal

Gazette des beaux-arts
October 1, 1905
(Ephrussi obituary)
National Gallery of Art, Washington, D.C.

Objets d'art, meubles, tableaux, sièges et tapisseries…
Sale catalogue, May 19, 1913
Galerie Georges Petit
Collection of Edmund de Waal

Tableaux anciens, objets d'art et d'ameublement des XVII et XVIIIᵉ siècles provenant de la collection de M. X. (**C. Ephrussi – written by hand**)
Sale catalogue, May 22, 1913
Galerie Georges Petit
Collection of Edmund de Waal

Georges Rivière
Renoir et ses amis
1921
H. Floury, Paris

HATS

Straw bonnet with black velvet and "wheat"
Late 1860s
Label: Feus Bées de S.M L'imperatrice mmes.
Hofele, Rue de la Paix, 7 Paris
Straw, silk, and velvet
Museum of the City of New York, Gift of Mrs.
William Hyde Wheeler, 1942

Collapsible top hat in black satin
1870s
Label: Amidon Mode De Paris
Silk, satin
Museum of the City of New York, Gift of Mrs.
Thomas L. Purdy, Evelyn P. Luquer, Lea S. Luquer,
and Thatcher Luquer, 1959

Hat with flowers and ribbon
1881
Label: Modes, Mon. Mivière, Rue de Caumartin,
10 Pres de Boul. Des Capucines, Paris
Leghorn, cambric
Museum of the City of New York, Gift of Mrs.
James Sullivan, 1927

**Bonnet in natural straw with green satin
ribbon and red flowers**
c. 1881
Label: "Aurora"
Plaited natural straw, embossed cotton sateen
blossoms, wool felt buds; silk satin ribbon
trim/ties
Museum of the City of New York, Gift of Mr. A.
Sanford Kellogg, 1978

Appendix

Pierre-Auguste Renoir, *Luncheon of the Boating Party* (*Le Déjeuner des canotiers*), 1880–1881

Provenance

1881, February 14, purchased
by Paul Durand-Ruel

1881, purchased from Durand-Ruel
by Ernest Balensi

1882, reacquired by Durand-Ruel

1923, July 9, Duncan and Marjorie Phillips
purchase *Le Déjeuner des canotiers* from Galerie
Durand-Ruel, Paris, for Phillips Memorial Gallery

**Exhibition history from date of completion
to date of acquisition by Phillips Memorial
Gallery**

Cercle des arts libéraux, Paris. Annual exhibition.
April 23–May 25, 1881 (as *Repas champêtre*).

Paris. *Septième exposition des artistes indépendants.*
March 1–31 (approx.), 1882. Cat. 140 (as *Un
Déjeuner à Bougival*).

Durand-Ruel, Paris. *Exposition des œuvres de P. A.
Renoir.* April 1–25, 1883. Cat. 37 (as *Dîner à
Chatou*).

The Foreign Exhibition Association, Boston.
*American Exhibition of Foreign Products, Arts and
Manufacturers.* September 1883. Cat. 26 (as
Boatman's Breakfast—Bougival).

American Art Association, New York. *Works in Oil
and Pastel by the Impressionists of Paris.* 1886. Cat.
185 (as *Le Déjeuner à Bougival*).

Durand-Ruel, Paris. *Exposition A. Renoir.* May
1892. Cat. 5 (as *Déjeuner à Bougival*).

Durand-Ruel, Paris. *Exposition de tableaux de
Monet, Pissarro, Renoir et Sisley.* April 1899.
Cat. 83 (as *Canotiers à Bougival*).

Petit Palais, Paris. *Salon d'automne, 2e exposition.*
October 15–November 15, 1904. Cat. 11.

Grafton Galleries, London. *Pictures by Boudin,
Cézanne, Degas, Manet, Monet, Morisot, Pissarro,
Renoir, and Sisley.* January–February 1905. Cat.
244 (as *A Lunch After Rowing*).

Kunsthaus, Zurich. *Französische Kunst des XIX und
XX Jahrhunderts.* October 5–November 15, 1917.
Cat. 167 (illus. as *Le Déjeuner des canotiers*).

Durand-Ruel, New York. *Seven Paintings by Renoir.*
January 1923. Unnumbered entry.

Selected Bibliography

Adler 1995
Kathleen Adler. "Renoir's *Portrait of Albert Cahen d'Anvers." The J. Paul Getty Museum Journal* 23 (1995): pp. 31–40.

André 1919
Albert André. *Renoir*. Paris: Crès & Cie, 1919.

André and Elder 1931
Albert André and Marc Elder. *L'Atelier de Renoir*. Paris: Bernheim-Jeune, 1931.

Arts Council 1985
Renoir. Exh. cat, Hayward Gallery, London; Galeries nationales du Grand Palais, Paris; and Museum of Fine Arts, Boston. London: Arts Council of Great Britain, 1985.

Bailey 1997
Colin B. Bailey. *Renoir's Portraits: Impressions of an Age*. New Haven and London: Yale University Press, 1997.

Bailey 2012
Colin B. Bailey. *Renoir, Impressionism, and Full-Length Painting*. New York: The Frick Collection, 2012.

Baudot 1949
Jeanne Baudot. *Renoir, ses amis, ses modèles*. Paris: Editions litteraires de France, 1949.

Benjamin and Prochaska 2003
Roger Benjamin and David Prochaska. *Renoir and Algeria*. New Haven: Yale University Press, 2003.

Berard 1938
Maurice Berard. *Renoir à Wargemont*. Paris: Larose, 1938.

Berard 1956
Maurice Berard. "Un diplomate ami de Renoir." *Revue d'histoire diplomatique*, July–September 1956, pp. 239–246.

Berard 1968
Maurice Berard. "Lettres à un ami [Renoir à Paul Berard]." *La Revue de Paris*, année 76 (December 1968): pp. 54–58.

Berson 1996
Ruth Berson. *The New Painting: Impressionism, 1874–1886*. Fine Arts Museums of San Francisco, 1996.

Besson 1929
Georges Besson. *Renoir*. Paris: G. Crès, 1929.

Blanche 1921
Jacques-Émile Blanche. "La technique de Renoir." *L'Amour de l'art*, February 1921, pp. 33–40.

Blanche 1927
Jacques-Émile Blanche. *Dieppe*. Paris: Emile-Paul Frères, 1927.

Blanche 1933
Jacques-Émile Blanche. "Renoir portraitiste." *L'Art vivant*, July 1933, p. 292.

Blanche 1949
Jacques-Émile Blanche. *La Pêche aux souvenirs*. Paris: Flammarion, 1949.

Bodelsen 1968
Merete Bodelsen. "Early Impressionist Sales 1874–94 in the Light of Some Unpublished 'Procès-Verbaux.'" *The Burlington Magazine* 110, no. 783 (1968): pp. 330–349.

Bodelsen 1970
Merete Bodelsen. "A Propos of the 'procès-verbaux' of the Impressionist Sales." *The Burlington Magazine* 112, no. 810 (1970): pp. 620–23.

Butler 2002
Augustin de Butler, ed. *Renoir: écrits, entretiens et lettres sur l'art*. Paris: Éditions de l'Amateur, 2002.

Callen 1978
Anthea Callen. *Renoir*. London: Oresko, 1978.

Carey 1981
Martha Carey, *Pierre-Auguste Renoir, The Luncheon of the Boating Party*, Washington, 1981.

Collins 2001
John B. Collins. "Seeking l'esprit gaulois: Renoir's *Bal du Moulin de la Galette* and Aspects of French Social History and Popular Culture." PhD diss., McGill University, 2001.

Davidson 1933
Angus Davidson. "A Renoir Portrait: Portrait of M. Lestringuez." *The Burlington Magazine*, December 1933, pp. 305–307.

Distel 1989
Anne Distel. *Les Collectionneurs des impressionnistes*. Lausanne: La Bibliotheque des Arts, 1989.

Distel 1990
Anne Distel. *Impressionism: The First Collectors*. New York: Harry N. Abrams, Inc., 1990.

Distel 1994
Anne Distel et al. *Gustave Caillebotte, Urban Impressionist*. Exh. cat., Galeries nationales du Grand Palais, Paris; Art Institute of Chicago; and Los Angeles County Museum of Art. Paris and Chicago, 1994.

Distel 1995
Anne Distel. *Renoir: A Sensuous Vision*. New York: Harry N. Abrams, 1995.

Distel 2009
Anne Distel. *Renoir*. Paris: Citadelles et Mazenod, 2009.

Dottin-Orsini 1991
Mireille Dottin-Orsini. "Jules Laforgue et Charles Ephrussi: le 'jeune homme si simple' et le 'bénédictin-dandy' de la Gazette des Beaux-Arts." *Gazette des beaux-arts* 117 (1991): pp. 233–240.

Duret 1924
Théodore Duret. *Renoir*. Paris: Bernheim-Jeune, 1924.

Duret 1937
Théodore Duret. *Renoir*. Translated by Madeleine Boyd. New York: Crown Publishers, 1937.

Fénéon 1921
Félix Fénéon. "Des peintres et leur modèle." *Le Bulletin de la vie artistique*, May 21, 1921, pp. 261–264.

Florisoone 1938
Michel Florisoone. "Renoir et la famille Charpentier: lettres inédites." *L'Amour de l'art* 19, no. 1 (February 1938): 31–40.

Fonsmark 2008
Anne-Birgitte Fonsmark et al. *Gustave Caillebotte*. Exh. cat., Kunsthalle Bremen. Ostfildern: Hatje Cantz, 2008.

Fosca 1976
François Fosca. *Renoir*. New York: Harry N. Abrams, Inc., 1976.

Gachet and Murer 1957
Paul Gachet and Eugène Murer. *Lettres impressionnistes (aux Dr Gachet et Dr Murer)*. Paris: Grasset, 1957.

Garb 1992
Tamar Garb. "Renoir and the Natural Woman." In *The Expanding Discourse: Feminism and Art History*, edited by Norma Broude and Mary Garrard. New York: Harper Collins, 1992.

House and Dayez-Distel 1985
John House and Anne Dayez-Distel. *Renoir*. Paris: Ministère de la culture, Éditions de la Réunion des musées nationaux and Museum of Fine Arts, Boston, 1985.

House 1994
John House, *Renoir, Master Impressionist*. Exh. cat., Queensland Art Gallery, Brisbane. Art Exhibitions Australia Limited, 1994.

House and Lucy 2012
John House and Martha Lucy. *Renoir in the Barnes Foundation*. New Haven: Yale University Press, 2012.

Jiminez 2001
Jill Berk Jiminez. *Dictionary of Artists' Models*. London: Fitzroy Dearborn Publishers, 2001.

Joëts 1935
Jules Joëts. "Les impressionnistes et Chocquet." *L'Amour de l'art*, April 1935, pp. 120–125.

Laforgue 1903
Jules Laforgue. *Œuvres complètes de Jules Laforgue: mélanges posthumes*. Paris: Mercure de France, 1903.

Lhote 1944
André Lhote. *Peintures de Renoir*. Paris: Les Éditions du Chêne, 1944.

Lhote 1883
Paul Lhote. "Mademoiselle Zélia." *La Vie moderne*, November 3, 1883, pp. 707–708.

Lloyd 2013
Christopher Lloyd et al. *Impressionists on the Water*. Exh. cat., Fine Arts Museums of San Francisco. New York: Skira/Rizzoli, 2013.

Mallarmé 1959
Stéphane Mallarmé. *Correspondance*, edited by L. J. Austin et al. Paris: Gallimard, 1959.

Manet 1979
Julie Manet. *Journal, 1893–1899: sa jeunesse parmi les peintres impressionnistes et les hommes de lettres*. Paris: C. Klincksieck, 1979.

Manet 1987
Julie Manet. *Journal*. Paris: Scala, 1987.

Marchesseau 2014
Daniel Marchesseau. *Pierre-Auguste Renoir: Revoir Renoir*. Exh. cat., Fondation Pierre Gianadda, Martigny, Switzerland, 2014.

Meier-Graefe 1912
Julius Meier-Graefe. *Auguste Renoir*. Translated by A. S. Maillet. Paris: H. Floury, 1912.

Meier-Graefe 1920
Julius Meier-Graefe. *Auguste Renoir*. Munich: R. Piper & Co., 1920.

Meier-Graefe 1929
Julius Meier-Graefe. *Renoir*. Leipzig: Klinkhardt & Biermann, 1929.

Moffett 1986
Charles S. Moffett et al. *The New Painting: Impressionism 1874–1886*. Exh. cat., National Gallery of Art, Washington, and Fine Arts Museums of San Francisco. San Francisco and Washington, 1986.

Moncade 1978
C. L. de Moncade. "Renoir et le Salon d'Automne." In White 1978.

Morton 2015
Mary Morton and George T.M. Shackelford. *Gustave Caillebotte: The Painter's Eye*, National Gallery of Art, Washington, and the Kimball Art Museum, Fort Worth, 2015.

Néret 2001
Gilles Neret. *Renoir: Painter of Happiness 1841–1919*. Cologne: Taschen Verlag, 2001.

Patry 2015
Sylvie Patry et al. *Discovering the Impressionists: Paul Durand-Ruel and the New Painting*. Exh. cat., Philadelphia Museum of Art; National Gallery, London; and Musée d'Orsay, Paris. Philadelphia, London, and Paris, 2015.

Perruchot 1964
Henri Perruchot. *La Vie de Renoir*. Paris: Hachette, 1964.

Rathbone 1996
Eliza E. Rathbone et al.
Impressionists on the Seine: A Celebration of Renoir's "Luncheon of the Boating Party." The Phillips Collection, Washington, D.C.: Counterpoint, 1996.

Renoir 1879
Edmond Renoir. "La cinquième exposition de La Vie moderne. P.-A. Renoir." *La Vie moderne*, June 19, 1879.

Renoir 1958
Jean Renoir, *Renoir, My Father*. Translated by Randolph and Dorothy Weaver. Boston and Toronto: Little Brown and Company, 1958.

Renoir 2011
Jean Renoir. *Renoir, My Father*. Translated by Randolph and Dorothy Weaver. New York: New York Review of Books, 2011.

Renoir 2012
Jean Renoir. Renoir, mon père. Paris, Gallimard, 2012.

Renoir and Florisoone 1938
Pierre-Auguste Renoir and Michel Florisoone. *Renoir*. Translated by George Frederick Lees. Paris: Hyperion, 1938.

Renoir and Vollard 1918
Pierre-Auguste Renoir and Ambroise Vollard. *Tableaux, pastels & dessins de Pierre-Auguste Renoir*. Paris: A. Vollard, 1918.

Rewald 1945
John Rewald. "Auguste Renoir and His Brother." *Gazette des beaux-arts* VI (March 1945): pp. 171–188.

Rewald 1973
John Rewald. *The History of impressionism*, 4th revised edition. New York: Museum of Modern Art, 1973.

Rivière 1877
Georges Rivière. "L'exposition des impressionnistes." *L'impressionniste: journal d'art*, April 6, 1877, pp. 2–6.

Rivière 1921
Georges Rivière. *Renoir et ses amis*. Paris: Floury, 1921.

Rivière 1925
Georges Rivière. "Renoir." *L'Art vivant*, July 1, 1925, pp. 1–6.

Robida 1958
Michel Robida. *Le Salon Charpentier et les impressionnistes*. Paris: La Bibliothèque des Arts, 1958.

Robida 1959
Michel Robida. *Renoir enfants*. Lausanne: International Art Book, 1959.

Simpson 1997
Marc Simpson. "The Earliest Public Exhibition of Renoir's *Luncheon of the Boating Party*." *The Burlington Magazine* 139, no. 1129 (1997): pp. 261–262.

Varnedoe 1980
J. Kirk T. Varnedoe. "The Artifice of Candor: Impressionism and Photography Reconsidered." *Art in America*, January 1980, pp. 66–78.

Varnedoe 1987
Kirk Varnedoe. *Gustave Caillebotte*, Yale University Press, New Haven and London, 1987.

Venturi 1939
Lionello Venturi. *Les Archives de l'impressionnisme*. Paris/New York: Durand-Ruel, 1939.

Vollard 1919
Ambroise Vollard. *La Vie et l'œuvre de Pierre-Auguste Renoir*. Paris: Ambroise Vollard, 1919.

Vollard 1925
Ambroise Vollard, *Renoir: An Intimate Record*. Translated by Harold L. Van Doren and Randolph T. Weaver. New York: A. A. Knopf, 1925.

Vollard 1938
Ambroise Vollard. *En écoutant Cézanne, Degas, Renoir*. Paris: B. Grasset, 1938.

Vollard 1990
Ambroise Vollard. *Renoir: An Intimate Record*. Translated by Harold L. Van Doren and Randolph T. Weaver. New York: Dover Publications Inc., 1990.

Wadley 1987
Nicholas Wadley. *Renoir: A Retrospective*. New York: Hugh Lauter Associates Inc., 1987.

White 1978
Barbara Ehrlich White, ed. *Impressionism in Perspective*. Englewood Cliffs, NJ: Prentice Hall, 1978.

White 1984
Barbara Ehrlich White. *Renoir: His Life, Art, and Letters*. New York: Harry N. Abrams, Inc., 1984.

Photography Credits

Index